PENGUIN BOOKS
THE FORTUNES OF MARY FORTUNE

Lucy Sussex was born in Christchurch, New Zealand
in 1957. After living in France and England she moved
to North Queensland in 1971. She has a BA (Hons)
in English and a MA in Librarianship from Monash
University and is now a research assistant at
Melbourne University.

Her other publications include stories and criticism
in the science fiction and fantasy field as well as a
children's book, *The Peace Garden* (OUP, 1989). She has
also written many articles and essays on Mary
Fortune for other publications, including *A Bright and
Fiery Troop* (Penguin, 1988).

Penguin Australian Women's Library

Series Editor: Dale Spender

The Penguin Australian Women's Library will make
available to readers a wealth of information through
the work of women writers of our past. It will include
the classic to the freshly re-discovered, individual
reprints to new anthologies, as well as up-to-date
critical re-appraisals of their work and lives as writers.

Other books in the Penguin Australian Women's Library

The Penguin Anthology of Australian Women's Writing
Edited by Dale Spender

Mr Hogarth's Will by Catherine Helen Spence
Introduced by Helen Thomson

Kirkham's Find by Mary Gaunt
Introduced by Kylie Tennant
Afterword by Dale Spender

A Bright and Fiery Troop:
Australian Women Writers of the Nineteenth Century
Edited by Debra Adelaide

Her Selection:
Writings by Nineteenth-Century Australian Women
Edited by Lynne Spender

The Peaceful Army edited by Flora Eldershaw
Introduced by Kylie Tennant and Dale Spender

The Letters of Rachel Henning
Edited by David Adams
Introduced by Dale Spender

Jungfrau by Dymphna Cusack
Introduced by Florence James

Series Editor: Dale Spender

Consultant: Helen Thomson

Advisory Board:
Debra Adelaide   Sue Martin
Kay Ferres   Lynne Spender
Sneja Gunew   Elizabeth Webby
Elizabeth Lawson

THE FORTUNES OF MARY FORTUNE

Edited with an Introduction by Lucy Sussex
Preface by Judith Brett

PENGUIN BOOKS
Penguin Australian Women's Library

Penguin Books Australia Ltd
487 Maroondah Highway, PO Box 257
Ringwood, Victoria, 3134, Australia
Penguin Books Ltd
Harmondsworth, Middlesex, England
Viking Penguin Inc.
40 West 23rd Street, New York. NY 10010, USA
Penguin Books Canada Limited
2801 John Street, Markham, Ontario, Canada, L3R 1B4
Penguin Books (N.Z.) Ltd
182–190 Wairau Road, Auckland 10, New Zealand

First published by Penguin Books Australia, 1989

Copyright Introduction © Lucy Sussex, 1989

Copyright Preface © Judith Brett, 1989

Typeset in 10/12 Andover by Midland Typesetters, Maryborough.
Made and printed in Australia by Australian Print Group, Maryborough, Victoria.

Fortune, Mary.
The Fortunes of Mary Fortune

ISBN 0 14 012302 4.

1. Australia – History. 2. Australia – Social life and customs. 3. Australia – Social conditions. I. Sussex, Lucy, 1957 –   . II. Title. (Series: Penguin Australian women's library).

A828'.1

CONTENTS

Part Two The Journalism

ACKNOWLEDGEMENTS

Thanks are due to the staff of the La Trobe library, Melbourne, particularly John Arnold and Richard Overall; the descendents of Percy Brett, especially Judith Brett, Rollo Brett, Margaret Dupleix and Pam Beattie; Doug Barbour, Dr Mary Lu MacDonald, Megan Collins, Brian Edwards and Hélène Martin for Canadian information; the Victorian Police Historical Unit; local historians Mrs Lee Gillespie, Kingower, and Raymond Bradfield, Castlemaine; Mrs Clarissa Tedder, Veronica Kelly and Elaine Zinkhan, for help with the John Oxley Library, Queensland; Dr Margot Sussex; Robyn Garden; Mary Cameron; Michele Field and Teresa Pitt, for their early encouragement of this project; George Turner, for his explanation of cherry-bobs; Doug Fortune (no relation) for a wonderful wild goose chase; Christine McGee and Carmel Egan, the *Australian*; Brian Matthews, for help at ASAL; David English; Dale Spender, Sue Martin and everyone at Penguin; Daisy Rose, for critical comments; and above all, to the three to whom this book is dedicated, Stephen Knight, Elizabeth Webby and Betty Gibson.

Preface

Most nineteenth-century women writers wrote from the centre of a domestic environment. They viewed the outside world from the security and the confines of the home, from behind its windows or from its verandah. Not so Mary Fortune. Her vantage point is the street, where she jostles with those around her – the overdressed prostitutes, the fighting schoolboys, the gossiping matrons and the dapper business men of colonial Melbourne. In the pieces collected here she does not present herself as having a home. From the street, from the camping grounds she shares with the swearing drivers in 'Fourteen Days on the Road' as she journeys unaccompanied in a carrier's dray, from the door of her tent as she surveys the chaotic life of the diggings, she always writes from the midst of a public space. Even when accompanied by her uncle on the goldfields, or by her son in 'How I Spent Christmas', she seems essentially alone, wryly observing the life around her and her own isolation amidst it.

Through the pieces collected here comes a lonely woman, but one who is self-sufficient in a world of strangers; who keeps her spirits up, not to say earns her living, from the continual observing and noting of the life around her. She is stranded on the outskirts of Benalla during her fourteen days on the road, while her driver does a side-trip to earn some extra money. 'But that enforced camp of three days was not lost after all. What a number of observations I made! What useful discoveries I therein laid up in the storehouse of my jumbled memory!'

In Mary Fortune's work, we have a different image of the woman writer from the more familiar one of the woman writing from the centre of the home, with her commitment to the domestic and private life as a source of judgement; and a different way of a woman constructing her sense of self through her writing. Where the woman diarist or letter writer is creating her own world inside a busy and perhaps confining domestic life, Mary Fortune, through her writing, is reaching out to the world around her, describing, reporting, making comments on the good sense or otherwise of this or that social arrangement.

The world which she observed was the chaotic world of colonial Victoria, a world of flux as people rushed from all parts of the globe to search for gold, in which social status, learning, skill meant little against the chance of a lucky find, and in which people lived makeshift lives, their close relationships strained often to breaking point. Later she wanders through the turbulent urban life of boom-time Melbourne. All this is presented from the woman's point of view, and she comments frequently on the vicissitudes of female respectability in the colonies. The women she encounters in her search for lodgings dramatise some of the possibilities: the landlady in stained black silk lying drunk in the gutter behind her Fitzroy house; the prim, suspicious old maid, the plainly dressed shopkeeper remembering the simple pleasures of her rural past; and her rude, foolish daughter bedecked with the frippery of a colonial girl.

Mary Fortune shares her street eye view of a chaotic public world with that quintessential representative of modernity, the detective as she shares some of his defining characteristics – his minimal private life, his sharp eye for human types and his simple faith in decent values to guide him through the moral uncertainties of a fragmented modern world, where people are not always as they seem. There xi

is much of this perspective in the examples of Mary Fortune's journalism collected here – she faces the disorder but her commitment to rectitude and respectability holds firm. It is not surprising that their author was attracted to the new genre of crime fiction.

There is, too, much of the stuff of detective fiction in Mary Fortune's own life – in her long anonymity behind the pseudonym of 'Waif Wander' and in the puzzles about her marriages which Lucy Sussex canvasses in her introduction. Briefly married to my great-grandfather, Mary Fortune's life had secrets, as did my great-grandfather's; something the descendants of his second marriage never suspected. Lucy Sussex's painstaking research has given my family a tantalising glimpse of its past; but far more importantly it has brought to the modern reader a new voice, a new writer to help us reach back to the experiences which shaped the society we live in today. The perspective this writer offers is excitingly modern – of the woman out in the street, making her way, lonely yes, but confident in the independence of her judgement and the strength of her pen.

Judith Brett.

WHAT THE MISCHIEF
DOES A BONNET WANT HERE?:
An Introduction to Mary Fortune (Waif Wander)

'I don't think I ever felt so small,' wrote Mary Fortune in 1870, '. . . as I did when I found myself stalking under that verandah (Melbourne's outdoor sharemarket), utterly unconscious of my whereabouts, until I found myself obliged to elbow my way amid a perfect crowd of gents, every one of whom seemed to be supplied with a pencil and a notebook, or something of the sort, and every one of whom looked at me fiercely, as though each should have said "What the mischief does a bonnet want here?" ('Under the Verandah', p. 599).

Little did these speculators and brokers know that the woman who had invaded their all-male domain was one of the most remarkable writers in nineteenth-century Australia. At the time of the encounter (which she duly wrote up and published) Mary Fortune had successfully occupied the largely masculine territory of Australian letters for five years, writing for the popular *Australian Journal* under the pseudonyms of Waif Wander and W. W. She was to publish in the magazine until 1910, contributing poetry, memoirs, novels, journalism and literally hundreds of short stories in the mystery genre. Some of her crime tales were collected in her only book, *The Detective's Album* (Melbourne, Clarson Massina, 1871) which was the first collection of such stories published in Australia. Yet, throughout her nearly fifty years of writing, Waif Wander was as anonymous to her readers as she was to the 'gents' under the verandah. It was known that Waif Wander/W. W. was a woman, and that was all.

It was conventional for nineteenth-century women writers to use pseudonyms, but few 'bonnets' wore such a deep veil of secrecy as did Mary Fortune. Only her editors and at least one friend knew her identity, and they concealed it during her lifetime. The enquiries of curious readers met with no response – Waif Wander, unlike Charlotte Brontë, never lifted her veil. She lived and died in complete obscurity, with not even an obituary in the *Australian Journal* to mark the end of her prolific career.

Identification was made only in the 1950s, by the book collector J. K. Moir. Realising that W.W. was a founding mother of crime writing (her stories are apparently the first short detective fiction by a woman) he decided to solve her mystery. After 'a great deal of hunting and luck' he obtained a letter to Minnie Furlong, the subject of several Waif Wander poems, which was signed M. H. Fortune. However, without the indexes to Australian records now available, he was unable to proceed further. It was only in 1987, the year that Waif Wander's stories began to reappear, in Fiona Giles' *From the Verandah* (Melbourne, McPhee Gribble/Penguin) and Elizabeth Webby and Lydia Wevers' *Happy Endings* (Sydney, Allen and Unwin) that, quite coincidentally, the name Mary Helena Fortune emerged from the shadows.

Who was this woman, who went walking down Collins Street in 1870, no doubt knitting up the plot of her latest crime story in her mind, only to find herself slap bang in the middle of a share mart? We would know little of her had she not, as in 'Under the Verandah', written about her experiences. That article, and some others from the period 1868–76, describe life in Roaring Melbourne from her inimitable viewpoint. Later, in 1882–3, she published the memoirs 'Twenty-Six Years Ago; Or, the Diggings from '55', which recount her first two years in Australia, spent on the Victorian goldfields. Besides the memoirs and journalism, there are numerous sly hints in the stories, showing that it was her game to write herself into her fiction. One example will suffice: the *Briseis*, the ship on which she and her son travelled to Australia, appears in her 1866 novel 'The Secrets of Balbrooke'.

Thus a paradox exists: an intensely private writer, avoiding any contact with her readers beyond the printed page, yet speaking directly to them about her life and opinions. The image that comes to mind is of a woman in purdah, shouting a speech from behind a brick wall. Nameless Waif Wander may have been, even faceless, but her personality is vividly expressed in her memoirs and journalism. To read these pieces now, more than a hundred years after their composition, is to meet with an individual.

She was born Mary Helena Wilson, probably in 1833, to George Wilson, a civil engineer, and his wife Eleanor (nee Atkinson). The couple were Scots-Irish Protestants, living in Belfast. If they had children besides Mary, they did not survive, and Eleanor Wilson appears not to have recovered from the birth. Waif Wander states, in the 1869 'How I spent Christmas' that she 'never knew either mother or sister or brother'.

Father and daughter emigrated to Canada, probably while Mary was very young, for though she describes Ireland as 'fair', it was Montreal, even after a decade in Australia, that was her 'home'. In 1851, while still in her teens, she married Joseph Fortune, twenty-two years of age, and to judge from his profession of surveyor, probably an associate of her father's. It has been suggested, by the Canadian academic Mary Lu MacDonald, that Fortune came from a French Catholic family. This point has not been verified yet, but their son Joseph George, born in 1852, was christened in a Protestant church.

At about this time, George Wilson set off to try his luck on the Victorian goldfields, and in 1855 Mary and the young Georgie joined him, travelling first to England, then to Australia. What happened to her husband is unclear, but for a young woman and child to travel thousands of miles alone suggests some upheaval, most likely the death of Joseph Fortune. In this case she would naturally return to her father's house, which had now become a tent.

Though George Wilson was an engineer, he was interested in literature, writing poetry to his little daughter. It was presumably his literary connections in the United Kingdom that gave Mary Fortune a commission to write about her destination, then of intense interest to the reading public. Possibly the *Ladies' Companion* hoped that Mary Fortune would be another Ellen Clacy, a young woman whose book *A Lady's Visit to the Gold-Diggings of Australia in 1852-3* had gone into several editions.

Mary and her child sailed from Glasgow in mid-1855, the ship depositing its cargo of salmon and whisky (not to mention a budding writer) in Melbourne that October. Straightaway she began taking notes, although the low rate of pay made writing them up hardly economic. However, she kept these notes throughout all her goldfields' wanderings, finally expanding them into 'Twenty-Six Years Ago', here reprinted for the first time since 1882-3.

These keen-eyed observations of early Victoria constitute a fascinating document, not only in themselves, but in what Waif Wander left out of them, in the interests of protecting her identity. Neither she nor her son were named, and George Wilson became James Grieve (not a reference to the eponymous species of apple, then not in existence), although she also calls him Uncle Barry. In addition the memoirs are partly fictionalised, a common Victorian genre, but in Mary Fortune's hands perhaps a device for further obfuscation.

Take the first instalment, 'Arrival in Melbourne'. The *Briseis* docked in Melbourne on 3 October 1855, and two days later Mary advertised for George Wilson in the 'Missing Friends, Messages, &c.' section of the *Argus*. This column was the usual place for friends and relatives to announce their arrival; but it also included advertisements for legatees, runaway spouses, non-paying clients of tradespeople, owners of rat-dogs, and the cryptic messages of secret lovers. The address she gave was not the Albion, but a cottage in Collingwood. Thus, either the Albion incident was fiction, or, as seems

more likely, after the 'wearisome' night there she took herself
and her child off to lodgings. She was, as the account of
the intruders makes clear, a 'nervous lady' – but not for
long.

Mary Fortune in fact advertised for her father three times,
the last time on 20 October. Communications with the
goldfields were difficult, and George Wilson was one of the
commonest names in Victoria – no less than eight men of
that name arrived in the colony in 1855 alone. It must have
been a worrying time for her, though no sign of this appears
in the memoirs. She went on expeditions around Melbourne
and attended the Free Presbyterian Church, noting perhaps
wistfully the theatrical entertainments, which she did not
sample.

The first instalment of the memoirs seems largely based
on her notes, but elements of fiction are present. She
introduces characters who will reappear in her narrative,
such as Mrs Blackett, who is later used to expand and explain
an arrest Mary Fortune witnessed in Taradale in early 1856.
The portrait was no doubt based on reality (Mary Fortune
admitted, in the 1871 'What Passed', that her fancy was
sparked by actual incidents), but presented as part of a
melodrama. Here the writer's hand is at work, working
experience into the tidy, all-threads tied form of the Victorian
novel.

The second instalment begins with Mary Fortune's first
observations of the goldfields. George Wilson, no longer an
engineer, was running a general store, something not
described in the memoirs but in her fiction:

Belette was a 'general storekeeper', and his shop was crowded
with articles of every variety, from a screw nail to a lady's
crinoline. The counter was untidily littered with a quantity
of drapery, tobacco, glasses, pewter pots, and bottles; and the
floor with gin cases, flour bags, bars of iron, and coils of rope,
not to mention many other things . . .

('Dora Carleton', 1866, p. 739)

Note the mention of gin cases. It was illegal to sell liquor
in unlicensed premises, but the practice was common, and
highly lucrative. As Mary Fortune noted in a 1905 story:
'Almost every tent was a shanty in those days, where

unlicensed drink was sold, for the few scattered troopers
did not trouble in hunting such delinquents' ('Queer Burke',
p. 686). In fact, one of the drinkers in Belette's store is a
policeman! The only hint of such activities in the memoirs
is the comment that their American cooking stove 'was
afterwards put to illegal use' – most likely, as part of a still.
If George Wilson was a sly-grogger, as seems probable, it
was no wonder his identity was concealed in an account
written for a nineteenth-century family journal.

Life in eastern Canada can hardly have prepared Mary
for the rough and tumble of goldfields life, but she
thoroughly enjoyed it: 'How often do I actually crave to
exchange our brick walls, and comfortably fitted-rooms, for
the old free life, and its canvas home!' ('Killed in the Shaft',
1871, p. 446). Her harshest condemnation in the memoirs
is reserved for those unable to adjust to the diggings, such
as the weepy Mrs Deasy. 'I never was happier in my life!'
Waif Wander tells her.

As new diggings were discovered and the old ones
exhausted, so George Wilson packed his tent and followed
his customers from rush to rush. After Kangaroo Flat,
'Grieve's store' moved to Buninyong, via Castlemaine, where
'M. H. F.' astounded the editor who had published her poems
by proving to be a woman! At about this time, she became
pregnant, giving birth to a son in late 1856. This child never
appears in the memoirs, although his birthplace (Ballarat
East) is the scene of the ruse to stop the drunk doctor
attending Mrs Mack's labour. This anecdote does not seem
to be Mary Fortune's experience disguised, for a Dr Curtayne
delivered her baby (and for his pains later appeared in her
1868 story 'The Fatal Penknife').

It was eight months before the child was registered,
perhaps with good reason, for the unnamed, unbaptised
baby was stated on the official form to be the son of Joseph
Fortune. Earlier it was surmised that Mary came to Australia
as a widow, something supported by Joseph's absence both
from the (unreliable) memoirs and from any Australian
records. Tentatively, it may be said that the child was
illegitimate – an explanation for Waif Wander's secrecy,
given the hypocritical morals of the time.

The memoirs end in Kingower in early 1857, the most

famous year in that remote goldfield's history, for the largest nugget then found, the 'Blanche Barkly', was unearthed there. Waif Wander was later to claim to have been a few feet away at the time (in the 1865 'Recollections of a Digger', p. 68). The following year little Georgie Fortune 'died of convulsions one hot summer day' ('Her Death Warrant', 1904, p. 102), probably from viral meningitis caused by the poor living conditions on the goldfields. Waif Wander was not to write of this tragedy for nearly fifty years.

Another event of 1858 was to recur in her fiction, intermittently, from the 1860s to the 1900s. In October Mary Fortune married Percy Brett, the young mounted constable in charge of the Kingower police station. The couple went to Dunolly to be married, although there was an Anglican minister at Kingower. Dunolly was then a 'gay Babel' of fun, full of amusements for a honeymooning pair, but there may have been darker reasons for the choice. The two witnesses were not from Kingower, but locals, including the Church of England schoolmaster, whose classes occupied the church during weekdays. Had the Bretts arrived in school hours, they would have been married during lessons, in the makeshift fashion of the diggings, where time and public buildings were scarce.

Mary and Percy Brett may have eloped, and certainly their marriage certificate is a peculiar document. The groom gave his age as twenty-four, one year younger than his wife; in fact he was twenty. Throughout his life Percy Brett was to be vague about his age, but nowhere else was he four years out. Mary declared that she was a widow, but did not give the date of death of her husband, nor listed her living and dead children, as was normally required for a remarriage. Her signature even differed from that which she had used earlier that year on George Fortune's death certificate.

The marriage was to be short-lived. Percy Brett left the police force in December 1858, possibly because of a fine by Inspector Samuel Stackpole Furnell (later to be Inspector S. S. F. and Samuel Stackpole Turnhill in Mary Fortune's writings). He moved to Urana, New South Wales, where in 1865 he eloped with the young Mary Leek. If the omissions in the marriage certificate of 1858 meant that Mary Fortune was not, as she claimed, a widow, then Brett was legally entitled to remarry. However, without Joseph Fortune's death date the question of bigamy (something not uncommon in colonial Australia) cannot be resolved. Brett's subsequent career included fathering eleven children, and becoming prominent in rural politics. He was also a bit-player in the story of the Kelly gang, and his former wife's fiction. There is no indication he and Mary Fortune ever met again, although in the 1890s his photo appeared in the *Town and Country Journal*, a magazine to which Waif Wander had contributed. One wonders if she saw it.

In 1865 she was still in the Kingower area, living in the quartz-mining town of Jericho (now Wehla). To the new *Australian Journal* she sent a poem under her old pen name of M. H. F. It was accepted, and she became a regular contributor to the magazine, adopting the self-descriptive pseudonym Waif Wander with her third submission. In 1866 alone she published three poems, fourteen short stories, three serialised novels, and the first instalment of a fourth. The reasons for this amazing spurt were probably both creative and financial. Her writing at this time was clearly aimed at a market, tending to be written in the ornately fashionable style, and about conventional subjects. 'I can't say that I ever felt any sympathy with the "bloated aristocrat"', Waif Wander wrote in 1876 ('My Friends and Acquaintances', p. 197), yet they litter the pages of these early works.

She had moved to Oxley, a wheat-growing area in what was later to be Kelly country. As with much else in her life, it is unknown what she was doing there, apart from cooking five meals a day for the threshers at Christmas ('Our Colonial Christmases', 1872, p. 256). However, her trip from Oxley to Melbourne in late 1868 was to result in 'Fourteen Days on the Roads', her first journalism. The young Marcus Clarke had set a precedent for reportage with much gusto and few furbelows. He was clearly the inspiration for her articles, most of which are collected here for the first time.

However, whereas Clarke used this form for colonial commentary, with Waif Wander it was a medium for self-revelation, within limits. She could not or would not write anything which would reveal her identity (although it was the clue that her son had never seen a ship, in 'How I Spent Christmas', that was vital to the Fortune-hunt), and her gender meant that certain topics were out of bounds. The 'Under the Verandah' column, by 'Atticus' was full of stockmarket gossip – her own, perhaps parodic piece of the same name dealt with an eccentric old woman. Nor could she say outright, as did male journalists, that the bedizened women in Bourke Street were prostitutes, for respectable women had to pretend innocence on such matters.

But what an individual, lively, opinionated, indeed modern voice is here revealed! She declared herself to be no refined lady, but an 'honest, downright, straightforward' woman, railed against the constricting female fashions, and even protested the ideal of a 'dependent and helpless feminity' (all quotes from 'Towzer & Co.'). A greater departure from the image of the Angel on the Hearth, those demure, doe-eyed, and silent women beloved of the Victorian orthodoxy, could hardly be imagined. It is not too great a claim that she likely influenced Louisa Lawson, an *Australian Journal* reader, who was later to voice similar sentiments in *The Dawn*, the first feminist paper in Australia.

The most personal of her journalism is 'How I Spent Christmas', a record for her readers of what she did on Christmas Day, 1868. The immense feasts of the colonial family, the food a replica of that at 'Home' in England, despite the Australian climate, were not for her – she wandered around Melbourne with her twelve-year-old son, melancholy, but determined to make the best of the day. In Sydney, as Veronica Kelly has discovered, a pantomime she had co-written, *Harlequin Little Bo Peep*, was playing. Perhaps this is the reason for the mention of pantomime posters in Melbourne, for she was unable to attend the performance. Her name was given in the Sydney advertisements as Waif Wander Esq., although the readers of her journalism would have known that the pseudonym concealed a woman.

From 'How I Spent Christmas' we know that she was supporting herself by her writing, and was proud of this fact; her tea tasted all the better for being bought with her own earnings. That this independence was due to her having no man to support her is clear. The mention of 'kinless' indicates that George Wilson had died, although his common name makes it difficult to establish exactly when. At the same time the low rate of pay for colonial writing meant that she must have needed extra income to survive. In 'My Lodger', an 1870 sequel to 'Looking for Lodgings', she claims to have taken in boarders, as did Louisa Lawson. 'The Spider and the Fly' may describe an actual job interview.

Self-reliant she was, but lonely. The Melbourne literati met socially at the famous Yorick club, but it was for men only. Marcus Clarke, Yorick co-founder, may have been her editor during his stint at the *Australian Journal*, but there is no evidence she was part of his free-wheeling fraternity. 'I do not owe a single "thank you" to one of my kind friends ... for an offer of treat or hospitality; nay, for even an expressed kindly wish during these festive times' she writes with some bitterness in 'How I Spent Christmas'. But in the next sentence she seems resigned to the isolation. 'God bless ye all, my dear friends, and grant me continued independence!'

Three of her articles, 'Fourteen Days', 'How I Spent Christmas' and 'Down Bourke Street' seem completely factual; the rest blend truth and fiction in a manner anticipating both her memoirs and the New Journalism. A case in point is 'The Spider and the Fly' in which what looks very much like an actual experience is structured so that it can be read either as a story or as a piece of investigative journalism. In the narrative, as Fiona Giles has already noted (*From the Verandah*, p. 5), she addresses an issue with which she was personally concerned: that of paid work for women, with a full awareness of the webs the Victorian society set for independent flies.

However, her accounts of such unmasculine pursuits as shopping at the Eastern Market and skirmishing with prospective landladies were to be short-lived. She concentrated on her less idiosyncratic crime writing, with only flashes of her personality visible between the lines, as when Sinclair, the male persona of her detective tales, describes his writing methods:

First I folded my margin down, and then I selected a pen,

and dipping it in the ink, wrote manfully, "The Detective's Album, by W. W.," and having done so much, I laid down my pen and lay back in my chair to admire the well-known heading

(From an untitled story in the *Australian Journal*, June 1878, p. 516)

The 'manfully' is obviously ironic.

From the 1870s to 1909, she wrote crime stories almost exclusively, one in nearly every issue of the *Australian Journal*. Her last novel, 'The Bushranger's Autobiography', featuring a hero with the appearance and early history of Percy Brett, appeared in the *Australian Journal* during 1871–2. Also in 1871 her one book, *The Detective's Album*, was published. Not a copy of this work seems to have survived.

The isolation, it appears, took its toll: in the last of her journalism, the 1876 'My Friends and Acquaintances' she described herself thus: 'I am what my friends – ahem – ! two-legged acquaintances (the article is, like 'Towzer', about dogs) call a "very eccentric person", and a "*rather* peculiar creature,"' (p. 197).

Old employees of the *Australian Journal* told J. K. Moir that Waif Wander was an alcoholic. Her letter to Minnie Furlong (c. 1909) reveals that she was losing her eyesight, and thus her small income, for she could not see to write. She was already impoverished, wearing cast-off clothes from Minnie and her husband, William Romuald Furlong, the composer. Her son was of no support to her, being mortally ill and preoccupied with thoughts of the 'hereafter'. Finally she asked the *Australian Journal* for an annuity, and thus her much-prized independence came to an end.

When this not-so-fortunate existence ended is unclear, and with it her works, some of them vividly expressing the woman, were forgotten. Several factors prevented their rediscovery until now: the pseudonym; the fact that most of the Fortune bibliography is crime fiction, until recently hardly thought of as 'literature'; the uneven quality of her work, caused by writing for a living; and the *Australian Journal*'s thorough overshadowing by the *Bulletin*.

Her crime writing needs an anthology of its own; in the meantime here is a volume of her more personal reflections, as much a record of an extraordinary woman as it is of extraordinary times in Australian history. It is to be hoped that with this book Mary Fortune will receive the recognition denied her in life, the recognition she craved, and deserved.

Time has not spared us a visual record of this writer, but by a curious accident one of her recipes has survived, published in the *Australian Journal* of 9 December 1865:

To one pound of buckwheat flour, add a little salt, and half a teaspoonful of carbonate of soda; mix thoroughly together, and make it into as thick a batter as can be stirred with some milk or buttermilk. Butter a shallow tin (it will not rise so well in a deep one), and bake in a quick oven. This preparation, only made thinner, and poured in spoonfuls on a hot plate – the top of a stove, for instance – forms the well-known 'Flap Jacks' of American cooking. For [Far?] more delicate ladies prepare it with eggs and cream or milk, and bake in the same way. Buckwheat is not good baked in any way from a thin dough.

(p. 239)

Enjoy – both eating and reading!

Lucy Sussex.

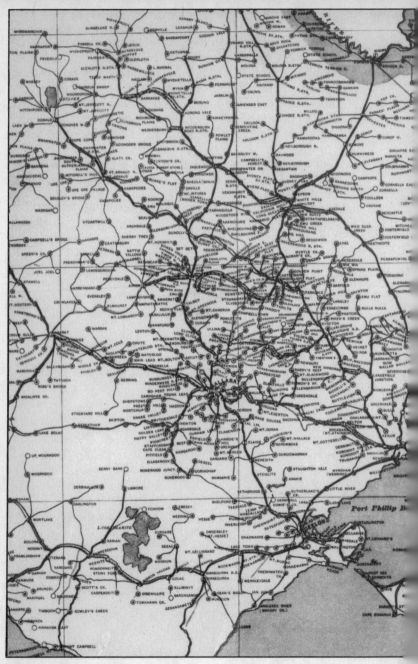

Detail of Railway, Postal & Telegraph Map of Victoria, 1887

PART ONE
THE MEMOIRS

Twenty-six Years Ago or The Diggings
from '55

ARRIVAL IN MELBOURNE

Twenty-six years is a long time to look back upon, and when those years have been passed in a series of frequent change of place and of circumstances and of people the time appears longer still. To me, indeed, standing here in the Bourke Street of today, and recalling my arrival in the colony, and the most different appearance of Melbourne in 1855, the past seems more like a bewildered dream than anything else; indeed, for my earlier impressions I might have been afraid to trust my memory in detail had it not been for notes made at the time, which I have fortunately retained, and which will greatly stimulate my recollection of my earliest colonial days.

I was not old at that distant date, and I had engaged myself to supply some papers, anent[1] the, then strange to England, Gold Land, for a London ladies' magazine called, I think, the *Ladies' Companion*. The notes I allude to were made with a view of fulfilling that engagement, but I need hardly say it never was fulfilled. Who would write pages at fifteen shillings when one paid nine shillings per day

3

for milk, and for a 'woman's' magazine, too! Nay, there was nothing of the namby-pamby elegance of ladies' literature in our stirring, hardy, and eventful life on the early goldfields.

It was toward the latter end of 1855 that I landed in Sandridge[2], and came up to Melbourne per train.[3] I distinctly recollect how inferior and dirty the railway carriages and the wooden stations seemed to me, after coming from lands where art and science appeared to have perfected themselves in the production of such conveniences; and I more than distinctly remember the almost impassable condition of Elizabeth Street, and the team of bullocks that hopelessly tried to drag a laden dray out of the clinging mud in the centre of the street (if street it could be called, when only scattered houses, and a here and there visible kerbstone, outlined a mass of glutinous clay), that was not, doubtless, at its best when I first saw it, as there had been a continuous downpour of rain on the previous night. I remember, too, the vacant allotments, half covered with empty bottles and valueless débris, where now stand the palatial buildings we read about and see, which are valued at hundreds of pounds per foot; and I also remember my first view of the Bourke Street of '55.

Up the hill to the east and up the hill westward it was a vista of nondescript and many sized tenements – shops of brick, shops of wood, and shops of iron, with nearly every one of the humbler sort shaded with awnings of calico or striped canvas, while flags of all colours floated from their poles or hung limply against them as the breeze served. It was a strange scene to me, but I had little opportunity then of studying it, for we had reached our hotel, and, in a perfect bewilderment, I was conscious that the landlord was looking at me doubtfully, yet sympathisingly, as he told me he could put me 'with the girls', as it would hardly be safe for me to occupy a room alone, if I was the least nervous. I wondered much, you may be certain, but gratefully accepted the good man's offer, and discovered before morning why it would not do to be nervous in the Albion Hotel[4] at night in 1855.

For it was in the Albion I spent my first night in Australia, and to this day there is but little difference in the outward appearance of that well-known hostelry, except, indeed, that time has, instead of giving it an evidence of years, rather beautified it with many additions of paint, and varnish, and plate glass, and filled up the vacant allotments around it with commercial establishments that may vie with those of many centuries-old cities. It was from the door of the Albion I started on my first coach journey to the diggings, and from the door of the Albion today start still 'Cobb and Co.'s coaches' to many a country or seaside resort, whose inhabitants, for the most part, know nothing of the Bourke Street of '55.

But to return to my arrival at the Albion, and my induction to the 'girls' room' in which I was to pass the night. It was yet early in the afternoon when I arrived, and it was the 'housekeeper' who took me upstairs to the sleeping apartment, which, it appeared, she shared with the barmaid, whose acquaintance I made later on. They were both Irish girls, and, in the case of the housekeeper, I may add that she was a decidedly superior and lady-like girl of twenty-three or four, with a most attractive face and figure, and kindly manners, that so won upon the heart of my nervous little first-born, that he permitted 'Miss Mac' to carry him downstairs to the bar, from whence he returned in good time, laden with lollies and tarts and 'tips', of various value, from, no doubt, admirers of kind and pretty Miss Mac. Meanwhile, as I enjoyed a cup of tea without the ship flavour, I took stock of the girls' room, with a great wonder at the incongruity of its few articles of furnishing and attire.

Today I should see nothing odd in the articles that then excited my astonishment, but, with my old-country ideas and prejudices unchanged by contact and familiarity with a state of affairs with which I was wholly unfamiliar, I stared to see black satin and black velvet dresses hanging on rusty nails against a rough, whitewashed wall, and a handsome cheval glass nearly reaching the low roof, and standing on an uncovered, and not over-cleanly, deal floor. The bedstead was of ordinary iron, uncurtained or unvalanced; there was a common wash-stand, with common ware, and an old chest of drawers behind the door, and also behind the door a single stretcher, which was to be mine during the, to me, unhappy night that was approaching. I have now enumerated every article in the 'girls' room', with one exception, to which, as it is of a delicate nature, I must devote another paragraph.

On the top of the drawers lay a gentleman's black hat of the genus – colonially yclept[5] – bell topper. There was nothing particular about the hat save that it occupied a place in the girls' room; but the fact of its being there urged me to the not unnatural conclusion that the said room must, during stress of business perhaps, have been occasionally vacated by the girls, especially as, during my arrangement of my intended couch, I discovered a common blue striped shirt folded under the pillow. Never connecting the wearer of the bell topper with the owner of the striped shirt, I concluded that the former had been honoured with the occupancy of the double iron bedstead, while the latter had to content himself with my stretcher as a place of rest. It remained for later experience to convince me that it was quite possible for a Victorian gentleman to don a cotton shirt – ay, and to work in it, as heartily as a genuine son of toil.

I had finished my tea and arrangements when Miss Mac returned, carrying my jubilant heir and his spoil. She was laughing all over her handsome face, and spoke as pleasantly as if she had known me for years.

'Come on, Mrs — ,' she said, 'there is a sight for a new chum just in front of the door! Come on, you can see from the drawing-room, and there isn't a soul to see you – hurry, or you'll miss the fun!'

Of course I obeyed, being only too ready to see some of the Victorian fun, and soon found myself witnessing, from one of the front windows, a scene which was, although common enough at that and earlier days in Melbourne, almost disgustingly ludicrous to my unaccustomed eye. Let me see if I can describe it.

In an open carriage of gorgeous colours, and drawn by a pair of good carriage horses, were seated, or standing, four persons, two females and two men. I am one of the most courteous of writers, as you old readers of the *Australian Journal* are well aware, but courtesy would be strained to the very rubicon of falsehood did I term anyone of the quartette in that carriage lady or gentleman. The women were red-faced, fat, and evidently vulgar; while the men

were epitomes of the very essence of purse-proud
clodhoppers, who had never known what it was to own
one pound until a lucky find on the goldfields enriched
them to their own ruin.

The women were both dressed in white of the richest
material, and both had apparently vied with each other in
donning the showiest and most expensive attire. One dress
was of white satin, trimmed with blonde and clusters of
flowers and ribbons; the other was of white watered silk.
The coarse, red shoulders of one woman were partially
shaded by a handsome lace shawl, which was fastened by
a huge colonial gold brooch, and festooned with a
ridiculously heavy gold chain; the other had draped around
her an expensive China crape scarf that was embroidered
showily in red and blue silk. The head-dresses of these
gorgeous dames consisted of white bonnets wreathed with
long white ostrich plumes, and each fat, rubicund face was
surrounded with a small forest of orange blossoms.

In contrast with their partners, the men's costumes were
the essence of simplicity; white duck trousers, with a scarlet
sash of silk at the waist, embroidered linen shirts and Panama
hats with blue veils, composed the full suit. Certainly there
were great rings on the gloveless hands, and heavy chains
around the thick throats, but no more; yet in every word
and movement could be traced the insolent pride of
Vulgarity who carries a roll of notes in his pocket, or, it
may be, in his fist.

It was certainly in his fist in one of the instances I am
describing, for one of the men as I first saw him, was standing
up in the vehicle and trying to steady himself with one
hand, while he waved a sheaf of notes toward the door
of the Albion in the other. He was gesticulating violently,
and evidently talking, though the words did not reach to
our altitude, while the women were shrieking with laughter,
and waving their laced handkerchiefs in a pretence to hide
their scarlet faces.

'What is the matter with the man?' I asked of Miss Mac,
'and what are those ridiculous-looking women exposing
themselves in public in that manner for?'

'What does he want?' the young lady repeated as well
as she could for laughter at my astonishment. 'Why, that's

a wedding party, and those elegant ladies are brides who have just been married.'

'Good gracious!' I exclaimed.

'Yes, and the men are two lucky diggers, just down from Fiery Creek[6] who never saw the women until yesterday. See, there is what the man wants.'

As she spoke a waiter hurried out and crossed the pavement with a tray in his hand, which tray he most obsequiously held at the door of the carriage until the tipsy bridegroom had managed to dispense the glasses of liquor it contained among his companions; that in doing so he should spill a considerable portion over the white satins and silks was not to be wondered at, and indeed occasioned nothing but reiterated shrieks of merriment from the wearers. The liquor disposed of, the glasses were returned, with some breakages, to the waiter; a handful of notes was flung in his face by the 'shoutee' as he fell back to his seat beside his bride, and the carriage was driven off amid the cheers of the small crowd that any scene will always collect in any street.

'The man is mad, assuredly,' was my comment as they disappeared.

'The sudden possession of gold has that effect very frequently,' said Miss Mac, 'but in this instance I should say his madness is the simple outcome of conceit and drink. I daresay he would be mean and miserable enough if he was poor and sober,' and I have no doubt that less truthful observations have been made than that one of pretty Miss Mac's.

Night came at last, and a wearisome night it was to me. The girls' room was situated at the back, and, as I afterwards discovered, over the kitchen. It had only one window, and that faced an adjutting portion of the hotel, or rather addition to it, in which, as the night deepened, a blaring band began to play, and the tramp of awful dancers' feet ushered in my first midnight in Melbourne. Tramp, tramp, tramp – thump, thump, thump – blare, blare, blare – laughter from various parts of the house, hoarse shoutings from goodness knows where, and the awful added noise of the Terpischoreans opposite, and so near to me, it was dreadful! Talk of the wild, dark, treacherous seas over which we had so lately crossed! Better the noise of a hundred storms than this of Bourke Street, in Melbourne.

To some such conclusion had I come when the band ceased, and other noises, suggestive of a break-up, came to my wearied ears. The doors were banged, and there was a scuffling somewhere on the stairs approaching my refuge, while I could hear a woman's laughter stifled, and a pleading voice, which I recognised as that of my friend, Miss Mac. Gradually those noises neared me until they were at the landing outside, and the bumps of struggling bodies were distinctly audible on the door itself. When I discovered, from the incisive assertions of some male voice, that I, myself, was the object of all this to-do, I was horrified, and felt so perfectly helpless that, had it not been for the rapid denouement, I believe I should have been new chum enough to faint. As it was, I covered my head up, and drew myself up as well behind the chest of drawers as I could, and listened, shivering.

'Oh, it's no use, Mary; I'm not to be put off. I'm determined on it, so you may as well give in. Let go, for see her I will!'

'Don't I tell you the poor lady is asleep,' Miss Mac cried, 'and the poor child, too. After such a long voyage, and their first night ashore, surely you would never be so cruel as to disturb them. Now, go to bed, Jack, like a good fellow!'

'Good fellow, be blowed!' was uttered in another voice. 'See this new arrival I will. I want to see what a woman looks like that hasn't been kiln-dried in this blessed climate. Stand out of the way, Jack!' and the door was dashed open with a burst. I could not, of course, see the crowd of faces that I knew were within a few feet of me, nor do I to this day know what occasioned the sudden lull and quiet departure of the boarders, unless it was the sight of my sleeping child's face. All I knew was that footsteps receded higher up the stairs; that the door was locked, and that, when I ventured to uncover my head, I was alone with the two 'girls'.

'Were you frightened?' asked the stranger, who was sitting on the edge of the double bed and dragging out many hairpins from an abundance of fiery red hair, that took the opportunity of tumbling down over her shoulders as she dragged. 'Arrah, they're quare divils; but there's no harm in 'em after all. Oh, lord, ain't I tired, Mary! Sure, I lades the life of a horse; an' if the master don't stop more in the bar I'll not stop in it neither.'

'Well, you'd better get to sleep now, at all events,' said Mary, 'for it's late, and you know the time you'll be routed out in the morning.'

'Late is it, you say? Faith, it's early, it is. I'll go bail that it's afther two. Divil sich a life any girl ever led before. Faith, I'm too sleepy to say me prayers. Goodnight, Mary!' and that was the last of the barmaid until the sun was brightening the clear sky of the following morning; then I was awakened by a sharp knocking at the door near my head.

'All right,' replied Miss Mac, and I opened my eyes to see that the housekeeper was already dressed most becomingly, yet simply, in black silk, with natty white laces at throat and wrist; and that she turned from the door to call the still sleeping barmaid.

'Mary, Mary, get up, do, the master's been calling you twice!'

'Let him call till he's tired!' returned the independent Mary, as she turned over lazily, 'divil a one fut I'll stir till I get me cup o' tay!'

Miss Mac threw up the window and bent her neat figure over the sill as she called to someone below:

'Cook, cook! send up Mary's cup of tea, quick – be sharp now!' and in due time the beverage appeared, and was handed to lazy Mary in bed by the obliging Miss Mac. Just at that moment when the barmaid was sitting up in bed, holding her tea in one hand, and trying to disengage her face from her dishevelled hair with the other, another furious knocking was made at the door by the impatient knuckles of the landlord.

'Is that girl coming down today, Miss Mac? The bar's full. Call her, I say! Mary, come down instantly!'

'Hum!' murmured Mary, the unimpressionable, as she coolly sipped her non-intoxicant beverage, 'tay's the finest thing out of a morning. I wouldn't call the Queen me cousin when I gets me cup o' tay of a morning. Arrah lave the dure alone, man; sure I'm comin' down,' and that was how the barmaid treated the landlord in '55.

Business on the same morning took me to the *Argus* office,

then on the same site it now occupies in Collins Street. In the first place, I had to insert a notice of my arrival in the *Argus* for the information of the relative I was about to join on the diggings; and, in the second, I had a letter of introduction from a Scotch literary gentleman to another gentleman named Semple, whose address was '*Argus* office', in those days. James Semple has years ago joined the ranks of the great army of the dead, and as he was solus here, as far as I know, it will do no harm for me to slightly allude to the strange career of a clever, but erratic character, whom some of my readers may perchance remember. He was, but a couple of years previous to my arrival in Melbourne, the ordained minister of a Scotch church in the ancient town of Peebles, but the pulpit was the last place a handsome young man who valued his position only as it afforded him facilities for pleasure, more especially in the shape of young ladies' society, should have occupied. Poor Semple was accused of other and more unbecoming vices too, and he lost his gown in consequence of them, leaving Scotland engaged to *two* women, with both of whom I was personally acquainted. Semple, was at the time I write of, sub-editor, I think, to the *Argus*, and correspondent to the *Sydney Morning Herald*. I understood that he was occupied on the *Mount Alexander Mail* at the time of his death, some years after.

All this, however, *par parenthèse*. Mr Semple was very genial and attentive to me during my short stay in town, and, when I left it, I never saw him more. I remember of Collins Street being then only some small cottages situated higher up than the *Argus* office, where now stand some handsome buildings, and I remember them because the verandah of one was literally covered with the creeping sarsaparilla in full purple bloom, that seemed lovely to me; and I recollect Dr Howitt's[7] corner, because near the garden fence was growing a young oak tree, which, I was told, was the only one in the colony. That must have been a mistake, however, as I know of an old oak now to which thirty years are accredited and vouched for by residents.

My visit to Fitzroy was made in a vehicle that was, I think, called a 'bus, but was neither, in size or comfort, anything to compare with our 'buses of today. I met in it, however, a character that I was to again see, under awful

circumstances, during one of the sad diggings tragedies it
has been my fate to witness, and which I shall record in
these papers, though it little entered either my mind or
that of the unhappy man himself to guess at the dark future
that awaited him. He was a sunburned, jolly-looking man,
of evidently the working class, and his great tangled beard
and long sun-dried hair told of a carelessness belonging
to the digger of the day. He was roughly dressed in a good
suit of slops, and his honest face was actually glowing with
happiness and honest pride. There were two or three women
in the conveyance as well as myself, and one of them, also
as well as myself, was in charge of a little boy, whose
wondering and inquiring eyes were fixed on the voluble
digger.

'Yes, ma'am, I'm not ashamed to say it; there's not a
happier man in the colony this day than Jack Dawson. That's
my name, ma'am, and I'm a mason by trade. I've just come
down from Fiery Creek with a belt full of gold. Thank God,
there'll be no sad faces in our home any more! I've plenty,
and to spare. See here!' and he drew a handful of sovereigns
from his pocket, shoving one each into the children's hands.
'Nay, missis, let the lad take it; I've got one o' my own
about his age, and it will be the sweetest music I ever heard
to hear him shout "Daddy!" when he sees me. I've been
six months away, and my lass doesn't expect me home today.
How surprised and glad she will be! my kind Nell! Look,
that's my cottage; but the door is shut – she must be out.'

As he spoke he was pointing toward a little wooden
tenement in Smith Street, Fitzroy, just as the vehicle was
stopping, and where we alighted. Not near, however, the
Smith Street of today, but amid a rutted track of stiff clay,
with an odd shop or so here and there. I think the Bricklayers'
Arms Hotel was there then, but I am not positive; but it
was but at a little distance that the digger stood knocking
impatiently at the inhospitable doorway. I had to pass it
on my way, and could not help witnessing the great agony
of a betrayed husband.

A woman, summoned by Dawson's repeated knocks, came
out of another cottage. When she recognised him, I saw
her draw back hurriedly, but she was too late, for the man
had seen her.

'Hallo, Mrs Bannon!' he cried, 'where's my wife? Where has Nell got to today, of all the days in the year?'

'Didn't you know, Jack?' the woman asked, with apparent hesitation. 'Nell has left this neighbourhood for some time.'

'What!' Oh! there was such an awful look of pain and fear in the poor man's face. 'I haven't got a letter from her for over two months, but, for God Almighty's sake, don't tell me that my Nell is dead?'

'I wish I could, Jack. Don't look like that, man, but come inside and I'll tell you all I know. Poor man, you were a good husband to her, but she didn't deserve you.'

'The child, my little lad Jack?' he asked, in a hoarse, low voice.

'She took him with her, Jack. Oh, don't take on, my poor fellow; believe me she was not worth it. Come inside.'

'Was it Bill Marsden?' he asked, as he laid his hand on the woman's shoulder and looked into her face strangely.

'It was, Jack. Come inside,' and she drew him into the cottage, and the door was shut between me and the stricken digger.

All this being entirely preliminary to the real subject of my future papers, viz., 'The Diggings from '55', I may pass over for the present my strange experiences during nearly three weeks of Melbourne life on my first arrival. I carried up to the diggings a few prominent memories of the city at that day, and it is strange to note with what pertinacity first and new impressions will cling to the brain upon which they have been photographed. I was two or three times in Chalmers' Church[8], then standing almost alone in the green, tree-dotted bush land where is now Fitzroy Gardens. On one of the occasions I was one of a wedding party, at which Dr Cairns[9] was the officiating minister, and on another I heard a clergyman preach a sermon, of which I can recall nothing, save his declaration that nothing had ever given him so great a realising idea of Heaven as the Crystal Palace in London. I remember seeing the walls and hoardings plastered over with delineations of a huge white spider's web, with a huge spider squatting in the middle of it on a black background, and an intimation that Coppin[10] was nightly in the habit of performing *his* spider dance – I presume in parody of the notorious Lola Montez, who was most likely then in the colony. And, speaking of theatrical affairs, I think that there was in those days a large canvas erection, called the Salle de Valentino[11] on Eastern Hill, somewhere about the place on which now stand our ugly Houses of Parliament, but what kind of entertainment it afforded the public I know not.

One other spot of lovely grass land was familiar to me in those old Melbourne days, and it is the Emerald Hill of today. We used to go from town in some kind of conveyance that, after passing the ruins and débris of old 'Canvas Town'[12], on the St Kilda Road, dropped us on a little way for our walk across the beautiful grassy slopes to the nucleus of Church Street, on the Hill. It was during one of those walks that I first saw the terrible bull-dog ants fighting an international war in groups of three and four around the entrances to their subterraneous dwellings. Ugh! what a horror-inspiring thing is a bull-dog ant. Of all colonial poisonous insects, and they are legion, I dread most the bull-dog ant for its ferocity, and the centipede for its loathsomely disgusting appearance.

At last I and my belongings started for the diggings in a coach, with four horses, belonging to the world-known firm of Messrs Cobb and Co. It was early in the morning of what proved a beautiful day, though our experience of travelling in '55 did not include any time to bestow on the beauties of Nature in any shape or form. I think it must have been six o'clock, or thereabouts, when the plunging horses darted away from the Albion Hotel, and tore up the western hill as if they had no Jehu[13] behind them, but they had, and as cool an American descendant of the son of Nimshi as ever fingered the ribbons and whip on a bush track. The broad-leaved, high-crowned hat, the olive-hued, clean-shaved cheeks, the pointed chin with its not too luxuriant goatee, and the slim muscular figure, were sufficient to denote the nationality of the man, even without his keen eye and reticent manner, or the significant drawl of the short replies he condescended to anxious or curious travellers.

Inside the coach we were four – five, indeed, with my youngster. There was another woman to keep me in countenance, and two men. The lady was about thirty-five, and seemed none of the most agreeably tempered women, and her whole anxiety during the journey was to prevent the dangerous jolting of a pretty little canary in a cage, who seemed the only living thing not incommoded by the terrible roughness of the primitive road we were rattled over. He, poor little chap, twittered and chirped at every jolt, and seemed to quite enjoy the rude swinging of his cage, which was suspended from the roof of the coach.

It took us all day to get over the seventy or eighty miles between Melbourne and Castlemaine, and, no matter how unsociable a woman may be, or how selfishly disposed, it would be almost impossible for two of the sex to sit opposite each other a whole day without some attempt at conversation being made; so, in the course of wearisome hours, my *vis-à-vis* and I began to discover a little about the private affairs of each other. She told me that her name was Mrs Blackett, and that her husband kept a hotel near Taradale, and on the side of the main track. She had been in Melbourne to visit a sister, she said, and the sister had presented her with the pretty canary.

The woman impressed me unfavourably in every way, and future events confirmed the justice of my impression. She had a restless eye, and a dark look, while an air of suspicion induced an almost perpetual frown. She left us at a roadside public, which I was fated again to re-visit, and where I was again to meet Mrs Blackett.

'Bedad, I'm glad the bird's gone!' exclaimed one of my jolly male fellow travellers, 'sure, I wouldn't say a word agin a lady, an' me bein' an Irishman, but that I may never if I ain't glad the bird's gone.'

'And I'm glad the woman's gone,' the other man said, with the air of a man that had the courage of his opinions. 'The sight of her scowling phiz has made me miserable all day.'

'Oych! sure it's the joults that's made me miserable,' the Irishman retorted. 'I'm a mass ov bruises, an' me head has fourteen or fifteen extra bumps on it since this mornin'. How are ye an' the little boy shtanding it all, ma'am?' – this to me – 'an' it's wonderin' I've been all the road if it's going to the diggings by yerself ye are?'

I assured him I was, and very much to my own

discomfiture, as I had hoped my relative would meet me in Melbourne.

'Is it Castlemaine or Forest Creek[14] ye're bound for?' he questioned again, with so kindly an air of interest that I foresaw help, and replied:

'No; I suppose I must change conveyances at Castlemaine, for I'm going to Kangaroo Flat.'[15]

'Whew!' was the whistled response, 'why, ma'am, dear, we won't get to Castlemaine till sundown, and there's no conveyance from Castlemaine to the Flat.[16] You'll have to stop at Castlemaine all night.'

'Oh, I couldn't!' for I remembered my experience at the Albion, 'I should be afraid, and it's only a short distance to Kangaroo Flat. Surely I'll manage somehow.'

'It's seven miles to the Flat, ma'am, and if it hadn't been for one thing you wouldn't have the ghost of a chance to get there this night' he said promptly, 'but it's lucky we talked about it, for I'll take you there myself.'

'You? Are you going there? I'm so glad!'

'Well, to tell you the truth,' explained the honest Irishman, as he scratched his brown, wavy hair, 'I did not mean to go home tonight, though I have me spring cart an' horse waitin' for me at the Hotel des Strangers; but, seeing as how you an' the child are situated, I'll drive you to the Flat.'

'Oh, thank you! But I am afraid, if I take advantage of your kindness, I shall be putting you to some inconvenience,' I said. 'You told me just now that it was not your intention to leave Castlemaine tonight.'

'An' I tould you the truth, ma'am, for I didn't; but – oh, I have it!' He suddenly interrupted himself with, 'I'll make her go down to the ball!' And the other passenger emitted a guffaw of laughter at the evident confusion of the good-natured digger.

'Well, what harm's in it, afther all, ma'am?' he explained, sheepishly. 'My little girl is here, in the hotel we stop at; an' I meant to stay there and have a look at her pretty face. Well, I'll enjoy her company, and take you to the Flat, too, ma'am, for I'll coax her to go to the ball.'

'Where is there to be a ball?'

'The grandest out an' outer is to come off at the Flat

tonight; and Polly – she's so fond of dancin', the darling. An', indeed, you needn't be afraid to trust yourself an' the little boy to me, ma'am, for Tom Slattery is as well known on the Flat as Fritz, the bellman.[17] May I ask who you are going to there, missis?'

'James Grieve, storekeeper,' I replied, 'he is my uncle, and he wrote to me to say that anyone would show me Grieve's Store.'

'Thunder an' 'ounds, are you the old gentleman's niece? Give us your hand, ma'am, an' welcome to the diggings. Why, the old man an' I are the best of friends, an' it'll go hard with me but I'll be a friend to his niece, too.'

Poor Tom Slattery, he kept his word, for he was a kind and true friend to me and mine for the rest of his too short life.

The memory of that terrible journey is as the memory of a nightmare to me. The crashing of the breaking branches under our wheels, as our cool Jehu drove his four-in-hand through the tangled mazes of the Black Forest, and the dangerous vicinity of the white gum trees, from whose tall trunks hung long strips of dead bark they were shedding as the snake sheds his skin. Great stretches of level country, without a growing stem, save those of the yet green grass blades, and without a dividing line or boundary save the running creek or the rifted gully. Flocks of sheep there were, with strangely dirty and dingy fleeces, and ranges of blue hazy hills in the distance, and, as for the rest, it is to me a blank, save one scene of plunging horses and broken traces on a bush track, where our Jehu seemed to thread the mazes of dead and living timber like a phantom driver with a team of phantom horses under his spirit power. One other memory I have of that journey to the diggings, and it is the memory of a pretty scene, though I had nearly forgotten it. Along the edge of a wooded slope, and among the beautiful green undergrowth, where one of the many tracks ran, we saw a conveyance, of strange and strong build, being driven with a velocity that seemed dangerous to us new chums, and behind and before it rode a mounted escort of red-coated soldiers. The rattle of its wheels as it passed us, the sharp crack of the driver's whip, the cheery salute as the clatter of hoofs and the cloud of dust they raised overtook us and disappeared, was like a vision or a dream. We had met the famous gold escort from Castlemaine.

The Castlemaine of that day was not much of a place as I recall it – a town of one street, with a few tolerable buildings, and a few odds and ends of various business places and private houses, but I saw little of it on that occasion. We stopped, when the sun was low, at a two-storied hotel, the very name of which I have forgotten,[18] and I was taken upstairs to a large barn-like room, where were several other women and children who had arrived, or were about departing, by other conveyances or coaches. They had mostly a bewildered, half-lost expression in their anxious faces, which, I daresay, I shared with them, for a woman, especially with little ones in charge, can scarcely be expected to feel safe or comfortable in a strange land, and among a class of people she has been told were as rough and knobby as the stones from among which they were rooting out their gold.

A waiter shortly made his appearance for 'orders', and told me privately that Mr Slattery had ordered tea for me, that Miss O'Connor would bring me herself. Now, that was so thoughtful of my fellow traveller that I felt doubly thankful that I had fallen in with him on my unprotected journey. Being so selfishly provided for, I had an opportunity of noting the arrangements going on for refreshment among my room mates. None of them seemed to be satisfactory, but the circumstances of a woman's order who sat next to me has remained impressed upon my mind, as it was my first realisation of the great difference of price in comestibles occasioned by the heavy freight, due to the terrible roads. The woman had ordered a small bottle of stout, and as it was supplied to her, drawn, and with a tumbler on a tray, she demanded to know what she had to pay.

'Four shillings, ma'am,' was the waiter's prompt reply.

'What! four shillings for a pint bottle of porter? You must be mistaken, man! Why, I could get it of the best Guinness's in Dublin for twopence.'

'Dublin is not Castlemaine, missis; and I'll trouble you to be quick, for they're shouting for me all over the house.'

The woman gave him the money with voluble protests

as to the imposition, and then she bent down her head and burst into tears!

'Whatever came over me at all to come to such an outlandish place!' she sobbed. 'I didn't know when I was well off, or I'd have stopped among my own people.'

Ah! many of us have come to the same conclusion many a hundred times since our voluntary expatriation.

It was a pleasant sight to see Mr Slattery's 'little girl', as she presently came to me with her grateful tea and ham sandwiches carefully arranged on a napkin-spread waiter for my especial delectation. A prettier girl than 'Polly' you need not wish to look at, and her happy and innocent-looking face was suffused with a conscious blush as she introduced herself.

'Tom, ma'am – I mean Mr Slattery – told me to bring you this, and – I'm going to the Flat ball!' and such a hearty burst of healthy laughter accompanied the information that it was infectious, for I laughed too.

'I am glad you are going,' I said, 'for I shall feel more comfortable, though I am sure your Tom is as good as gold.'

'He is, indeed, and so good-natured. Now, take your tea if you please, ma'am – there are some biscuits for the little boy, and the cart will be at the door in a few moments.'

Such a radiant picture of loving, happy youth was Castlemaine Polly – her pretty, plump figure, attired in a light coloured dress, all decorated with ribbons of a bright blue, that just matched the hue of her sparkling eyes, and her fair wavy hair, pushing little coaxing tendrils all over her low white forehead. Often and often afterward I recalled pretty Polly as I saw her then for the first time.

Let me pass over the six or seven miles' drive, that was so much enjoyed by the betrothed pair that I was naturally left in the shade; and it was much to my satisfaction that I was, for, as the twilight deepened, and my sleeping boy lay snugly and quiet in my arms, I began to realise that I was on the borders of a new life. All the perils of the sea were over, and it lay an impassable barrier between me and the old happy Canadian life. What fate was to be for me and mine in this land of gold over which the shadows of night were slowly dropping? Could the question have then been answered, would I have stopped and retraced my steps? Alas! it is impossible to say, for human nature is a strange thing, and the unknown and untried has always attractions for the sanguine and the young.

Long before Mr Slattery's spring cart drove around the hill that bent the road to a sharp curve, on entering the diggings, the noises of a prosperous 'rush' came for the first time to my ears. German bands were crashing out familiar dance music, dogs were barking, men were shouting, and now and then a sonorous bell rang, while, in the interludes or temporary lulls, hundreds of firearms were being let off – crack, crack, crack – in every direction. This was a nightly custom, I afterwards discovered, for every digger had his revolver and some of them two, and it was considered a double precaution to discharge them every evening, in order to ensure their being in working trim, as well as to let all whom it might concern know that the owner was in a position to defend the gold he had worked so hard to obtain.

All at once we turned the corner, and burst upon my astonished gaze the 'street' of an Australian goldfield. The best idea I can give of it is a rough and almost impassable road, outlined by huge lanterns of various sizes and forms. The places of business (and, indeed, all were places of business in one way or other) were entirely of calico, and mostly unlined, so that the lights inside shone through them brightly, and cast the moving shadows of dancers and drinkers and fighters on the canvas as on the sheet from a magic lantern. The noise was wonderful. Every tent was open almost the entire end that always faced the road, and, as we passed, there was always the opposite bar, with its crowd of men laughing or drinking, or throwing dice for drinks. It was a terrible scene to me, and if I had any ideas of a Pandemonium, they must have been realised there. Suddenly there was a lull, the bands ceased in the immediate neighbourhood of the spot we had reached, the men crowded to the openings of the tents, and a bell rang violently. As it ceased I heard a voice cry – and it was the voice of the bellman:

'Wanted, two young ladies to attend the finest ball ever held on the goldfields of Victoria!'

'It is Fritz,' said Slattery, laughingly. 'Hullo, Fritz, what is it that's wanted?'

'Two young ladies,' replied Fritz 'but I see you've got one there, so I'll only call for one now.'

'Bad manners to your impudence, Fritz, I want my own young lady for myself.'

'Oh, you do, do you? Don't you wish you may keep her;' and a laugh went up from a dozen throats, in which laugh good-natured little Polly joined heartily herself, and we continued our drive to my destination.

'Grieve's Store; here you are, ma'am, and here is the old gentleman himself, God bless him! Ah! if you knew how he has been longing for you and the child, missis – poor, lonely old man – I'm so glad! See, his face is like the face of a picture with the sun on it, and he's speechless with joy!'

Yes, that was it, speechless with joy, and so was I to see the dear old face I had come thousands of miles to see. He lifted out my child and held him in his arms until I stood beside him, when he peered into my face to read the record of years. 'Thank God,' he murmured, as big drops rolled down his cheeks; and that was my welcome to the diggings.

And now that I have fairly reached them, I will leave to my next paper my first impressions of my unusual surroundings, and a description by daylight of Kangaroo Flat and its workers.

NOTES

1. About, concerning.
2. Now Port Melbourne.
3. The first railway line in Victoria. Despite its 'dirtiness' it had only been open since September of the previous year.
4. At 33 Bourke Street, proprietors Watson and Campbell.
5. Called.
6. Now Beaufort.
7. Godfrey Howitt (1800–73), brother and brother-in-law of the writers William and Mary Howitt.
8. Chalmer's Church was opened in October 1855, and was then a wooden building, described as 'handsome', which held a thousand worshippers.

9. Adam Cairns (1802-81) the formidable spokesman for the Presbyterian Church in Victoria.

10. George Seith Coppin (1819-1906) actor, entrepreneur and politician. His Spider Dance, which involved Cupid drinking a Brandy Spider and getting the 'staggers' was a parody of the notorious Lola Montez dance, regarded at the time as obscene. She had, while in Victoria, appeared at the Theatre Royal, owned by Coppin's rival, John Black. Montez's last performance in Melbourne was on 24 September 1855.

11. The Salle de Valentino was licensed to present singing and dancing.

12. Canvas Town was a tent city between Emerald Hill (South Melbourne) and St Kilda Road which housed immigrants unable to find lodgings in goldfields Melbourne.

13. A common term for a coachman, from the biblical Jehu, noted for driving a chariot at speed.

14. Now Chewton.

15. Not the Kangaroo Flat near Bendigo, but a diggings seven miles from Castlemaine. The name was subsequently changed to Tarilta. Not a trace now remains of the thriving settlement of 1855, which boasted hotels, bowling alleys, libraries, schools, and a fair amount of armed robbery and horse-stealing.

16. Incorrect, for in October 1855 a Mr Brown began to operate a spring cart service from Castlemaine to Kangaroo Flat twice daily. It met the Melbourne coaches and claimed to get its passengers to the One and All hotel, Kangaroo Flat, before sundown.

17. A mishearing, for the bellman (Town Crier) of Kangaroo Flat was William Fitzgerald, known as 'Old Fitz'. Like Mary Fortune, he travelled to the Avoca region, becoming a noted eccentric in Dunolly before being incarcerated as a dangerous lunatic in 1861.

18. The coach terminus at Castlemaine was the Victoria Hotel.

KANGAROO FLAT

To fall asleep and dream dreams that change as quickly as the forms in an unsteady kaleidoscope, and to awaken with a bewildered feeling that you are not yourself but have changed places with some other identity, must be a sensation akin to that I experienced when I opened my eyes in the morning after my first sleep on the diggings. I had been too tired the night before than to thankfully follow my child to bed without finding enough energy to even wonder at my strange, not to say uncouth surroundings, and in the morning the extraordinary and unaccustomed objects that presented themselves to me suggested the dregs of a nightmare.

To convince myself that I was awake I got up and dressed myself. I was surrounded on all sides by a calico wall that rendered windows quite unnecessary. The bedstead was of mill-sawn quartering, with posts sunk into the ground and high enough to be nailed to the 'tie beam' that held together the wall-plates of the tent. The table was a couple of boards supported by brackets instead of legs, and seats there were none save 'cases', which I may, *en passant*, assure the reader were *not* empty. There was an enclosure yclept a chimney on one side of the apartment, and the said chimney was formed of bullock hide that had been green when first stretched on the frame to which it was nailed, but which was when I first saw it as dry as parchment and as tightly strained as the sheepskin on a drum. Such, with the exception of the carpet, was the form and furniture of my first home on the diggings.

And the carpet deserves a new paragraph. When I first began to move about on or *in* it – the latter being the most appropriate preposition – I was exceedingly puzzled, not to say annoyed, for my boots were of light kid and did not take kindly to a contact with twelve inches in depth of 'tailings'. Nor were the tailings those later years have made us accustomed to as the sandy refuse of quartz crushings; they were tailings from the 'hoppers' of 'cradles'[1] and consisted of large and small water-worn pebbles that never set into a mass, and move about unreliably with every pressure of the foot.

Never shall I forget my first look at the diggings by daylight, or the first breakfast partaken of on them. It was from a back entrance that I saw the piles of uprooted soil, where the diggers were burrowing like moles, and heard the monotonous rock of a hundred cradles that went 'swish, swish' down by the creek that wound through the Flat. It was from thence also that I saw the long double lines of business tents that formed the street, and the waving of gay flags of all nationalities, from the rough flag poles in front of store, or restaurant, or billiard-room, or what-not. It was from thence, too, that I laughed at and commented on the extraordinary display of constructive and adaptive ability displayed in the material and formation of the hundreds of odd chimneys within my view.

A sketch of them must suffice. Some were of broken-up wine or porter cases, or shingle intermingled with bits of tin boxes, flattened out with pains and patience, others of sods or rough stones piled carelessly together.

Some had frames of wood, and were filled up with 'wattle and dab', and some of any kind of foundation with two or three flour barrels with their ends knocked out piled one on the other to form a flue. I saw one made of bottles – literally bottles (empty you may be assured), built up firmly and scientifically, 'heads and tails', to form a shelter for the useful little fire that was burning within.

But there was no fire burning in our bullock-hide chimney, for no cooking went on in our establishment. Breakfast was brought over from a restaurant on the opposite side of the 'street', and served on the queer table in my sleeping apartment for myself and my scion. There was no place else to serve it, unless on the store counter, which, considering all things, would have been rather too public a place in which to eat. The waiter was a seedy-looking individual in seedy pants that had once been black, and a seedy shirt that had once been white, and he showed so evident an interest in my personal appearance by staring at me that he nearly served a dish of chops on my unsteady carpet. To make room for his plates he swept away with his hand and arm to one end of the board a heap of nondescript and, to me, unknown articles; but when I pushed a case toward the extraordinary set out and sat down, I took a list of the articles on that table down in black and white for the intended reading of the English public who patronised the *Ladies' Magazine* I told you of in my first paper.

The breakfast consisted of the said plate of chops, that were burnt into cinders and swimming in fat, several thick slices of dirty-looking bread, and about a pound of *awful* butter rolled up in a bit of green paper that I afterwards discovered to be a part of an ancient play bill. Two enamelled dinner plates that had seen rough usage and fire, black-handled and stained knives and forks, two enamelled cups without saucers, and a *billy* full of tea completed the preparations for breakfast. There was no milk or eggs procurable, but it did not so happen often during my later life on the diggings.

And the items of household property that had been forced to give way to the requirements of our appetite – just let me once more record them as the necessaries and luxuries of an old single man on the diggings of '55. A hank of sailor's twine cut and plaited carefully, a large sail needle, a small ditto, a tomahawk and a bag of nails, a sailor's thimble, some trouser buttons, and a huge pair of tailor's scissors, a pint pot with a glass bottom, a bar of soap, an almanac, several lumps of washing soda, and a bit of unbleached calico; some scattered pins and tacks, among which were lying loosely several golden sovereigns, a pair of gold scales with their tiny weights beside them, and several bits of rusty and bent hoop iron lying comfortably on last mail's *Illustrated London News*. This incongruous list comprises most of the goods on that wonderful table, but there were others and many of them, though I need not now swell the list.

When we had gained courage to face the front door and I had peeped out, my first question was if everybody was yet asleep, and my good old uncle laughed to himself.

'What makes you think so?' he asked.

'Because there is not a soul to be seen in the street or at the doors. Last night there were little crowds at every tent.'

'Why, the population is all out of town just now, you see, for the diggers are our real population, so that nothing in the way of business is done while they are at work. They had all started off long before you awoke, and you will hear and see them both at sundown, or before, when they come back to their tents.'

'But the business people themselves – where are they?'

'The few who have wives or sisters about them are digging too, and you may see that many of the shanties are shut. What, indeed, is the use of keeping an open door when there is no one to enter it? Besides, it is a very hot day, and those who are willing to take their chance of business without rocking a digger's cradle, too, are lying down to recruit their energies for the hurry burry of the night. By-the-by, your friend Slattery called this morning to ask for you, and said he would call again when he came back from Castlemaine – he's gone to drive back his Polly, you know – and he took in an order to S — for me. Now that you have really come to me we must have your room lined, and some comforts round you.'

Quickly the day passed in wonders and fresh wonders at each new aspect of life that presented itself to me, but one of the most interesting to me was a new arrival.

'Now you will have an opportunity of seeing what you will experience when this rush is over, viz., the process of camping and pitching tents from the beginning. Here's a man and wife apparently going to camp close beside us.'

The intelligence took me quickly to a slit cut in the calico wall for ventilation purposes, which slit was in the usual fashion, kept open by a bit of wood with notched ends. From this point of observation I saw a loaded dray at the side of the vacant patch close beside us, and a coarse looking as well as indolent looking man pretending to help the owner and driver of the dray to unload and place the things on the ground.

'We are unfortunate,' was my experienced relative's comment as he saw some kegs and cases that told no tales to me. 'It is going to be a grog shanty, pure and simple, and if one may judge from the faces of both husband and wife, I should guess that they would be anything but comfortable neighbours.'

The observation made me more closely observe the female, who was engaged in carrying such articles as she was able to carry from the dray to a place farther back from the street. She was twenty-two or so, and decidedly good-looking, as far as features went, but an expression of dogged sulkiness spoiled a face that might otherwise have been attractive. Her hair was dark and coarse, but twisted into natural thick curls and hanging down over her back more than half way to her waist. Dark eyes with heavy black brows and lashes, a complexion like milk with a suspicious looking bloom on both cheeks and lips, and a figure good though rather too redundant, made a presentable whole, had it not been, as I said, for the 'dour' look in the whole face and action;

for even her very movements were eloquent of a sullen disinclination to her task.

During the erection of the tent, in which the man was assisted by the driver of the dray, I watched the woman with interest and some sympathy. The drayman had built a fire for her, and arranged some stones to set her cooking utensils on, but it was evident that she had had no experience of cooking, and the result pleased her man so little that he rapped out foul words at her, that only deepened the look of determination and sullenness in her countenance, but she replied never a word.

'Her husband has been on the diggings before, but she has not,' was my friend's decision, 'and I'm afraid the poor thing has made an uneasy bed for herself.'

'From her manner I should judge that she was not a woman likely to endure any uneasiness long without at least an attempt at change. I never saw repressed temper so plainly exhibited before,' was my own verdict.

'He has been in the store for nails, and told me his name was Anstead. He talked of getting a billiard table.'

And that was our first meeting with a couple who were the principal actors in a dreadful tragedy not very long after.

Our first day on the diggings was a hot one – intensely hot to me, but I was not yet inured to it; as the sun dipped towards the west, however, great tumuli gathered up, and white piles whose shadows deepened as they grew and overcast the blazing sky refreshingly.

'We are in for a thunderstorm tonight,' the dear old man said, as he looked toward the west, 'and if it comes down heavily the rain will be a godsend to the diggers.'

'Why to the diggers?'

'Because many of them have had to pile their stuff for want of water, as my books can testify.'

'Pile their stuff?' I repeated, wonderingly.

'Which means leave it in a heap with the gold in it because they have no water to cradle it, and the result is that I and other business people have to give credit until the water is available.'

'And where do they get water, I mean for washing their "stuff", as you call it?'

'In the creek while the deep holes are full. Why, do you know what we are paying for water now? I have to cart it, or buy it, at sixpence a bucket.'

'Buy water! Oh, what a dreadful country!' I thought, as I watched with an increasing interest the gathering clouds, while dear old Daddy – as my young one already called him – was more anxious by far in the rapid erection of our new neighbour's tent.

'If they do not get covered in before the storm breaks it will be uncomfortable for the woman,' he said. 'There would be nothing but under the dray for it, I'm afraid.'

'Goodness! couldn't they get beds or shelter anywhere?'

'The man wouldn't leave his property, and, if I read him aright, he would think a good many times ere he let the woman out of his sight.'

Little by little the frame of sawn timber was erected and fitted, and then the canvas cover was drawn over and fastened down to logs of wood that had been procured for the purpose, and laid from corner post to corner post round the foundation on three sides; then all hands carried into the shelter all the property which could be arranged in it, and so was formed that poor creature's first home on the diggings.

But ere the storm burst, or the dark clouds had exhibited any immediate signs of discharging their contents on the hot, thirsty earth, the diggers began to pour back from their labours at tub or cradle or pick and shovel, across the lead in little bands down from the almost empty creek and across the spur of the Big Hill[2] until the street was alive with movement and loud voices. Shanty and restaurant keepers, store owners and boarding house people, all buzzed out of their tents to greet the diggers and hear of the day's luck. Dogs, that were chained at nearly every little tent, barked a joyous welcome to their returning masters, who stopped in crowds opposite a 'brewery', where was prepared and sold a strong hop beer, which was the only beer available on the diggings in '55, unless, indeed, bottled and imported ale and porter. How well would it have been had such a state of things continued until this day! How much less accommodation would have been required in asylum, gaol and churchyard!

Almost every man carried his tin billy, which served to hold or make his dinner-tea in, and bring home the gold, if he had been lucky and had any to bring home; nor was there any secrecy as to their success in those days. Nothing was more common than to see a man handing his billy round for examination; or two or three interested parties fingering his nuggets and 'hefting' them eagerly, while the jubilant owner 'shouted' for all hands. At one time the front of that brewery was a picture, as a couple of hundred of eagerly thirsty men stood and waited patiently for the grateful pint they so much appreciated after their day's work in the droughting sun, and it was with much merry joking and laughter the full pints were passed through the crowd from hand to hand, and, in some cases, over the heads of those unfortunate enough to have failed in their efforts to gain admittance to the limited 'bar'. The wholesome drink was sixpence per glass or pint, and was sold to business people in bulk, as colonial is now, for the purpose of retailing at a profit.

'Where?' I asked, unbelievingly, as I scanned this mob of thirsty souls – *'where* are all the *gentlemen* we had supposed to have become diggers?'

'Do you recognise none?' my uncle asked, laughingly.

'No, indeed; each one seems coarser and rougher than another.'

'Appearances in that case are truly deceitful. Surely you did not expect to see gentlemen doing diggers' work in dinner costume, or with their faces shaven and their hair perfumed?'

'Not exactly; but those great brown men, with beards all over their chests, and such rough, ill-fitting shirts and common pants, surely not even such a change would entirely hide the gentleman?'

'It does so, you see, that is, as far as appearance is

concerned; but you soon recognise the educated man when he speaks. There are amid that very crowd many a man who has taken his degree and abandoned a good profession, at least *pro tem.*, in the pursuit of sudden wealth. Just observe that party of four who are coming toward us, most probably to sell their gold to me; the one at the right who has the pick over his shoulder is a Glasgow MD; the next to him a barrister who has left his briefs in London. The tall one is a Philadelphia Yankee, who came out with capital to speculate in stage-coaching or railways, or something, but who threw up the idea for digging.'

'And the fourth?' I questioned, for I was observant of the fourth as being of a type entirely different from his companions. He was of medium height, and rather thin, but of handsome features, in which was a despairing melancholy, which exhibited itself in slow and heartless movements, as he appeared instinctively to follow his friends.

'The fourth? Oh, the fourth is "Captain George", as they call him. He was captain of a mine in some Cornish tin mines at home, and knows all about underground working. I have an interesting story of him to tell you, but I must go into the store now.'

I was sitting by my ventilated slit, that I may call my window, when my relative left, and the new tent next door had an opening, which was eventually to serve for a back door, at a point within my view. Mrs Anstead, as we presumed was her name, was standing outside this opening, shaking some bits of drugget[3], as the quartette were passing, and I saw that the men noticed her as a new arrival and scanned her with passing interest; but with one it was more than a passing interest, and that one was Captain George.

As this young man's eyes fell upon her he half stopped, stared, and then went on again; only all at once an irresistible desire to address the woman seemed to seize him, and he turned sharply and walked directly to the new tent. Mrs Anstead saw him, dropped the carpet, and while her face grew so suddenly suffused up to the very roots of her black hair she tried to draw back into the shelter of her doorway. I could not hear what was said, but I could see with what determined force he held her until some few words were exchanged, when a hurried embrace concluded the interview and he was gone.

She looked behind her into the interior of the tent fearfully, and then, as if reassured and certain of privacy, she leaned her red face on her hand as it rested against the quartering doorpost, and I could see that her limbs were trembling weakly; but soon there was a loud, rough call, and she started guiltily as she hurried into the tent.

Here was my first experience of intrigue on the diggings, and it puzzled me so much that I thought a great deal more of Captain George and the story I was to hear about him than I should otherwise have done.

At the first leisure moment I reminded Uncle Barry[4] that he had promised to tell me something interesting of Captain George but I told nothing then of what I had seen myself. We were in the store at the time, and at the back part where were stores of barrels, and boxes and bags.

'Ay,' said the old man as he sat down near the partition, which was at the bottom a strip of Indian matting, 'I must tell you about it. Some three or four weeks ago the Captain and his party struck gold, and when it was divided among the four each had a good many ounces. The result was that Captain George got on the spree, as they call it, and spent a great deal of money foolishly.

'He was here one night, laying in some groceries, and he paid me out of a little chamois leather bag that are much patronised by diggers as purses, and he was very much intoxicated. He was quite able to carry his things to his tent that is just at the back, so I thought no more of it until next morning early, when he came into the store, suffering from the effects of drink and the loss of his purse.

' "You had it here last night," I told him, "but I did not notice what you did with it after you paid for the things"; and I began looking around the outside floor of the shop, which is, as you see, tailings the same as in your room. Now I know you want to ask me why I chose so uncomfortable a flooring, so I may as well tell you that it was to disappoint the fleas that are a perfect Egyptian plague in this country; for, you see, I make a daily practice of slouching the tailings with quantities of water that sinks through and cleans the pebbles. Well, when Captain George was gone, looking very disconsolate and woe-begone, I went and filled my water buckets down at the creek, and began throwing it about the floor.

'I had a little spaniel sort of dog then, who was a great pet and a good watch – she's on a visit to a digger's tent just now, for I had overfed her and mange was threatening – and as I was throwing my second or third dipper full about, she got in the way of the water and made a sudden movement to escape. The movement disturbed the loose pebbles, and I saw something glittering among the wet stones; picking it up, I found it was a heavy colonial gold ring, and I was confounded, for the Captain had told me what was in the purse he had lost, and one of the valuables was just such a ring.

' "You must have dropped it from the purse when you were settling with me," I said to him when I gave him the ring; but never from that day to this has Captain George found his purse or got one pennyweight of gold, and the want of money has made an unfavourable change in him. He is very proud, and cannot bear the idea of being dependent on his mates when he should have had as much money as they, only for his own folly in taking too much drink. But speaking of the little dog reminds me that she will soon be coming back, and I may as well turn out her bed.'

As the dear old man spoke, he stooped and drew from under the loose matting that formed part of the partition an empty wine case, in which were several woollen socks, and some old flannel flattened down by the evident pressure of the little animal, whose hairs were very plentifully sticking on the woollen things.

'She's the queerest little animal,' said the old gentleman

as he lifted out the articles preparatory to turning the box upside down and knocking it several times against the pailings, 'every sock of mine she can find she always drags to her box to make a bed, and doesn't content herself with old ones either. See here now, there's a new sock I've been looking everywhere for; but in the name of goodness what is this!'

Uncle Barry was staring down into the now empty case with such a look of surprise, not to say horror, in his countenance, that of course I stared too, and there I saw a chamois leather bag embroidered and scolloped round the mouth, in scarlet silk, but soiled and flattened by the repeated weight of the animal who had lain upon it so long.

'I am almost speechless with amazement!' cried uncle, as he lifted the article. 'It is Captain George's lost purse! But how came it there? The dog of course. She has a habit of considering all loose articles as toward her own comfort for bedding. How glad the poor fellow will be! Let me see that the contents are all right,' and he emptied out several folded and flattened notes, and two small nuggets, all of which represented a sum of which even a lucky digger had no need to be ashamed. I was glad for the loser's sake; but had I guessed at what would result from the discovery of the lost purse, far rather would I have seen it empty and in atoms before its recovery from the dog's lair.

Well, there came on a heavy storm ere sunset, and such a downpour of rain as few, but those who have seen, accredit the quickly gathered clouds with. It was like an extended waterspout, a continuous, heavy sheet, that in a trice soaked the hundreds of men forced to encounter it in self-defence. On the side of the street next the hitherto nearly empty creek especially, every tent and tenement was threatened with being swept bodily away by the great rushing streams of rain water that gathered from the hill sides and dashed across the street to the lower level of the creek and made a way through or between the tents as they found easiest admittance. Picks and shovels were in anxious requisition, and men with old coats over their heads, or bags and sacks, ay, and blankets and bits of drugget, were picking here or shovelling there, while kneedeep in water, trying to guide the torrents past their own tenements or out of them where they had gained an entrance. Our carpet of tailings was a great advantage in the very partial encroachment the water made upon us, but the most of our trouble was from the element to which our bullock-hide chimney formed a regular funnel to pour volumes into my 'room', and the result was that Uncle Barry insisted upon me and my young one getting up *on* the bed, and camping there until the flood had partially subsided.

And subside it did, almost as quickly as it had appeared; but we were released from our temporary retreat sooner than we might otherwise have been by a scene that a 'new chum' must be afforded an opportunity to witness.

'Come and see; I never saw such a sight before,' was my summons, accompanied with a hearty laugh, and before it had ceased I was peering out at a portion of the creek behind our dwelling, where the still flowing streams that came from all the higher ground seemed with one accord to concentrate, each sweeping before it such multitudes of *corks* that the foam of their disturbed course seemed to be literally of corks ere they escaped and were dashed into the quieter bosom of the flooded creek.

It was a strange sight indeed when, by the eddying and swirling water, the thousands of new and scarcely discoloured corks were swept into an embayed bend of the creek and still obeying the impulse of the miniature whirlpools they had just escaped, collecting in swirling groups that finally amalgamated into one grand whole as it was still augmented by the arrival of fresh detachments of corks brought down by two-and-twenties in the still lively freshets. There in the comparatively quiet water they crushed against one another, or bobbed up and down in a jerky, uncomfortable fashion, until the surface was completely covered, and so thickly that no individual cork had room to assert itself or make visible protest against the attempted encroachment of a neighbour.

Having sufficiently observed this army of corks, and wondered to realise the quantity of liquors that must have been imbibed by the diggers to supply the material for such a display, I had time to bestow on any other new and wonderful phase of a life on the diggings which might present itself, and the first that did present itself was the position of our new neighbours the Ansteads. Their place was in a pitiful condition. The empty space on which it had been erected was a level slope, very favourable to the downward tendency of the storm water, and the tent having impeded its way, great heaps of refuse of all kinds were dashed in and left against the logs to which the canvas was nailed. In the rising breeze, too, the sides and roof, too hastily covered in to have been properly stretched, flapped their wet surfaces to and fro, making a melancholy sound very unsuggestive of comfort. Of the woman I saw nothing at that time, but the man was popping in and out, busying himself with what seemed to be preparations for business.

'Yes,' said old Uncle Barry, 'he is going to open this evening. It seems he has fallen over an old acquaintance in one of our lucky diggers, who is going to bring a party to give him a start.'

'What do you mean by giving him a start?' I asked.

'Why, putting some money in Anstead's pocket by spending it in drink. And who do you think they have got hold of already? Why, Captain George, and I'm very sorry I gave him that purse so soon.'

'Captain George!' I thought of what a meeting I had witnessed between him and Mrs Anstead. 'Is *he* an acquaintance of the man's then?'

'No; Anstead himself was in the store a little ago and he asked me who and what the young man was. It seems he had been "shouting" so freely in the new tent that he was quite interested in him.' And again I thought of the meeting I had seen and the hypocrisy that must be enacting in that new tent.

And now came the hours of life and profit for the alert

business folk of the diggings. With cleansed hands and faces, and stomachs fortified by a good supper of their own preparing, the diggers strolled from tent to tent and talked and smoked until the usual number of friends were enrolled to form a party to some favourite billiard room or store, or dancing saloon, where, as night crept over the sky, one by one the tents were illuminated and burst into the visible outline of great lanterns, as I had first described them. Bands and violins and flutinas[5] and barrel organs crashed out music of some kind or other, while shouts and roars of coarse laughter, or coarser anathema, were bandied in the bars by violently gesticulating and, you may be sure, successful diggers. The effect of the bounding shadows on the unlined calico walls of the dancing rooms was ludicrous, especially in so dark a night as the one I write of proved to be; but as loud voices began to be heard in Anstead's, I turned my attention there by means of my original window.

The new tent was blazing with light, and a broad stream of it was flashing so directly into my ventilator that I was obliged to hang some drapery over it, through the folds of which I might see without being seen. When I *could* look I soon discovered the cause of the light.

In consequence of the rubbish brought down by the flood and deposited against Anstead's tent, he had been obliged to, at least, temporarily change the position of his entrance, and a portion of the calico directly facing us was untacked and raised, exposing almost the whole interior. Opposite was a rough wooden counter, half covered with bottles and tumblers, and behind it stood Anstead himself in the glory of rejoicing anticipations and a white shirt, while in front were grouped six or seven men, one of them being Captain George.

I examined him with interest as he lounged with apparent ease against the 'bar', holding between two fingers of a well-formed hand a yet unkindled cigar. He was a finely-built young fellow of scarcely thirty, and had as handsome and manly a countenance as one could wish to see, evincing honest purpose and good sound principle; not that I could read either one or the other in the face at that moment I speak of, but I thought such expressions might have been seen there at another and more propitious time.

'Oh yes!' one of the men said, as he drained his glass. 'You must get up another tent, Anstead – a billiard or a dance room, one or the other. See how well you did at Forest Creek, that girl Nell was a fortune to you there. What has become of her?'

'Don't know at all,' was the reply, but I, hidden from him, yet seeing every look and movement so close to me, noticed the half frown and look of intelligence and warning cast into the interior of the tent, and I knew that Anstead was giving his acquaintance a hint as to the unwelcome tendency of the conversation, which was immediately checked as far as the first speaker was concerned.

'If you are speaking of Nell Ray, I can tell you where she is,' observed Captain George, with apparent off-handedness. 'She's barmaid up at the Bull and Mouth.'

'Here!' exclaimed Anstead, gaping in disagreeable surprise at the informant.

'Yes, here on the Flat, and nowhere else. She's a famous draw, and knows you are here, or coming; for I heard her telling Dark Joe that she wanted to see you only this very evening as I was having a drink at the Bull and Mouth.'

'Did you know her before?'

'Yes, when she was with you at Forest Creek. You and I did not happen to become acquainted, but I met her at three or four dances.'

As he spoke, the young man's eyes were fixed on the advancing form of the woman Anstead, and I saw her husband turn a sharp look to her face as Captain George ceased to speak. The woman's whole appearance had undergone a change since I had last seen her, not only in attire, but in the expression of her features and movements. She was dressed absurdly from my point of view, but most attractively as far as might be toward influencing male admiration, and her eyes were glowing with a sense of her own good looks, of which her consciousness was fully evinced by the affected toss of her long perfumed ringlets, and the occasional dropping of her dark eyes to exhibit more fully the length of heavy lashes she could rest on a plainly rouged cheek; but at the moment I noted her she had stopped, and turned a bold face from one to another as she asked:

'Who was speaking of Nell Ray?'

There was a pause, for Anstead was stooping down to place some article under the counter, and when he lifted his face it was very red, and had a dark look under the heavy brows that was not pleasant to look upon.

'Did you speak, Margaret?' he asked, as he turned his stern face abruptly toward her.

'I did, and you heard me. I was asking who spoke of Nell Ray.'

'What do you know of her?'

'What's that to you?'

The short retort was given with a look in the speaker's eyes that might have suggested the danger signals on a railway engine, so lurid were they and so full of suggestive anger, and Anstead was urged to a point of rage beyond which he lost entirely all control over his fearful temper.

'If you have had any acquaintance with the woman you speak of, it is not to your credit, and you will drop it, or I'll drop you!' he said, between his clenched teeth.

'You!' she cried, with bitter scorn, '*you* will drop me! Take care that you don't find the boot on the other foot.'

Anstead stepped from behind his counter and struck the woman violently, and the next moment was felled to the ground himself by the strong arm of Captain George, who stood over him exhibiting every symptom of repeating his blow, when he was dragged off by those around.

'I'll never stand by and see a coward ill-use a woman!' he shouted; but just then he saw the woman swaying unsteadily as she held her dress up to her face to stop the blood that dripped from it, and caught her in his arms ere she fell. Perhaps the prostrate man witnessed this as the others raised him and made him sit down on a box – indeed, that he did has been almost a certainty to me for ever afterwards.

Uncle, being busy in the store, did not notice the noise next door, and just then he called me for some purpose. When I went back for another peep at the Ansteads, the canvas was dropped, and only a faint light showed through the back of the tent.

It was not to be wondered at that I slept ill on that night; my unusual excitement in consequence of the strange scenes I had witnessed during the day as well as the noises of the night around me, duly considered, it is wonderful that I slept as I did; but when one by one the bands ceased and the noises of loud-voiced men on their way homeward grew less frequent, when the dogs at their master's return ceased to bark and strain at their chains, I slept nor wakened until the sun was high, and the street once more enjoying its quiet of yesterday.

'I have really slept in,' I half apologised as I noted the time when breakfast was cleared away.

'You are earlier than our new friends next door after all,' returned the old gentleman. 'If they had not been such new arrivals, I should say they had made a moonlight flitting of it.'

'But the tent is not down.'

'No.' And what is stranger still, a faint light could yet be seen, even in the broad daylight, apparently of a candle or lamp yet burning where I had last observed it in the back of the tent. I went to the back curiously, but could see nothing save that all the openings in Anstead's tent were closed, nor was there one sign of life about it.

As the day advanced and that light still burned inside the closed tent, my curiosity began to be shared by many in the street; and when a mounted trooper made his appearance riding down toward us he was stopped by half-a-dozen of the neighbouring business folk who, as we could judge from their pointing and looking toward Anstead's, were trying to inoculate the policeman with their own suspicions that all was not right. Presently the man dismounted and led his horse toward 'Grieve's

Store', while the half-dozen men followed, and collected others as they went, talked loudly and in groups around the new tent, awaiting the anticipated official visit to satisfy their curiosity.

'Have you seen or heard anything of these people this morning?' the policeman asked of my uncle.

'Nothing whatever. The place has been shut as you see it all the morning.'

'Who saw any of them last night?' and an appeal was made to those awaiting the issue.

'I had a drink there at about nine o'clock,' one man replied; 'Dan Marney took me in.'

'Was everything right then?'

'There was nothing wrong as far as I saw, but I heard there was some quarrel among them afterwards. But here's Marney himself passing to the blacksmith's. Hallo, Dan, come here!'

Dan came, with two picks that required 'pointing' slung across his shoulder, and I recognised his face as one I had seen in Anstead's when the man had been struck down. It was he who strode first to the closed place and ripped down the temporary door leading into the bar, which he entered, followed by the trooper.

'I saw him strike her, and Captain George knock him down for it; but the woman may be hurt, for Anstead is a dangerous man when his temper is up,' was what Marney had said ere he entered, and the sequel sadly proved the reality of his fears.

When the man had fairly entered, a rush of others was made closer to the tent, when a loud cry from Marney drew as many as could gain entrance inside. But the particulars of what they saw I must, of course, relate from hearsay. The woman Anstead,[6] or whatever had been her name, was lying on the floor close to the back door, with a bundle gripped to one side and a knife in her breast. She was stone dead, with every limb and feature stiffened into rigidity, while the little lamp of oil yet burned, and threw its weak light on the awful face from which light had passed for ever. Her dress had been changed, for she wore warmer things, and had on both bonnet and shawl, while the bundle was found to contain necessary articles of a woman's attire.

'Poor soul, she has been on the bolt, and he found it out,' was the prompt verdict of one as the policeman cleared the tent.

'But where is Captain George?' asked Marney; 'he might be able to throw some light on this awful affair.'

Even as the man was speaking the young man who was known as Captain George made his appearance down the street, and, as it was afterwards discovered, he was on his way to Anstead's, after a visit to Nell Ray at the Bull and Mouth. His face grew white as a corpse when he saw the agitated crowd and the policeman driving it back from the death-sacred premises; but he rushed to the tent and grasped the calico of the door.

'What is the matter here?' he asked, hoarsely, for an awful dread rendered his voice almost powerless. 'Tell me, I say, has anything happened?'

'Murder has happened,' replied the trooper, tersely, 'and I understand that you might give some information of the doings last night. Did you see Anstead strike the woman?'

'I did, and I knocked him down for doing it.'

'And when did you see him last?'

'See him last? I didn't see him at all after I felled him. Margaret was hurt, and she told me she would leave him that very night and go to Nelly Ray, and then some of the fellows dragged me out. I had been drinking – I was not sober. Good God!' he suddenly added, as he looked round and saw the horrified faces near him, 'is the man dead? Have I killed him?'

With these words he disappeared into the interior of the tent to see what dreadful thing it contained, and a second after there was a cry that was almost a shout, and Captain George reappeared.

'He has murdered her!' he shouted, 'and as the living Lord is above, me I will avenge her! What are ye all standing there like fools for, instead of hunting for the monster while you can stand or walk? Is a poor woman to be killed in our midst while we, who call ourselves men, look on and let the murderer escape? By the God above me I will drag him to light, though it be from the hole of a bandicoot!'

The hint was taken, and search for Anstead became the order of the day. Every place of business, every claim and shaft, every bend and nook of creek and hill was tramped over by willing men, eager to see justice done on the wretch who had shed blood at their very doors, as it were; and that it was a woman's blood did not render them any the less rancorous or anxious to succeed in arresting Anstead. But it was all in vain, for night fell yet the murderer was free.

This was an unhappy interruption to my interest in my first neighbour on the diggings, and I was truly relieved when the body was removed to the next 'hotel' to await an inquest. It was dreadful to know that, hidden only by the still calico, that awfully rigid form was lying within, and I found myself wondering if the red painted spots were still visible on the cheeks of the dead, or if the long curls were dabbled in the stream that cruel knife had drawn from her breast.

One sad face bent over the dead woman ere she was borne away, and they told me it was the face of Nell Ray. She came in company with the policeman who had charge of the body; a young, good-looking woman in the showy and extravagant dress of a barmaid of the day, and with the unmistakable and repellant air of one whose life had been passed amid scenes and in company to which womanly modesty and gentleness were no password. It was, however, Nell Ray, and she had been a town acquaintance of the dead woman's.

If it was genuine grief that affected her and drew the heavy sobs from her heaving chest, some feelings powerful enough to simulate it shook every nerve in her body, so that she hardly dared to cross the threshold to look in the face of her dead companion. Did the wretched survivor look back on the life she had shared with the silent woman, and dread the day when she too should have to account for the deeds done in the flesh? or did she fear, shudderingly, her own fate in the

unknown future? These are questions I cannot expect
a reply to, but when she came out and went away with
her handkerchief to her face the girl tottered in her walk
as one just rising from a bed of sickness.

The inquest was held and an open verdict returned.
The body was buried, the tent and its contents disposed
of and removed, and glad were we when once more the
spot where it had stood was vacant, and only suggestive
by its memories of the tragedy so lately acted upon it,
and you may believe that when I got up a morning or
two after, I was interested and curious to know something
of a little black tent that had arisen like a mushroom
in the night.

'Another!' I cried.

'Yes, indeed, but a very different sort of folk I should
say,' returned Uncle Barry. 'You'll be amused to see such
queer folk on the diggings.'

'Who or what are they, uncle?'

'An old Irishman and his wife. They might have been
caught in the bogs yesterday, they are so inimitably Irish;
but here she comes to call on you by all that's laughable.'

We were standing at the back door when uncle spoke
and retired, leaving me to meet an old woman with short
wincy petticoats and a great white muslin cap, whose
borders flapped around a shrewd-looking, wizened
visage. A pair of brass-rimmed spectacles were mounted
on her nose, and she had a tin pannikin in one wrinkled
and knotted hand.

'Good marnin' to ye, mam, an' sure it's lucky I am
to be camped near a dacent lady like yourself, an' luk
at the bewcheful child ye have, mam – a little b'y, praises
be to God, an' the very image of the father, I'll go bail!
Seein' ye at the dure, mam, I med bould to come over
an' pass the time ov day, for sure there's nothin' like
bein' nabourly always, more specially here where there's
so few famales at all.'

'You came in the night?' I asked, by way of encouraging
an amusing conversation.

'Be moonlight this mornin' early, mam. Oych sure it
doesn't take ten minutes to whip down the little tent,

an' whip it up agin! an' th' ould man's handy at that same.'

'Have you been long on the diggings?'

'A follyin' 'em iver since the first month, alanna. We was in Milburne whin they first broke out, an' had a bit of a horse an' cart, so we had nothin' to do but buy the bit ov a tint an' shtart. Oh, bedad! it's not a bad way o' livin' at all, when there's only our own four bones to provide for.'

'Does your husband dig?'

'Faith you may take your davy o' that, mam, an' he's not an onlucky hand when all's come an' gone. But betune you an' me an' the post, asthore, I doesn't do bad meself wid a bottle in the corner – sellin' it on the shly, you understand; not a sowl suspects the like of a little place like ours, an' many a bright bit ov goold I've med out o' the corner keg.'

'But how do people know that you sell it?'

'Oych! what fools they are. A'most every digger knows us now, an' one tells another. There's many quiet min as would sooner sit down wid their drink an' a pack ov cards to enjoy themselves in a place like mine, than go where the dancin' an' screechin' and shoutin' ud be goin' on. Bless you, ma'am, I've seen hundreds of pounds change hands onder that bit of dirty calico.' And she waved the pannikin triumphantly toward her domicile. 'Well, ma'am, I'll say good mornin' an' good luck. I see it's a shtore ye have, an' I'll be in to get a bit o' tay an' a grain o' sugar wid ye, for I b'lieve well in always dalin' wid a nabour.'

This was my introduction to a character which I afterwards discovered to be as well known on many diggings as even Fritz the bellringer; and before they had been many days camped near us all their old patrons had discovered 'Mother O'Brien' and 'Old Dan' to our sorrow, for it was with very little of the boasted quiet their business was done, the patrons being, of course, nearly all countrymen of their own.

There was always something fresh going on at Mother O'Brien's. Sometimes it was a drinking or a gambling bout, sometimes a noisy political argument, and sometimes a fiddle turned up somehow, and the step dancing continued until the performers were unable to stand, and very often each and all of the entertainments ended with a free fight, in which the wonderful old woman always performed with applause and to some purpose, as she 'whaled' them all out of the confined premises with the broomstick she kept for the purpose.

'Git out, ye lot o' crazy omethauns an' square it in the road!' she would scream, when her patience and her customer's money were quite exhausted. 'A dirty, ondacent, onmannerly lot to be smashin' an ould woman's bits o' property that a-way! Clear now, and may the divil drive betther sinse into ye afore mornin'!'

Before a fortnight had elapsed after our arrival on the diggings, and in consequence of continued complaints on my part as to the meals served from the restaurant, I was indulged with utensils to commence cooking for myself and the child, for Uncle Barry knew too well what would be the consequent result to desist having his own meals at the table of the restaurant. One day he went to the 'Johnny All Sorts' of the Flat, and purchased some of the most extraordinary iron articles I had ever beheld – particularly, I only remember two, and these two were a frying pan and a camp oven. The latter article was nearly two feet in diameter, and utterly beyond my strength in the matter of weight; and the frying pan was of a corresponding size, with a great strong handle nearly a yard and a half in length. I stared at these wonderful things on their arrival, and asked what they were.

'You would try cooking for yourself,' said Uncle Barry, 'and I've got you what material I could, this is a frying pan, you see.'

'A frying pan! a new kind of warming-pan I should say.'

'Oh, you don't understand the long handle! Well, my girl, when you have camped out once or twice and have to cook at the great log fire, you may find out the utility of the long handle, that is to say, if you are not a salamander.'

'Oh no, I shan't – at least by experience, I couldn't lift the thing; and as for that awful-looking pot-concern, who *could* manage it?'

'I can, it is a first-rate camp oven, and all I can say is that if you will make the puddings and pies, *I* will cook them.'

But it so happened that the unwieldy ironmongery was never used by us, and my first essay at tart-making, for which we – that is, I and the child – were intensely longing, was baked over a fire in the bullock-hide chimney on a short-handled frying pan, and the fruit it contained was bottled preserved gooseberries, the only fruit then obtainable on the Flat.

And with reference to the want of pastry, I may here note the fact that it was nearing Christmas time, when our ears were gladdened by the news that a real live pieman had arrived on the diggings, and when we heard his 'Hot pies! hot pies!' every night after that, it was with a delight which could not be realised by any save those who have experienced the want of change in the dietary of the early days. I never saw the man, so do not know how he carried them round; but half-a-dozen were nightly brought in to us by the dear old uncle, and received with a joyous welcome. There were both meat and apple tarts, something in size and appearance like the ones now procurable in some parts of Melbourne at one penny each, the price then being sixpence each.

I think I will conclude this paper by the relation of an event that has some connection with the tragedy enacted at Anstead's tent. Captain George, after an ineffectual and continued search for the murderer, returned to his work; but he was ever after a changed man, nothing could arouse him from the silent melancholy that had fallen over him like a cloud, yet he haunted the bar of the Bull and Mouth. Many had it that his attraction was Nell Ray, with whom he was formerly acquainted, as we know; while others insisted that he was jealous of the girl, whom he closely watched, without, however, paying her any extra or noticeable attentions; but not one suspected his real object, which the result elucidated.

One night the bar at the Bull and Mouth was pretty full, and a strong business doing. Amid the loud talking and laughter, Captain George leant silently against the counter, smoking, and watching every movement of Nell Ray, as, in her usual showy array of ribbons and jewellery, she dispensed the drink and her smiles and 'chaff' together, taking the money with an alertness that entitled her to what she really possessed – the confidence of her employers. To anyone who had made her a study, as Captain George had, it was evident that the girl was unusually absent, and that her sharp eyes wandered more frequently to the door than her business required – the same close observer, too, might have seen that ever and always the young man's eyes followed the direction of hers.

It was late, and business in full swing, when a swagman entered the bar and asked for a drink. He was a dark-skinned man, who might have been taken for a foreigner, and his hair and beard were both so voluminous that scarcely an inch of his features were visible. He carried a light swag, and asked if he could have a bed.

'It's rather late to camp out,' he explained. 'I lost my way, and that made me late.'

Nell Ray poured out his drink, but the Captain saw that her hand trembled as she did so, and as he closely scanned the man his heart gave a great bound of triumph.

'I don't know about the bed – I will see,' she said, as the man lifted the glass and swallowed its contents at a gulp, and asked for another, and something to eat.

'You had better go into the dining-room,' Nell said, in a low voice, 'and I will tell the waiter to serve you.'

'No, he don't; we will serve him here!' shouted Captain George, as with one bound he was by the newcomer's side, and had him by the throat. 'Shut the door, mates! it is Anstead the murderer!' and at the cry the wretched man was seized and pinioned by half-a-dozen strong arms.

'Are you sure? How do you know? Don't ill-use the man he may be innocent!' cried some of the excited bystanders.

'Innocent! Look at him, the coward! Innocent, with a face like that?' and as he spoke Captain George tore the false beard and black wig from his head.

'It was these that ruined him and you, Nell Ray!' he continued. 'By accident I discovered that you had sent an order down by one of the carters to a town hairdresser, and when I knew of the false beard[7] I guessed the rest. You have harboured and hidden him ever since he dipped his hands in the blood of a woman you called friend! Pah! and that is what they call woman's love!'

The assertion proved to be true, and the girl had to leave the Flat. She had supplied him with food and disguise in the gully where he had hidden, and, when discovered, he was risking an escape to town, where he might ship for some safer land.

What punishment, if any, was meted out to the man Anstead I never knew. In the rapid changes of locality and scene we half forgot the events on the Flat, and never happened to see or hear the case alluded to afterwards.

NOTES

1.   A cradle was a box set on rockers, much used on alluvial goldfields. Gold-bearing dirt was placed in the hopper, a sieve on top of the cradle, and then washed to extract the gold. Tailings were the residue of the process.
2.   Kangaroo Hill.
3.   Drugget was a coarse fabric used to protect carpets, or as in this case, as a carpet itself.
4.   Apparently forgetting she had previously referred to him as James Grieve.
5.   A type of accordion, resembling the concertina.
6.   This incident was apparently based on the murder of Sarah Williams by her de facto husband William Jones, which occurred on Kangaroo Flat on 26 November 1855.
7.   A reversal of the actual incident – when William Jones was arrested for the murder of Sarah Williams, he shaved his whiskers off to prevent recognition.

BUNINYONG

Toward the end of the year '55 Kangaroo Flat, as a goldfield and 'rush' began to show signs of a rapid decay, and many of the business people began to follow the example of the miners and look out for 'fresh fields and pastures new'. About this time there was a choice of minor rushes at Taradale and its vicinity, to which much of the floating population drifted temporarily, until the greater extent and attractive promise of the Ballarat 'White Hills' absorbed all interest, and drew everyone toward Ballarat. There is no magnet so powerful as the one made of gold.

Grieve's Store was among the first to strike tent poles and 'load up', and then began my first experience of travelling on the summit of a heavily loaded bullock dray. I have a few items of interest to record of a short stay near Castlemaine – a stay chiefly occasioned by 'my first connection with the Press', a very high-sounding phrase, but rather too much so for my slight connection with the *Mount Alexander Mail*.

Coming almost directly from America, and being young you know, perhaps it was natural that, in a new land and among scenes in which law was of but little account, I should bloom in the Poet's Corner as a thorough Democrat. At all events, some pieces of mine[1] were printed in the sheet I have alluded to, of which Mr Saint (Charles,[2] I think) was the editor or proprietor, or both. Some of the rhymes I have alluded to I have since reprinted,[3] but with changes that redeemed them from the Republican taint.

The lines I write of were printed with my own initials attached, and just before I left the 'Flat' a line was addressed to me in the answer to correspondent's corner of the *Mount Alexander Mail*.[4] The line was a request that 'M.H.F.' would call at this office at his earliest convenience. I was very much tickled at the personal pronoun, and curious too, so I took the opportunity of passing through Castlemaine to call at the office in question.

My recollection of the office is but slight, but I think it was even then a two storey building, and that from the desk in a corner of a large and almost empty room I was interviewed by a man who stared in open-eyed wonder at me and my youngster, whom I led by the hand.

'Are *you* "M.H.F."?' he questioned with evident disbelief.

'Yes.'

'I can hardly credit it. You had better see Mr Saint; but as for the request that M.H.F. would call, we want a reporter and sub-editor, and thought he might suit.'

I was fortunate enough afterwards to see Mr Saint, and to spend a very pleasant evening with Mr and Mrs Saint in their cottage home.

But another sensation awaited us at Castlemaine. My dear old relative had some business to transact about stores in the township, and not having been able to accomplish it in time a camp was decided upon; so the bullocks were unyoked, and the round military travelling tent duly pitched in a snug bit of bush land on the

outskirts of the township. This information I should have
given you in an earlier paragraph, for it was after it had
been made that Mr Saint suggested a visit to the Police
Court on the following morning.

'Everything is so new to you that you cannot fail to
be interested,' he said, 'and the affair is creating quite
a sensation.'

'What is it?' I asked.

'A number of persons arrested and had up for sly-
grog selling, that is, selling drink without paying a licence.
There is a great deal of talk and not a little indignation
about it, for it is reported that the people were arrested
before they were out of bed, and actually marched to
the Sawpit Gully[5] in handcuffs. The scene will be a curious
one and Aspinall[6] is engaged for most of the prisoners.'

So we all went toward the Police Court on the following
morning. Only with a few of the noticeable particulars
of the police premises does my memory serve me with
after so many years, and one of the most noticeable was
the lock-up, around which were several of the prisoners'
friends communicating with the prisoners through the
open crevices between the log walls. It was a strange
idea of a prison to me, where plugs and cakes of tobacco
were freely passed in, and consultations held under the
very nose of the man on guard.

The Court itself was held in a large room that to
my eyes appeared very rough, even to the fabrication
of the very bench and tables. We were accommodated
in a corner not far from the door, and Aspinall sat
or stood, as his business required, almost directly in
front of us. The wide fame his great talent in the
line of his profession won for him in later years, as
well as his unhappy fate, has kept alive my recollection
of his appearance at that early day; and I remember
him as a young man of very fair complexion, and
rosy cheeks, who was an excellent pleader and examiner,
and who seemed to possess a keen sense of the ridiculous
which he could scarcely restrain from exhibiting itself
at *mal apropos* times and seasons. One other thing I
noticed, he had a habit of pulling the lobe of one

ear as he spoke, and I have often wondered since if that habit grew with him.

The prisoners stood at the end of the long table, at which both Crown Prosecutor and Aspinall sat, and I know nothing of the affair, except that there were a number of them, some of whom were females. The result was invariably, 'Fined fifty pounds,' on which Aspinall stood up, with a broad smile on his good looking face, and intimated, 'I give notice of appeal,' when he sat down, as he had risen, with the jerky rapidity of a Jack-in-the-box.

But all this is *par parenthèse*, the deepest interest of the whole being to me a woman's face, who was brought up on the same charge of selling spirituous liquor without a licence. The face was not a pleasant one naturally, and a black eye with some minor contusions did not improve it; but my interest was that I recognised it in spite of all: it was that of Mrs Blackett, my fellow traveller in the coach from Melbourne. She looked like a silent fury as she stood there for the short time her case occupied, and when the inevitable verdict and 'give notice of appeal' was pronounced, she strode out looking as dangerous a woman as one could well imagine.

'If you would like to have a look at the new rush before going, I shall be glad of your company,' said one of the merchants who supplied Grieve's Store. 'I am just going out to Taradale and Yankee Point.'

'Well, it would do no harm to take a peep,' said the old man, 'though I have no faith in the ground.'

So behold us on our way to Taradale, via Sawpit Gully, in the merchant's trap.

It was after lunch that we started, and, as the distance was but seven miles or so, we arrived in the vicinity of the public-house, where the coach had dropped Mrs Blackett and her canary, early in the afternoon. Before entering it, however, I saw a scene so strangely illustrative of what might happen to a lady in those days that I must tell you of it.

A bullock dray, empty, blocked up the narrow roadway, by either side of which the ground was honeycombed with holes sunk by the fast departing miners. In this dray was a woman, whose face could not be distinguished in consequence of her skirt of black damask satin being turned over her head, doubtless to save her light bonnet from the awful dust of a hot summer road. As we were met by shouts to 'pull up', and saw a lot of men holding the wheels and trying to unyoke the bullocks, of which there were eight, apparently wild and rampagous animals, we were naturally alarmed and full of inquiry.

'Anything wrong? Anyone hurt?'

'No, thank goodness, but that poor woman has had a narrow squeak of it.'

'How?'

'Well, you see, the man took her as passenger to Taradale, as the dray was empty, and she sat on the old tarpaulin he had in the bottom of the dray. The tarpaulin slipped gradually and got caught in the wheel, every turn dragging it round the barrel of the wheel until the woman's petticoats were caught, and she was dragged down to the rail and jammed there. Nothing saved her but her dress being turned over her head, for, see, she has slipped out of the petticoats and left them behind.'

'A narrow squeak' sure enough, and greatly put out the refined-looking young woman did look, as, after having performed so delicate a part of disrobing before a lot of rough-looking men, she hastened into the hotel with only the black satin skirt and mantilla hanging loosely about her. Some time after the petticoats, in a sadly mangled condition, were brought in to her carefully bundled up under a digger's arm.

Our friend having some business to transact at the Taradale Hotel, we went in, for the sun was broiling hot, and any shade welcome. Some speculation had taken place among us as to whether Mrs Blackett had got bail and returned, but our first step into the hotel set that at rest, for the woman was behind the bar, and the little canary was twittering a welcome from his cage behind. I have often thought since that the wretched being must have had some soft spot in her hard, vicious heart, or even the little canary would not have loved her; but her memory, as I saw her last, haunted me for years.

We were shown into a small parlour, of which the door opened directly into the bar, and from which a view straight through the bar to even the road outside the house could be commanded. I watched the woman Blackett with much and painful interest, her whole appearance being so woefully changed for the worse since I had encountered her in the coach. As she talked with the friend who had driven us out, she loudly declaimed as to her inability to pay his account for spirits, etc., and told him insolently to ask the loafing wretch whose laziness had exposed her to that day's loss and disgrace for the money due. Every now and then an awful fury, that seemed beyond her control, rushed into her bruised face, with a flow of hot blood which she did not subdue by repeated applications to a glass that stood near her on the counter.

'There he is, curse him!' she shrieked, as a quiet-looking man, with a pale, sad-looking face entered behind the bar; 'there he is, the lazy wretch that can't serve a glass, or earn a penny, while I am made a laughing-stock for the whole country. Ask him for your money, for you'll get none from me.'

'My dear, what can *I* do?' pleaded the husband with humble deprecation. 'You will not let me interfere in the business anyway. Mr S — knows very well that I should be glad to pay him, but I never *have* any money.'

'No, curse you, and never had! Poor, miserable, skulking hound, my black curse on the day I first saw your hungry face,' and the wretched being lifted the glass she had been drinking from and hurled it at her husband's head. The glass struck the man on the forehead, and a gush of blood darkened his face in a second. She looked at him for a moment in an awful, dazed sort of way, laid the hand she had hurled the glass with on the counter, then staggered and fell in a great huddled heap on the floor.

Pitying hands led the blood-blinded man to a seat and wet the wound on his forehead, while others administered stimulants, etc., and it was he himself who first pointed to the prone figure.

'Lift her up,' he whispered weakly, for he was a nervous man, and was shaking like a leaf.

'Not I, let her lie till she gets sober!' several replied with disgust, but the poor man still repeated 'Lift her up,' and at last she was lifted up – a dead woman, with that face I have told you of that haunted my dreams for years after.

Our eventual journey to the White Hills, Buninyong, was one to be remembered, especially now that steam and steel rails make the miles so seemingly short. We were many days in accomplishing it, in consequence of straying bullocks and tedious, bad roads, and minor and manifold accidents concurrent on travelling in those days. But we were not alone in our disasters, for after the first camping out we were joined by six or seven other drays, laden dangerously high, an unexperienced eye might reasonably think, and among those who became our fellow-travellers we found several of our late acquaintances from the Flat.

First and foremost there was Fritz the Bellringer, who was already a character, and a noted one, among the diggers of the day. He travelled with a restaurant keeper, with whom he boarded, and had his bell conveniently at hand among the piled up properties on his especial dray. This dray was the leader of the file by acclamation, and every camping place was chosen by Fritz, and announced to all those behind by a sonorous peal on his big bell, as well as a laughable accompanying shout on his own part.

'Roll up, roll up, mates! here's the finest camping ground on this side [of] the Snowy Ranges, and not a snake or a centipede or a darned fly nearer than the Pacific Ocean! Roll up, mates, and take the ladies down without letting them fall, for they're delicate articles and easily injured! Roll up, ladies and gentlemen, roll up!'

Somewhat like this were Fritz's cheering shouts as, weary with heat and dust, and cramp and not unfrequently thirst, we women and children 'rolled up' on the tops of high-loaded and crawling drays, and the very bullocks got to know and welcome the sound of the bell that told of unyoking and rest and feed and, above all, of water.

Pleasant reminiscences are these 'campings out' when the evenings were cool and pleasant, and the nights still and dewy; but to know and feel all their strange delight one must be suddenly plunged into them from a previous life in the so-called enjoyment of an existence in which the conveniences of life were not valued without its luxuries. To lounge on rugs under the canopy of a pale heaven, broken only by the spreading branches of rustling trees; to see the gleaming of creek or dark waterhole in its denser shadows of bush and bank; to hear the bullock bells 'tinkle tinkling', as the grateful beasts cropped the grass for acres around our temporary shelters; and listen to the sighing or rustle of leaves above us was a pleasant thing, and every puff of sweet night air brings the remembrance to me still.

There was certainly another side to the picture, which was far from an agreeable one, even to the youngest and most light-hearted among the travellers from rush to rush on the diggings. There were rainstorms that drenched the unhappy women and children, who, perched on the top of a rough loading, were exposed to wet and its consequent chill, and had often to change their attire hurriedly with only the screen afforded by the trunk of some great old tree, for there was no hope of a stoppage until water was reached. But we got used to all such discomforts, and I have slept well many a time with an umbrella propped up over my pillow to catch the drip from a thin calico roof, and with the wet side of the tent flapping and bulging in the wind against my bedding.

It was on a cool and enjoyable evening, however, that our party was joined by a solitary man who came tramping into our camp at sundown with a swag over his shoulder. We were in scattered groups, each family or party of mates being collected together and resting on the grass after the fatigue of the day. The two or three women among them were only too glad to stretch their limbs by washing and putting away in the 'tucker boxes' the few tin utensils used in the rude yet enjoyable meal that was just over, and the man I have alluded to marched toward the embers of a fire, tossed his swag to the grass, unslung his billy from his belt, and went down to fill it at the creek. The smoking and lounging men lifted up their heads as he passed, and gave him a 'Good evening, mate', or 'A hot day for travelling, mate', but none recognised him, nor did he appear to recognise anyone either, though he looked keenly at each group as he passed it.

'Darn it, I've seen that chap somewheres or other,' said a man near us, as the stranger returned from the creek and settled his billy on the fire. And the speaker sat up and spoke further.

'What rushes have you been at, mate? I seem to know your face, yet I can't bring it to mind where I saw it before.'

'I don't wonder at that,' was the low-toned reply 'for I sometimes don't know it myself. When I get a glimpse of it in the creek, I sometimes think it must belong to some other man.'

'Your face?'

'Yes, mate, my face.'

'Been working in the deep sinking?'

'No.'

'You look so white like; but I know I saw you somewhere.'

'On Fiery Creek, maybe?'

'So it was! Good heavens, you're never Jolly Jack Dawson, as used to be the life of the lucky four!'

'Ha, ha! Yes, I'm Jolly Jack Dawson!'

The awful scorn of himself, as it were, implied in the tones of the man's mocking, hollow laugh was painful to hear, as was the sight of the haggard face with the dusty, tangled beard and sunken eyes; but it was with the deepest pity I recognised my Fiery Creek digger who had gone so joyously home to Collingwood, only to find a desecrated hearth and the tidings of a faithless wife and a lost child – unhappy being, he looked as if years of misery had passed over him since I saw him last!

'You are greatly changed, mate, down on your luck, eh?'

'Yes, down on my luck.'

There was silence as the Fiery Creek man opened his swag and made his tea. The one who had accosted him smoked on until Dawson had fairly settled to his supper and made some progress in it, when he all at once set down the billy and laid his hunk of cold meat and bread on the grass beside him.

'Are you shaping for Buninyong?' he asked with some interest, as he looked in our fellow traveller's face.

'Yes, all of us we're bound for the White Hills or the Black Lead.'

'So am I.'

He lifted the food again and began to thoughtfully cut it with the jack-knife he held in his hand.

'There's a great rush there?' he said in a questioning way.

'I believe you, one of the greatest we've seen yet; why, man, there's thousands and thousands!'

'Ay!' and his dim eyes brightened with a fierce light. 'I shall most likely find them there.'

'You're looking for some old mates, I guess?'

'Mates! Yes, I am looking for a mate I had on Fiery – did you ever happen to come across him – one Bill Marsden!'

'Bill Marsden? No. Mates, did ever any of ye come across one Bill Marsden?'

'Bill Marsden?' was echoed by them all, but followed by the same negative as a reply, and then the newcomer was silent and unresponsive, until he rolled himself in his blankets and lay down to sleep – if sleep it was – until the sun aroused him to a fresh day.

On this journey we passed through Creswick Creek and Ballarat, the former an almost deserted digging at the time, with only piles of 'stuff', and tumble-down, makeshift chimneys to remind those among us who had a short time previously been among the thousands who rushed to the alluvial diggings there. As for Ballarat, I have never forgotten the strange appearance it presented, as from our camp on the brow of a hill we looked down upon it just ere dusk had been swallowed up in perfect darkness, save for the light of glimmering stars that shone coldly above it. It appeared to occupy a great saucer-shaped valley, which lay among the rises, and to be composed of thousands of canvas tents that were huddled together beneath our eyes, in the bottom of the valley, and crept in white shoals up every surrounding slope until miles were covered with the gradually darkening tenements. Then, one by one, and score by score, and hundred by hundred, gleams and glimmers and floods of light burst from the illuminated canvas dwellings, until the whole space was clustered with ghostly lanterns, as from every hillside and lower level the pop-pop, crack-crack, ping-ping of thousands of firearms suggested the dropping *feu de joie* of a review.

'If it wasn't for the braying bands and joyous laughter we can hear even from this, you would fancy the whole population were preparing for war or actually engaged in it,' I remarked.

'When, as a fact, every man is simply letting all whom it may concern know that he is prepared to defend the gold he has won,' returned my uncle. 'It is a custom with diggers to fire off and reload their guns or revolvers every evening.'

There was even then, however, in Ballarat a nucleus of brick houses of business, and some attempt at street formation, and both are recalled to me by the fact that in one of them was purchased a brown silk umbrella for my use. It is strange with what tenacity apparently trivial circumstances will cling to the memory, when much of far greater importance escapes us into oblivion. The very price of that umbrella remains impressed on me, and considering the high prices of that day and the heavy cartage which occasioned them, I do not see that, in the article of umbrellas, we have gained much of a reduction in twenty-six or twenty-seven years, for the price of my brown silk umbrella was one pound only.

But let us get to the White Hills rush. Along the dreary, dusty road, and beneath the broiling sun, and in a hot wind, of which we experience but a faint imitation in the hot winds of today, let us get among the disordered tents and crowded slopes, where the drays were camped and disloaded in a confusion and with a noise quite unimaginable to one who has not witnessed some such scene. Let us try if we can to distinguish among the miles of heaped-up pipe-clay, from which the rush took its name, the hundreds of gay flags fluttering or drooping from their poles, the thousands of windlasses and moving diggers' forms, the strange hum of a busy multitude, and the astonished and bewildered faces of newcomers who, like myself, had not hitherto seen a 'great rush' – let us get there and find ourself camped for the night almost among the very holes where miners were working, while already the men of our party were driving in posts and raising rafters for Grieve's Store.

It was a pleasant experience to sit or stand at the open side of our temporary shelter, and idly watch the scores of busy workers within view. There were some odd scenes exposed to the public in those days, and even refined women got accustomed to perform wholly domestic duties without even a screen between them and the moving, talking, laughing, eating, or working population around them. On the occasion I write of one party at a short distance were busily getting up the wooden frame of a tent, while a young woman was coolly washing a baby near an American cooking stove that was set up on the unsheltered ground and on which several pots were bubbling and steaming in the process of cooking.

The noise was shocking, and toward evening deafening. Hammering, chopping, bellringing, band-playing, shouting, laughing, fighting, and singing were all represented horridly in the babel of a new rush, and one heard and saw as in a dream in which the dreamer's identity is lost. Every now and then a hearty response would greet the welcome of some friends who had unexpectedly met in the working hive of all nations; or the oaths and whipcrack of a bullock driver denoted the arrival of another team laden with stores and canvas. But until near sundown the creaking of windlasses and distant swish, swish, swish of diggers' cradles went on unbrokenly, and there was a lull in the noise until the hungry were fed and the weary refreshed and ready for the dancing saloon, the billiard table, or the bar.

'Oych then, ma'am dear, is this yourself?' was my first morning greeting as I lifted the calico to emerge into the morning. 'An bedad it's in the hoigth av luck we are to be camped close again ye wance more! Oh alanna asthore, isn't it the wild, awful life intirely intirely? Sure what wid climbin' up and tumblin' down aff that ondacent ould dray every bit o' me is black an' blue, savin' yer presence.'

'Oh, there you are, I do declare!' I couldn't help exclaiming, as I saw Mrs O'Brien standing near the identical old dirty tent that had neighboured us on the Flat. 'How ever did you get here at all?'

'Git here is it, ma'am? Arrah, why wouldn't I git here as well as anyone? Thanks be to God, I'm as hearty as a buck, and thim that takes me ould bones for bein' worn out 'ud find thimselves mistaken wid the weight ov me hand on 'em! Arrah, where are they all runnin' to, Pat? Pat Carrol, I say! what's the mather wid ye all?'

'Rush oh!' answered the running Pat in a shout. 'Send Dan out wid the drop, bedad he'll sell it.'

'Dan! Dan I say! Run, ye ould divil! there's a rush down the Black Lade way. Off wid ye an' see if it's worth while taking the dray out. Hocks! there they go! Run, yer sowl, or ye'll be late!'

As Mother O'Brien shouted and clapped her hands, the end of a small tent at a little distance was drawn back, and a good-looking young fellow, rather dandily dressed for a new rush, stepped out into the air. He had a pipe in his mouth, and seemed rather conscious, not to say conceited, of his really fine build.

'A rush?' he said to the old woman. 'Where this time?'

'Black Lade way, Bill. Are ye goin'?'

'Going be blamed,' said he. 'Have you got the keg opened yet, old woman?'

'That I have, Bill. Och, it'll go hard, but I'll sell the drop in spite of all the informin' thraps in Australy!'

'Turn us out a nobbler then,' and the idle-looking

speaker sauntered toward O'Brien's shanty.

I was watching with a natural interest the different scenes of busy life within view, when the old woman again appeared in front of her tent, and addressed me in what is termed in her country a 'pig's whisper'.

'Oych! isn't he the divil?'

'Who?' I asked.

'Bill,' she replied. 'Look over at his tint, bad cess to me if the rogue isn't married.'

I looked toward the tent from which the young man she had called Bill had so lately emerged, and, sure enough, there stood at the opening a good-looking woman of about twenty-five. She was tastefully dressed, and had, I think, the finest head of brown hair I ever saw, so rippled and waved that it caught the sun in its shimmering gloss; but in that woman's face was a sad unrest as she gazed after the retreating form of the man 'Bill'.

'She's a fine looking girl,' said old Mrs O'Brien, 'but she has the sorrow in her face. God help her! and what cud she expect wid a man like Bill Marsden?'

'Bill Marsden!' I echoed.

'Ay. Do you know him, asthore?'

'No, but somehow the name is familiar to me.'

'Well, it might if you'd been at Forest Creek, or Barker's[7] or Daisy Hill,[8] or Maryboro'; but you warn't. Oh, a lazy, rollickin' chap was always the same Bill, an' sich a lad among the women that it's little I thought he'd ever get married. Oych! sind I may live if there isn't a child in it too, an' over to spake to her I must go.'

Yes, a little sad-faced boy of maybe four years had crept out, and was peeping around him shyly, holding on at the same time to the skirt of his mother's dress. You may believe with what a painful interest I scanned the wretched wife's face when I guessed she it was who had dishonoured her child, and his father who had returned so happily to pour his gold in her lap from his fortunate sojourn at Fiery Creek, and on whose track the forsaken husband was even then following with what dread intentions I could but guess shudderingly.

I saw her start as old Mrs O'Brien's foot sounded in her approach, and then turn quickly inside her tent and drop the calico over the entrance.

'Bad cess to her!' grunted the old woman, as she tossed up her broad muslin cap borders with a jerk of her shrivelled chin. 'Who the mischief is me lady that dacent nabours aren't good enough to spake to her? Faugh! that for her pride, an' I'll tell Bill what I think of her an' her manners before I'm a day oulder. That's his claim where the blue flag's flyin'.'

Some days elapsed after this, and in the whirl of incessant noise and change, and work too, I saw little of my neighbours except at a distance; but there began to be an apparent dullness in business of all kinds, and an unhealthy restlessness among the diggers themselves that were only too easily read by an old worker.

'Another shift, lassie,' uncle had said more than once, 'for White Hills is done for, and we have only to look out and choose one of the new rushes. What do you say for a try at the Green Hills?'

What could I say? I was a new chum and a greenhorn, and had no experience of diggings or digging ways.

'Our friend, old Dan O'Brien, has dropped on something good, I understand, and is going to shift to it tomorrow.'

'Dropped on something good?'

'In other words, the old man has been prospecting – '

'Prospecting?' interrupted I. 'What's that?'

'Ha! ha! What fun it is to talk with a new chum!' laughed the good old gentleman. 'Prospecting means digging in *hopes* of finding gold, and dropping on something is *finding* what a digger has been prospecting for.'

'So old Mr O'Brien has been lucky, then?'

'Anythin' has he, me dear,' interrupted Mrs O'Brien, 'an' sure it's come over to bid ye down tint and come over before every claim 'll be taken up. Lard, if ye ony seed the crowds o' min wid the corner pegs up like threes in a wood, an' the diggers at work widout bit or sup, they're that ager. Oych! come an at wance, ashthore, an' be in it wid the best ov 'em. I'm off meself like a shat, an' plaze God, I'll impty ever keg in the place afore mornin'.'

'Shall you go, uncle?'

'Yes, to see it; but the men who know old Dan are very shy of believing about his golden claim. A party are going over tomorrow to spy out the nakedness of the land, and if you are not afraid to be alone in a crowd, I think I'll go and have a look too.'

Afraid? Of course I was not afraid! What was there to be afraid of? The assistant at Grieve's Store took charge of the strange amalgamation of goods under our humble roof, and I and my boy amused ourselves by watching what was going on through the interstices of a saplin erection at the back of the storeroom, which served as a sort of kitchen and scullery, and abutted so close on the lead that every word of the men at the nearest windlasses could be distinctly heard by us.

Opposite the very door of this tenement was the claim over which floated the blue flag pointed out to me by Mrs O'Brien as that of Bill Marsden, and past it also wound the tortuous half-path, half-road, half-street, upon which the sinking had encroached to occasion many a diverted track from tent or shaft. I could lift my head from my book or my work and see Bill Marsden when it was his shift on top, and many an interested gaze I directed toward the tent where the unhappy companion of his sin lived on, while her little sad-faced boy stood or sat beside her, but without any semblance of childhood's happiness in his little countenance or subdued demeanour.

'That woman is utterly miserable,' I had said to myself more than once, as I saw her pale, despairing face quiver with pain when Bill would roughly push the child out of his way or only half suppress an oath at her maternal folly, as he called it. But how could I pity her – I, who had seen her husband when he went home rejoicing, to find a disgraced home, and when he followed as the avenger the woman who had deceived him? Often, too, I had noted the woman's terrified look as some sudden voice that reminded her of him would break from a new party, when she would shrink inside as if fearful to be seen.

On this afternoon Bill was not on top, it was a mate of his and a stranger to me. I can recall this man, at one moment idly leaning on the windlass as he waited the signal to 'haul up', and the next I saw him start and shrink back from the shaft, and finally almost run from the spot.

It seemed but a moment, when a great crowd of men had gathered around with excited shouts and serious faces.

'What's up?'

'Jones' claim fallen in. Look out! see, it's giving way under Marsden's.'

'Anyone below in Jones'?'

'Thank God, no.'

'Bill? where's Bill? Connerford, where is Bill?' This was to the man who had been at the windlass, and who now became visible as, with a ghastly white face, he came to the front, and shaped a reply with trembling lips to the shouts around him.

'Where is Bill? Where is Bill Marsden?'

'Down below,' replied Connerford, 'down in the back drive. God help him. I heard a fall of stuff just as the windlass slewed.'

'What's wrong here? Stand back, mates, and let me in. What is it?'

'Ground given way and a man buried.'

'And you all standing here to let him smother! Give way, mates, and work. Bolster up that windlass, and if there's a man's heart among ye stand by to haul up.'

'Hold, mate, don't you see the stuff sinking bodily? You are going to certain death yourself.'

'If you are too cowardly to lower me I can lower myself, and perhaps for shame's sake ye will then man the windlass.'

As the speaker uttered the words, he had torn off his coat and seized the insecure rope; before they were finished he had disappeared down the fatal shaft and then, with a hoarse shout, there were half-a-dozen volunteers for the dangerous honour of standing by to haul up.

I had risen to my feet, and in panting terror was staring at that awful scene; for it was my Fiery Creek man who had ventured his own to save his rival's life. Even in the dread pause, while the men above whispered their fears, and the surface began to crack visibly, and settle slowly but surely, I found time to glance towards Marsden's tent opposite. *She* was standing at the door, with the pallor of fear and death on her face, and her little boy was clinging to her skirts, crying bitterly. In this case were the wages of sin to be literally death?

That was what I asked myself when a ringing cheer broke from every throat, as the rope grew taut and hearty arms began to wind up and hold firm the tottering windlass, and at its sound the wrteched woman snatched her child up in her arms, and darting from the tent crossed the lead and struggled to the front in the crowd of anxious miners. They gave way to her, and in many a sunburned face might be read the reply put to some stranger's question, 'Is she his wife?' Even at such a moment how hard must it have been to bear that frown of avoidance and disapproval in the face of honest men!

A second of anxiety when you could hear, not only the creak of the shaky windlass, but the hard breathings of the men who drew Jack Dawson and his heavy burden to the surface; but when he appeared with his enemy's form hanging limply over his strong arms, such a shout went up as might have put life in any half-dead man, and Bill Marsden opened his eyes. Scarcely had his preserver secured foothold on firm ground when, with a rumble as of underground thunder, the whole claim caved in, and my Fiery Creek digger and his faithless wife stood face to face! At the first look he recognised her, and then with an awful cry he threw the clay-soiled figure almost at her feet.

'I did not know it was he!' he cried, with an awfully fierce light in his hollow eyes, 'he was not worth saving, but let him live to avenge me on you! Faithless and vile that you are, give me my child!' and the little boy put out his arms and shouted 'Daddy! daddy!' while a very radiance of happiness lit up the little pale face.

The father took him roughly from her apparently helpless arms, and as he went away with the boy in his arms the men made way sympathetically, and Marsden struggled to his feet. She put out her arm to steady or assist him, and he struck her, though not heavily, in the face. Yes, after all and before all these men the betrayer of his friend and of her honour struck and spoke vile words to her.

'That's what I get through you!' he said beneath his clenched teeth, as the men fell back as from things accursed. 'Go, and let me never see your shameless face again, for under roof of mine you don't shelter again!' and the woman grew as one stricken senseless as she found herself alone, and everyone dropping from her as from one visibly infected with sin. Then some woman came and led her away by the arm, she staggering in her steps as though from the influence of drink. I saw her months after at the bar of a restaurant selling drink to a crowd of flattering diggers, with a haggard painted face and much jewellery; but my Fiery Creek man and his little boy I never saw again.

'And what do you think of old Dave's rush, Mr Grieve?' was the oft-repeated question of diggers who, knowing of his visit to the new rush, had dropped into the store in the evening to hear his opinion.

'I don't know what to think of it; there's three or four hundred men on the place, and I daresay fifty places of business, but I couldn't hear of any gold being got except in the prospecting claim.'

'Old Dave's?'

'Yes, he's got a countryman working with him.'

'I've just come in from there,' another and a new arrival volunteered, 'and when I left the diggers were inclined to mutiny.'

'Mutiny?'

'Ay, there's not a spec been got out of Dave's claim, and they're beginning to suspect he's salted it. Morris and Tyler expected to bottom early tomorrow, and if they bottom a duffer Dave's claim will be rushed for examination. I am going out again to see the fun, for I believe it's a regular piece of salting.'

'What does all that mean?' I asked at the first opportunity.

'What does all what mean?'

'Salting and shicers and duffers.'

'Oh! why it means trouble for our friends the O'Briens, I think,' the old man replied merrily. 'They suspect him of salting his claim, that is, of putting gold in the ground himself to cause a rush.'

'With what object?'

'His own benefit of course. The old woman sells drink you see. Well, they are almost first on the ground when it is rushed, and hundreds of men will get their refreshment there; but if they all bottom duffers and shicers (which means don't find any gold where they ought to find it), they will go down and root in the old man's claim to see if there *is* any there.'

'And then?'

'And then, if they don't get any, they will in all probability punish old Dan. It is no joke for a lot of people to be deceived into shifting their household gods and goods to no purpose, and if the O'Briens get off with the loss of all they possess, they may consider themselves well off.'

The actual result of old Dan's rush I may relate from the description of eyewitnesses. It seemed that there was a regular stir at the place from the early morning, and that as soon as Dan left for the claim a sort of guard was put over the movements of 'Mother O'Brien', for the old dame was supposed to be far more wide awake than even her husband, and quite able to sneak out of the affair with the proceeds of their roguery intact.

The men on watch were a Scotchman and an Englishman named respectively Munro and Dallas, and both of them were very decidedly awake to the charms of a full bottle. It was a treat to the initiated to see these two lounging about old Biddy in the earlier part of the day, and lounging inside near the kegs when the darling influence had fully exerted itself on each swimming brain.

'D'ye think th' ould body has ony suspicion?' the Scotchman asked, as he squinted over his glass at the alert movements of Mother O'Brien.

'Suspicions be blowed! what do I care? Push over the bottle!' was all the reply he got.

'She's kickin' up an awfu' dust out by, Dallas, an' there she gangs syne wi' a gey dirty feather bed on her back. Whaur ye ganin' wi' the bed, Biddy?'

'Oych, sure it's a fine day, thanks be to God for that same, an' the air'll drive away the moths. Arrah now, Misther Munro, asthore, did you iver see a finer feather bed in your life?'

'It's a gey fat ane ony how. Fegs! old Dan's bones lie soft eneuch for a better man.'

'Bether man inyagh! Show him to me! An' why shouldn't ould bones lie as saft as young wans av they arn it decently?'

'What do you call decently, auld wife?' asked Munro, who in his anger began to recall what he was on duty for, 'vara honest an' decent it is to empty the diggers' pockets by salting a claim! Dallas, man, rouse up! here's the boys comin'!'

And coming they were sure enough, with a murmur and a shout and an oath from scores of throats at one instant, and repetitions of, 'Tar and feather the old schemer!' 'Douse him in the creek!' 'Make a bonfire of him!' etc., etc., until it was impossible for the old woman to doubt that it was at the devoted head of her old Dan the threats were levelled. Falling back helplessly on the valued feather bed, she set up such a 'Phillillillew!' that every voice was stilled to listen to it, and then re-arose a grand chorus of mocking laughter as Dan was tossed from the rail on which they had ignominiously ridden him into the very lap of his terrified spouse.

'Who's laughing?' shouted a black-looking, stalwart digger, with an angry face and evil expression. 'This is no laughing matter. I spent my last shilling to shift here, and fill the pockets of this lying old — , and by — he'll be as poor as I am before I leave this! Get up out o' that, you thieving old salter, and you, missus, turn out your stock, and hand round the grog.'

'Oh lord, sure it isn't ruinin' a poor ould crathur you'd be, gintlemin, an' she a'most gone wid the rhumatiz? Arrah, Misther Munro, say a word for me, there's the ould man a'most dead wid the fright. Spake up for me for the love o' God!'

'Speak up for you! You old schemer, I'll speak up for you!' was the unexpected assurance of Dallas, as he flung his glass at Biddy's head. 'I believe she's drugged me, for I can hardly see out of my eyes. Here, lend a hand, Munro, and let us spile the grog.'

'Roll it out, I say,' shouted the dark ringleader. 'A drink all round, and then we'll spile them, roll it out!'

'Oh, for the love of heaven, an' the sake of your own poor sowl, misther, don't ruin a dacent ould couple that never harmed chick or child,' and Biddy wrung her hands, and ran to and fro distractedly, while her stock of drink was ruthlessly drank and destroyed by the disappointed men.

'You *will* have it you are decent and honest, eh? Why your wretched old villain has confessed to salting the claim, and swears you told him to do it. Look at him. He looks like an honest man, doesn't he? No mercy, boys, smash and rip all before ye!'

'And I know what I'll rip,' cried tipsy Munro, as he plunged upon the feather bed, amid the shouts and screams of Biddy, who tried to save the cherished luxury. 'No — old salting schemer shall lie in feathers while a hard-working man has to be content with his blanket and a sheet of bark. Hurroo! hurroo!'

'Oh, vo, vo, me feather bed, me bewcheful bed, wid not a feather in it but goose's, an' every wan ov em picked an' sthriped! Meila murther! meila murther! An' is it sthandin' around an' laughin' at the like ye'd be, an' the blessed sun shinin' in the blessed heavens above!'

'Tipperary and the blue sky over us!' cried Munro, as he cut gashes in the tick, and scattered arms full of feathers around him, covering friends and enemies in a clinging white, as of a snow-storm. Then, as the half-amused and half-angry men ran, shook themselves, and in all ways tried to get rid of the feathers a gentle wind (that was hot) would catch and lift up a light cloud of them, to make room for the next contribution from the destroyed bed.

'That you may never die in a bed!' shrieked the irate woman at last, when her empty kegs were rolling down the hill, and Munro emerged from the remains of the tick, with his red beard one mass of down, and his red, hatless head ditto. 'May the pains an' horrors get hould av ye on a cowld shtone, and my curse be the last sound ye'll know when yer masther the divil drags the lost soul out o' yer carcass! An' as for you, ye murtherin', black-faced villain, gallows is written in yer eyes, an' plaze the Lord I'll live to see the hangman's grip an yer throath!'

The man she addressed in her desperate anger shrank back at her words, and his dark face grew darker as though his conscience echoed the old woman's curse; Munro, too, slouched away as one by one the diggers left the O'Briens alone. And that was the end of 'Old Dave's rush'.

The White Hills and Black Lead soon became almost deserted, while several spots in the neighbourhood were tried as rushes with more or less success, but I think that the Green Hills was the only one that survived to even retain its name until now. It was a couple of miles or so from Buninyong, and about three from the part of the White Hills where we had camped.

It was in lovely weather that we once more removed and planted our tents on the Green Hills. I remember the bright greenness of the smooth hills we wound through to our destination and the pretty glimpse we got of the first white tents among the trees as we neared the River Leigh, the Yarrawee of the Black man. Here it was that we climbed to the lonely grave that has found a place in many of my previous sketches during all those years, and which I daresay has long ago disappeared in every trace.

I don't know who pointed it out to us, but as the drays

rolled easily on the short journey, we left them and walked up the easily sloping grass until about half-way up to the summit we reached the grave of no one knew whom. A hillock with a rich grassy coverlid, and a little English rose bush without a bud or flower, a large stone laid against the head, and a time-stained and rotting fence of rough, axe split rails, was the last resting-place of the nameless stranger. How much might be written here of the unknown tenant of that lonely grave! How many fancies might be recorded of his birth, or parentage, or country! How we might wonder as to his life, where it was passed; or his death, how he died, and how futile and foolish it would all be! Little recked the sleeper who listened to the rose leaves rustling over his bed, or who passed them by unheedingly and if his story is worth knowing we may be assured that we shall know it where nothing is hidden.

The Green Hills were not a financial success, but I think it was while simply waiting for a more attractive goldfield to turn up that many business people held on after most of the miners had left. The place did not indeed present the usual features of a rush from the beginning, as it only attracted its hundreds and I should not perhaps be able to say that there was deep sinking there, had it not been for the shafts sunk and worked both by day and night so close to our back door that a man could have thrown a stone into one of the claims.

The nearest of these claims was worked by a party of four and of the four Con the Devil was the most prominent member. A young and handsome Irishman, his fun and pranks, that extended themselves more especially in the direction of practical joking, had gained him the *soubriquet* I have penned, and he was one of those noisy spirits who could no more be quiet or silent than headache smitten. If no worse luck had befallen Con than the fulfilment of my heartfelt wishes for his toning down, he would certainly have had more aches than one when it came to be his turn for 'night-shift' work. I suppose it was pumping they were, but Con's stentorian leadership of tramping choruses was nearly suggestive of seamen's 'Capstan bars'. Hour after hour and night after night it went on until other miners followed the fashion, and made sleep impossible for the unfortunates in their vicinity until their throats got sore toward morning.

At this quiet season on the Green Hills our end of the street was more like a very quiet and friendly suburb than anything else. There was the billiard room, yclept Jones' opposite, and Mrs Mack's the restaurant ditto. There was a quiet store or two and notably 'the doctor's', next door to Grieve's; and these, with many more, were in the friendly habit of gossiping across the street as they waited for the very occasional customers, and the doings of one side were as patent to the other as though one roof had sheltered them both.

I don't know what the community would have done without the doctor, and the *Buninyong Advertiser*. The former kept up the fun with his drunken absurdities, and the latter published occasional squibs in the shape of 'Sketches', of which W.W. was not wholly guiltless. Mrs Mack, being in an interesting way, and dependent on the doctor for attendance during an interesting event, took it as a necessity that he should be shepherded, and so occasioned much liveliness and laughter in our wide circle; but Con was her right-hand dependence in seeing that the professional imbibed no more than he could sleep off again. But I am bound to add that 'the Devil' proved indeed a broken reed to lean on, for he generally got as much fun out of the doctor's failings as kept us continually lively.

Poor Dr — was an elderly man with an exceedingly fine head of iron-grey hair and whiskers to match. I don't know that he had ever been to say a man of ability in his profession, and at the time I speak of he was in an almost continual muddle and had the strangest look when he turned out after a long sleep. At such times his round eyes appeared rounder still behind his round silver-rimmed spectacles as, without putting even a cover on his curly and untidy head, he would start across to 'Jones'' for a reviver or two; even then he would mutter

anathemas to himself as he went back and found Mrs
Mack watching him with more and more anxiety as 'her
time' drew nearer.

'Doctor, there's Mrs Mack watching you!' some
mischievous person would call out to him as he was
making his way to Jones' for a fourth or fifth reviver,
and the poor man would gnash his teeth and rumple
his hair up on end worse than ever, with a –

' — Mrs Mack! she sent for me three times last night
for nothing! If I knew when she was going to be really
wanting me, I'd get as drunk as a fiddler and keep so!
Boys, couldn't you coax some fool of a medical man to
squat here for a bit and give me a chance, eh?'

Well the doctor had his way about Mrs Mack, that
is to say, after a fashion. Con the Devil had scraped up
an intimate acquaintance with Mrs Mack's eldest, a young
scamp of about ten years, as full of mischief as Con
himself. In consideration of certain tips, this Mack boy
kept a strict watch over the state of his mother's health,
and the result was that on a certain day Con the Devil
was afflicted with a most obstinate toothache. Work might
go to the deuce, he declared, and out of the doctor's
surgery he would not stir. Have the tooth out? Not he,
indeed; it was sound as a bell, and medicated cognac
was the tip for *his* complaint. So the cognac was supplied
ad libitum, and the doctor medicated it – and himself.

I wondered what was in the wind that evening as a
crowd of laughing men gathered at Jones' place and the
poor doctor's.

'Whatever is it?' I asked, just as Con the Devil appeared
and shouted out, 'Come on boys! The doctor's dead, and
we'll have a jolly wake over him!'

'Dead?' I said.

'Dead drunk, poor man,' uncle explained. 'Con has been
keeping him on it all day because Mrs Mack is ill.'

'What a shame!' many said, but a good many more
were of opinion that it was a charity to prevent an
incapable man from committing manslaughter.

The next scene I personally witnessed of the Con
comedy was a strange one. On a sort of handbarrow

of rough material and construction, and borne on the shoulders of four men, lay the doctor on the broad of his back, with his grey hair all frizzed round his face, and his mouth wide open, and his eyes fast shut. There was no necessity for his friends being alarmed on his account, for his snores were evident as distant and regular thunder, though not even the shouts of Con and other wild spirits could awake him.

They carried him in procession down and up the street, and at last landed him for a wake on Jones' billiard table. Such a spree as was that night held around the doctor's insensible body has not been known there since, I know, and a queer scene it was, as witnessed from our verandah about ten o'clock.

The billiard table was reversed, and a white 'fly' spread over it, while upon the fly reposed the doctor, at full length, with some torches stuck around him, and a plate of snuff on his breast. The space around him on table and floor was littered with tumblers and diggers, whose loud laughter and jokes at last aroused the debauched medico.

'Where am I!' he shouted, as he started up like a Jack-in-the-box and stared around him.

'Where you ought to be, doctor! Ha, ha, ha, why you're dead!'

'Dead and be – ahemed – to you. Give me a drink!'

'To be sure, doctor. Con, give the doctor a drain.'

'Not I! A drain, indeed? There's poor Mrs Mack calling out blue murder for him!'

'Mrs Mack be – ahemed! Give me a drink!'

At this stage the curtain fell between the public and Jones', but when next the doctor came to himself he was chained up at Mrs Mack's dog kennel, and Mrs Mack's dog keeping grave watch over him, with the doctor's striped Kilmarnock night-cap securely fastened on his canine head. To the last day of his acquaintance one had only to speak of the 'doctor's wake' to see at least a semblance of his old spirits exhibited by Con the Devil.

NOTES

1. 'Song of the Gold Diggers', 'To ****', and 'Climb Up the Hill', published 14, 21 and 28 December 1855.
2. Charles Abraham Saint, proprietor of the *Mount Alexander Mail* until 1865, and afterwards of newspapers in Hong Kong and Gippsland. He died aged 63 in 1886.
3. 'Climb Up the Hill' was reprinted as 'Excelsior' in the *Australian Journal* (November 1880) without the references to 'serfdom' and 'No one need grovel here' of the original.
4. In the issue for 28 December 1855.
5. Sawpit Gully is now Elphinstone.
6. Butler Cole Aspinall (1830–75), barrister, journalist and politician, most famous as a defence lawyer at the Eureka trials.
7. Barker's Creek at Castlemaine.
8. Now Amherst.

CHINAMAN'S FLAT

Our next move was to the new rush at Chinaman's Flat,[1] via Daisy Hill and Maryborough, and a most unpleasant journey it proved. It was in the hottest days of a hot summer, and was a series of misfortunes of one kind or another. Fortunately none of them were very serious, decidedly the worst being an enforced encampment of four days on the then Ballarat racecourse, in consequence of all the bullocks of the party being lost.

I shall never forget that wretched camping ground, or the frightful hot winds we had to endure there. Persons who had no experience of outdoor life in our Victorian interior some twenty-six years ago can get but a faint idea of the hot winds of that time in the hot winds of today, and never had I a better opportunity of feeling them than during those days in a shelterless camp.

There was not a tree or a shrub on the burnt up level course, and not a roof save that of a sort of roadside store or inn, which we could just discern on a bleak track that had no charms for the wearied eye. Bullock drivers had a way of keeping their loads together in those days when it not unfrequently happened that a loaded dray got 'bogged', and rendered it necessary for the bullocks of one dray to be yoked to help those of another out of the mire; so there were five or six drays together, making a total of some fifty bullocks, who took it into their wise heads to leave on a private pleasure excursion, while we awaited their leisure in the delightful enjoyment of camping out on a shadowless plain.

There was then literally no shelter save what we could get under the respective drays, for during the heat of the day no human being could have existed in our military-looking tent. From early morning to late evening we sat or lay and panted under our drays, when every recurring puff of hot air felt as though coming through the blast pipe of a furnace, and could only endure, as best we might, in hopes that the men might that day be successful and find the truant animals.

There being, as I have said, five or six drays, our party made up pretty strong; that is to say, we might have been a dozen in all, including two women and three children, beside myself and youngster[2], and you may be sure that very little of each one's appearance or characteristics was left unnoticed during our enforced stay in that place.

It was on the second morning that my attention was first particularly drawn to one of my female fellow travellers. It was the morning custom of all to perform their ablutions in or at the nearest water, and far pleasanter it was than any dabble in a luxurious bedroom could ever be. Before the sun had arisen further than to lay long shadows across the gliding creek or waterhole, rippled by the cool morning breeze; before the dewdrops had evaporated, or the freshness of night airs had forsaken the welcome fluid, its touch on the heated forehead of the miserable mosquito-pestered campers out was worth gold, and it was at such a time that I first saw Ann Rashbone.

A steep banked creek was behind our camp, and down it the cattle had worn a broad track diagonally to the water, and from it a little footpath led to the creek higher up, where clearer and purer water was obtainable. As I reached this nook on the morning in question, I saw a young woman with a baby in her arms standing on the very brink of the water, and in so dangerous a position that I involuntarily seized her by the skirts and dragged her back.

'You will fall in,' I cried as I did so, and she turned on me a white face and a great pair of blue wild-looking eyes, and stared at me with an unpleasant persistence.

'Are you going to tell?' she whispered at last in the strangest hollow voice.

'Tell what? I have nothing to tell.'

'Haven't you? Mike would kill me,' and then she seemed to be-think her of the baby, and looked down upon it with a gathering frown on her low forehead. She was not handsome, nor was she plain, but she was just such a girl of twenty as you might see any day in an English country village to which the so called improvements of the day had never penetrated.

'Is the little baby yours?' I asked, as her frown grew into a scowl.

'No, it is Mike's. I am Ann Rashbone.'

'What are you telling the lady sich a pack of lies for?' cried a voice close behind us, and a stout, elderly woman, with a white cap, and a little shawl crossed over the front of her green wincey gown, snatched the child from the girl's arms and began to scold and tidy the infant's wraps with the greatest volubility and fuss.

'Ann Rashbone indeed! I wonder you're not ashamed of yourself! She's my son's honest wife, ma'am, for all she wants to shame us all that-a-way. Go up to the dray wid you, or Mike'll be coming afther you. Huzho babby, huzho. Ann Rashbone indeed! Did any one iver hear the like in all their born days!'

'Is the baby hers, then?' I asked, as the girl moved listlessly up the incline with the heavy frown still on her face.

'Av coorse it is, missis; but the crathur has got it into her head that it doesn't belong to her at all, but I often heard tell av the like – I mane girls going a bit aff their heads when they had the first increase.'

Of course I was interested in the trio that formed that family after this encounter, and had too much opportunity of studying them during our enforced detention. 'Mike', the man, was a stout built man of thirty-five or so, with a dark-looking, lowering countenance, and heavy black brows and whiskers. Mike Connel's hat was always well down over his face, and his eyes rarely lifted from the ground, when they were it was with a furtive suspicious glance that, when it rested on her, seemed to shrivel his unhappy young wife as though he had struck her.

It was impossible not to notice that she was dreadfully afraid of him, and that if ever he had cared for the girl his affection had not lasted. There were times when I believe he could have killed her had it not been for the consequences and the watchful admonitions of his doting mother and, between them, they watched every movement of poor Ann as if they suspected her of some evil intent.

It was some time, however, before I observed that she was not allowed to have the baby, save when her mother-in-law was at her side or not far away, and then she held the poor innocent with a horrified distaste that would exhibit itself. After events made it all plain to me, but at first I could not at all understand such apparently unnatural conduct on the part of a mother. Mrs Connel did her best to hide the strange truth; but it was soon patent in the camp that Ann was an object of watchful distrust to both her husband and his mother, while she herself hated both them and the child she held as if it was an object disgusting to the touch.

The Connel's dray was camped next to ours, and to the east of it, so that it was but natural they should affect the shade thrown by the vehicle during the early forenoon hours. I got used to seeing Ann sit idly on the burnt grass and look at nothing in the distance with eyes that seemed to grow larger in size and paler in hue with every day. She never seemed to notice the watch she was always the object of, but no sooner did she get a moment's liberty than she took advantage of it to start up and stare frowningly at the poor child, if he happened to be lying asleep or awake in the shade where his basket cradle was wont to be placed.

On one of these occasions I was startled by her seizing the child by its garments, and running to me with it hanging doubled up limply like a bundle of clothing.

'Take this child – take it at once,' she said, imperatively, as she dropped it on my lap.

'Do you want to get rid of it?' I asked, as I straightened the poor thing, who was about three months old, and an unhappy, puny looking little creature.

'It is Mike's,' she replied with apparent indifference, 'and my name is Ann Rashbone.'

'I thought your name was Ann Connel?'

'No! I hate that name, and that child is Mike's. Are you going to tell?'

'You had better take the baby, for here is your mother-in-law coming,' and like a frightened child she snatched it and returned to her own premises.

'I don't know what's best to do with her,' Mrs Connel said to me as she watched my face suspiciously to discover what effect her words might have on me.

'Do with her? What do you mean?'

'My son's wife, missis, that's just gone from you; sure she's gettin' worse every day.'

'How worse?'

'Arrah, what's the use of strivin' to hide it? Sure anyone wid ears an' eyes can take notice of it; the poor crathur's quite gone in her head.'

'Do you think she is out of her mind really?'

'What else can anyone think when she denies her own man, an' is set on killin' her own child?'

'Killing her own child!' I repeated with horror, but recalling too well the strange actions of the woman Ann. 'If you think that, surely it is not safe to allow the poor creature to be at liberty?'

'Faith an' it isn't, an' we mane to hand her over to the police on the first chance; but sure it isn't so aisy to prove the like of insanity to their satisfaction, bad cess to 'em.'

It was, under the circumstances, only prudent to avoid any intercourse with the Connels, and it was arranged that our dray should never camp near theirs again, so that until we reached Chinaman's Flat, and I witnessed the sad *denouement*, I saw little of Ann Rashbone, as she persisted in calling herself.

We passed, on our way, through several 'dead diggings' and among the rest that part of Maryborough that had been forsaken in the formation of that nucleus that has resulted in the prosperous town of today. A deserted claim is, to me, a more melancholy sight than a graveyard, for in the latter the suggestive mounds are symbols of a dreamless rest after the weariness of life is over for ever; while in the deserted and grass-grown shafts, the broken and weather-stained windlass supports, the fallen chimneys, and the blackened rags of calico fluttering from decaying rafter or wallplate, one reads but the record of disappointment and unrest. Among my memories of the ruin and decay of deserted diggings, I must class as the most prominent those of Forest Creek, which I have neglected to mention as the once prosperous almost addenda of Castlemaine; but old Maryborough looked sad enough too in '56.

Chinaman's Flat promised well when we pitched our tents at the side of a long straggling street of business places, but it did not fulfil its promise, and many stores, etc., that were put up there were moved again without having opened. Grieve's Store *did* open, and in a larger and more pretentious style, for I had actually a rough boarded floor and a real table, not to speak at all of the convenient little American cooking stove that was afterwards put to illegal use.

The water at Chinaman's Flat was the most grievous want; it had to be carted some distance, and was sold according to market rates, at from sixpence per bucket to four shillings a barrel, and such water! I often smile at our growls anent the present Yan Yean, and the necessity for filtering. As a rule, the water on diggings was so dense that you could see the suspended matter floating over and over each other in it like clouds of smoke. There was one rule in choosing when a choice was possible. We avoided red water and clear water (as being brackish), and selected that which seemed mixed with whitening when we could get it, yet I cannot remember of any illness in those busy days when people seemed to have really no time to die.

Before we had time to see the roof fairly over our heads we discovered, to our dismay that once more we had the O'Briens as neighbours.

'That I may never see glory if it isn't yourself an' the darlin' asthore machree of a b'y!' she exclaimed, as she set eyes on me, and ran across, clapping her hands in the height of her pretended satisfaction. 'An' how's yourself an th' ould gintleman? Oych, sure, here we are the same as ever, Dan an' myself, only for the ruin that blaggard Scotchman done on us, and may the curse o' heaven folly the same man day an' night till he raches his dirty grave is my prayer on my bended knees. I'm doubled wid pains an' aches since he destroyed me bewcheful feather bed – the divil roast him wid feathers, the murtherin' robber!'

'Have you ever seen him since?' I asked.

'Seen him is it? I have so, ma'am. We've follied on his thrack, pit be pit, and here he is on Chinaman's – and so beggora is Dan O'Brien's friends!' she added, with such a vicious emphasis that I should have been sorry to be in Munro's shoes.

An older acquaintance than Mrs O'Brien turned up in Slattery of Kangaroo Flat, who shook hands all round with such a radiant face as it did one good even to look at.

'And she's here!' he whispered to me, 'not a stone's throw from you! Do you see that white tent on the rise above you? Well that's mine, and there she is at the door, God bless her!'

'I am very glad indeed! When and where were you married?'

'Here at Maryborough a month ago. You see Polly has

some relations there, and it was handy for her to stop at while I was getting the place ready for her. You will come over and see her when you get settled, missis?'

'Indeed you may be sure of that,' and I went more than once to see the happiest little wife in Australia. She was prettier than ever, and as fresh and sweet as any rose, while her strong affection for her good husband was artlessly exhibited in every sentence from her lips. The beloved 'Tom' was ever on the smiling lips, and Chinaman's Flat has always been a saddened memory to me for little Polly Slattery's sake.

It turned out that Ann Rashbone and her unpleasing relatives were not far away from us either, and that Mrs Connel was a 'towney' or neighbour of Mrs O'Brien's at home. I got familiar with her husband's face too, as he took a fancy to deal at Grieve's Store, as well as to sell his gold there, of which he seemed to obtain a puzzling quantity.

Apropos of that fact there was a talk between uncle and I one evening about a fortnight after we had commenced business at Chinaman's.

'That Connel has been in again with some very fine nuggety gold, and from what I could hear and see some of the boys are keeping a watch on him,' uncle said.

'What for?' I asked.

'To find out where he's getting the gold. It seems that Connel is not in any of the known ground, and the diggers don't think it fair that he should keep a good thing to himself.'

'Neither it is. What harm would it do him to let some others work there too? Is Connel all alone?'

'No, he is not a hatter; he has gone mates with a Scotchman named Munro. I have been wondering if it was the O'Briens' Munro.'

'Well if it should be he is big enough to take care of himself at any rate.'

'Ay, against old Dan or Biddy, but the O'Briens are friends with a very shady lot of loafers here.'

This information made me feel more interested in Connel's movements than I should otherwise have been, and when I went up with my boy one lovely afternoon to have a walk with pretty Polly Slattery, she told me something that had tragical consequences afterwards. We had climbed the hill and turned down the other side, when she pointed to a little gully on our right.

'You would think this was a regular bush spot without a soul nearer than the Flat wouldn't you? Well you'd be mistaken, for there are men working among the scrub; but I only found it out this morning, and I'm afraid Tom will be angry with me when I tell him what I did.'

'What awful thing did you do then, Polly?'

'Tracked and watched them. You see Tom goes early to work, and as I was up the slope this morning to get some light wood for the camp oven, I saw first one man creeping through the scrub and then another. Well, of course as I'm a digger's wife I am interested in prospectors, and I followed on without them taking any notice of me, but the fun of it was I was caught myself!'

'Caught!'

'Yes. I was peeping between the bushes and as quiet as a mouse, when I heard a step, and in a second that old woman behind you was staring at me quite as frightened as I was myself.'

'Do you mean Mrs O'Brien?' I asked.

'Yes, indeed, and she asked me what I was doing there, so I told her that I expected my business was pretty much the same as her own, when she laughed and asked me not to tell I had seen her, for the old man would kill her if he knew.'

'As if she wouldn't go straight home and tell him!'

'Of course! The place will be rushed tomorrow.'

'Did you know the men?'

'Oh yes, one was Connel, that poor crazy girl's husband, and the other was Scotch Munro, a beast of a man that we knew on Forest Creek.'

Connel's prospecting neighbourhood was not rushed on the following morning, however, for a terrible incident prevented him from going to work, and Munro had apparently disappeared. And the sad news was brought to me by Mrs O'Brien herself, who was in a terrible state of excitement and trembling as if suddenly aged.

'Oh vo-vo! nothin' but misforthens an' misery! Did you hear the news? That unforthunat Ann Rashbone has done for the child at last.'

'What!'

'Arrah sure it's thrue, alanna, an' more's the pity, the crathur has throttled the babby all out, an' the father's gone for the police.'

Here was indeed dreadful news, but it was only too true. Ann Rashbone had murdered her little child. Strange stories of the ill-treatment she had received from Connel and his hard mother during her married life cropped out afterwards, and laid her insanity and its sad consequences at their door, but we saw the last of Ann Rashbone as she was taken away in a spring cart in charge of two policemen. She died very soon afterwards in an asylum at Castlemaine.

Connel and his mother accompanied the poor girl so far on her way, and when day after day went on and neither Connel or his mate Munro turned up, there began to be a sort of undercurrent of guesses as to the locality of the Irishman's successful prospecting.

'How is it that you don't tell?' I asked Slattery one day.

'Because I'm doing ripping where I am, Mrs — , and when my claim's worked out, I want to keep Connel's gully for myself; but what beats me is why old Dan isn't there, as Mrs O'Brien knows of it.'

''Tis strange,' observed Uncle Barry, 'and there is beginning to be some fuss about Munro it is said. It seems that he has left tent and blankets, and gold too, and never told anyone of an intention to leave.'

'In that case someone is bound to have a hunt for the gully and find it, so I may as well go out and mark out a claim in the morning.'

That was what Slattery said, and when I went up the hill for our usual walk Polly proposed that we should make our way alone to Connel's gully.

'It's not far,' she said with one of her merry musical laughs, 'and it'll be such fun! I'll peg out a claim and when Tom goes out in the morning he'll think someone has been before him!'

Over the hill and down the wooded slope to the right we came upon such a small gully as may be seen almost anywhere in Victoria, a distended cleft in the hill as it were, with its sloping sides and broad bottom covered with grass and granite boulders and scattered undergrowth; under and in the shade of a number of tall saplins lay, upon the otherwise undisturbed sward, the heaped-up 'stuff' that marked the mouth of the prospectors' shaft, and toward it Polly's agile figure led the way.

'It's not deep,' she said as she peeped down, 'but they have been filling it up again. That doesn't look as if they had bottomed on gold, does it?'

At the question I also looked down and saw, at about the distance of ten or a dozen feet, a heap of loose soil, through which part of a large stone seemed to have gradually penetrated as the soil settled; but before I had time to remark on the fact of the soil having been plainly shovelled back into the hole from the surface on which we stood, we heard the sound of voices, and lo, down the slope came a dozen men, headed by Tom Slattery.

'Bless us, Tom!' exclaimed Polly, as she drew back in astonishment. 'You have really caught me, for I was just going to peg out a claim for myself!'

'Come back, Polly dear,' he almost whispered, 'this, I am afraid, is no place for you. Some whispers of foul play to Munro have got about, and see at that!'

He was pointing toward the shaft, round which the men were gathering excitedly, and from which a swarm of flies were emerging with an angry buzz as we retreated to some little distance. In vain I begged of poor Polly to leave the gully altogether, for she took no heed of me save to shake her pretty head as she sat down upon a log with an awful horror in her big blue eyes.

'I *must* see it,' she said at last as I persisted in trying to pull her away, and so I sat down beside her, and witnessed one of the most dreadful scenes of my digging life.

After a short consultation, and many looks down that fatal shaft, one of the men went down by the steps in the shaft, carrying a rope with him, and then a shovel was sent down. The men were greatly excited, yet spoke in subdued tones that might be styled the buzz of human bees in their anger at finding their hive desecrated. It was such a strange contrast that one spot in which angry men were collected, and the green-growing verdure of the lonely gully where the birds were flitting and chirupping in the gum tree branches. Again, as many hands seized one end of the rope, and put their strength to raise some object beneath, I would have taken the now trembling girl away, but she only stood up and held on to me in silence, while her eyes were fixed on the open shaft below us.

A moment of throbbing and terrified suspense, and then the crushed and clay-stained body of a man was laid upon the fresh grass. Even from where I stood I could see the awful white face, and the crooked, rigid limbs, and the great, damp, red beard of the dead man.

'It is Munro!' gasped Polly, as she turned suddenly and commenced to go homeward, as if flying from the dreadful sight and that night saw poor, tender-hearted Polly raving in the wild delirium of a fever, in which she was always reviewing again Connel's gully, and the dead body of the murdered Munro; for that he had been foully slain there was no doubt, though no one more than guessed that the O'Briens had avenged their loss at Dan's Rush.

'Oyeh, is it dead he is? Well, well, an' it's glad I am that it wasn't a bether man that went! Throwed the big stone down an him whin he was at work, is it? Faix then he must have died hard wid his skull broke, and the divil a feather bed onder him. Bedad it's glad I am that we're goin' out o' this onlucky place,' was what she said as they were packing up for a move.

'Do you think he won't haunt you?' I could not help asking, 'and very little comfort you would have in the best of beds if James Munro's spirit stands beside it night after night until the day you die yourself.'

'The Lord betune us and all harum,' she murmured, as she devoutly crossed herself and went abruptly away; but I saw before she went that her face had turned white as clay, and her wrinkled hands were trembling like leaves in the breeze.

We got acquainted about this time with a man who had got the soubriquet of 'Lazy Joe' from his idle, lounging ways and extreme disinclination to movement of any kind. He boarded at a sort of restaurant that rejoiced in the appropriate title of 'Spell O!' which was under the supervision of a very fat widow woman named Collins. Mrs Collins being without legitimate male assistance, took kindly to Lazy Joe's aptitude for rest, and little by little turned it to such good account that he became her right-hand man, and ultimately her husband, and it was he who, coming on his own business one morning, told me the sad news that Polly Slattery was missing.

'Missing!' I cried,' how can it be possible? I saw her last evening when Dr Alcorn was there, and she was quite delirious, poor thing. How could she have gone away?'

'I can tell you when she went, for Mrs Collins was up at the tent. Slattery had to go in for medicine to Maryborough, and he got the old woman's horse, so she went up to stay by Polly 'till he came back, and when she went up there was no one in the tent, for Polly was gone.'

'Has Slattery come back?'

'No, but they're expecting him every minute, and his mates have turned out to hunt the hill for Polly.'

I waited to hear no more, but went quickly up to the well-known little white tent, and there I found poor Tom Slattery with his dying darling in his arms. They had found her in her nightdress, and with cruelly scratched bare feet and hands, lying by Connel's claim, and even at that supreme hour she was murmuring broken words about the dead man and the rough way to Connel's gully. Poor, gentle-hearted little Polly! Tom laid her in

Maryborough cemetery, and went away to face the empty life before him with a half-broken heart that refused to be comforted.

Still the sounds of pick and shovel did not cease though Polly died, and the rush at Chinaman's was far past its best. Diggers did not stop in their search for gold to even weep over the graves of their friends, and dance and song and fights and drinks went on as usual, and Lazy Joe got married. It was his wedding he was telling about when Polly's loss was made known to me.

'You see we're doing nothing on the Flat, and the boys are dropping off up Inkerman[3] and Kingower way, so we think it best to have the wedding come off before we go, and while there's idle time,' he said drawlingly, and with his shoulder propped up against the post, 'and now the missis is going to give a grand spree over it that'll be a sort of advertisement of the partnership like, so we hope both yourself and Mr Grieve will drop over and show your good wishes.'

Well, we did not exhibit our good wishes by a personal attendance at the entertainment, which became the great topic of conversation on the Flat for some days before and after the event, and, to the great delight of many, who should put in an appearance just then but Jack the Devil[4] of the Green Hills. We had left him behind at Ballarat, but he soon found out Grieve's Store in company with some old friends, and there he heard the tidings of the coming wedding.

'Lazy Joe going to marry a widow!' he cried, in unbelief, 'a fat old widow with tin! Whew! Ain't I glad I'm in time!'

'Do you know Joe?'

'Know him? I should think I do! But *she* doesn't, or I'll swear she wouldn't marry him! Lazy? ha! ha! did any of ye ever see Joe drunk?'

'Drunk? no. He doesn't drink at all.'

'He daren't, but he'll drink with me, and I'll show you some fun at the widow's wedding.'

Jack's jolly practical jokes were too well known and appreciated not to cause an increased interest in the coming spree, and every item of the preparations were retailed critically by the Devil himself for public information. He would mount a box or barrel, as a rostrum, and shout:

'Come here, boys, till I tell ye about the wedding!' when a mob of laughter-loving diggers would gather and listen to him with delight.

'The gown? Why, man, there never was seen the like of it since Mrs Collins was young, and that was before any of you were born. It's exactly the colour of an opening rose bud, and trimmed with flounces up to *here*. There's bows on it, mates, that are made every one with half-a-fathom of white ribbon, and twisted in the regular true-lover's-knot style. Oh, that I may never, but I wish I was in Joe's shoes! But I have one great fault with that dress, gentleman,' he would add, with great solemnity, '*it won't wash.*'

'One doesn't want a wedding dress to wash,' some silly would say, to be overwhelmed by another solemn, '*It won't wash!*' from the Devil, and 'I wonder what Jack means about the wedding gown not washing,' or 'He's up to one of his old tricks,' began to be common utterances of his friends.

Well, the great day came at last, and Jack, as best man, was, in truth, the picture of a jolly, handsome young digger, and, oh, didn't he make fierce love to the triumphant bridesmaids, who each one believed herself the most favoured; but, closely as he was watched, no one could see that Jack was trying to make Lazy Joe drink more than was good for him. One or two ventured to remind him of the fun he promised them, and got for an answer that solemn shake of the head, and a woeful, '*What a pity that gown won't wash!*' so they gave it up as a bad job, and waited as best they could his own time.

And truly it was not hard to wait, for the entertainment was given on a large and lavish scale. The party went to Maryborough to be married, and returned amid such hurrahing and firing of guns that half the business population on the Flat ran to their doors to witness the triumphant entry. Amid a cloud of dust and smoke rattled down the street the several vehicles composing the procession, the bride and bridegroom, with Jack the Devil and the bridesmaids, occupying a roomy waggonette in front, and three or four spring carts, threatening at each turn to run into and overturn each other. To anyone not used to sprees on the diggings the whole party must have seemed mad enough to be escaped lunatics, such hurrahing, and shouting, and firing, as they kept up. Every vehicle was decorated with green branches and coloured flags, that in which Jack was more especially proving his taste and determination to outdo the others by an exhibition of his decorative ability.

And then the reception as the half-distracted horses dashed up to the 'Spell O', the shouts, the hurrahs, the firing, the music that welcomed the descending bride; the overdone fuss with which that rogue the Devil helped the ladies to alight; the winks with which he replied to sly questions as to Joe's sobriety must have been seen to be appreciated, you know; but certainly so brilliant an affair was never seen on Chinaman's Flat before or since.

The 'fly' had been removed from the big roof of the late Mrs Collins' restaurant, and erected as a separate building, whose walls were filled in with a screen of green boughs, and here it was that the supper was laid and the dancing accomplished. The marriage had taken place in the afternoon, so that the fun began almost immediately on the return of the party, when some forty or fifty diggers, with only a very bare sprinkling of sweethearts or wives, sat down to the smoking and creaking boards, literally, for the tables were a rough, unplaned wood, and only temporary, as they were to be struck and carried out as soon as the meal was over.

And such a meal as no words can adequately describe; what with corks popping, and shouts of laughter, and singing of jolly good fellows, we could hear the noise too distinctly even at the store, and I daresay it was about nine o'clock before the tables were dismantled, and the two fiddlers struck up.

The new Mrs Joe's dress was the theme of universal admiration, and freely commented on.

'Looks stunnin'. A pity she's so fat, eh?'

'Pink silk don't you call it?'

'Ay, fifteen shillings a yard, if it cost a penny.'

'What do you think of Joe, mate?'

'Blessed if I know, I never saw him so quiet. I suppose he's too lazy to laugh.'

'Too sulky you mean; if ever I saw a man in a scot, he's one. I say, Jack, what's the matter with Joe?'

'It's a pity that gown won't wash!' replied the Devil, as he laid his finger knowingly along his nose, and went off on fresh mischief intent.

The bridegroom's conduct was indeed odd, to say the least of it. He sat at a table that had been left at the side of the booth as a handy and suggestive hint to the guests of the evening, for you must not by any means suppose that even a wedding in those days was not looked upon as a business matter to a certain extent. The table I allude to, then, was amply supplied with bottles, and from it the bride and her maids graciously and encouragingly dispensed the drinks 'shouted' and paid for by the guests. At this table sat Joe, as I have said, with his fingers clasped around a full glass that stood at his hand, and his eyes rolling from one to the other with an accompanying scowl that had caused the above remarks among the men.

It was observed that Jack was closely watching Joe, and was often obliged to hide his hilarity among the friendly bushes. One of the friends could not hold in any longer, and went up to the Devil as he was indulging his uproarious mirth among the leaves.

'What the deuce is up?' this mate asked, with some warmth. 'I call it a — shame for you to be keeping all the fun to yourself this way.'

'Oh Lord, watch Joe!' exclaimed the almost choking Jack.

'Watch him? Why we have been watching him all night. What's up with the fool? I never saw such a murdering scowl on a man's face.'

'Ha! ha! ha!' reiterated Jack, 'he's going to begin. Oh, watch him!'

Just as the Devil spoke it happened. Lazy Joe had been silently scowling at the company so long that even the busy bride began to notice the strangeness of his behaviour, and made her way toward him with her silk dress spreading around her like the tail of a peacock, and her expansive bosom covered with white satin ribbons and pink silk. She was not a bad-looking woman, though much older than Joe, and the plump hand she laid on the table near him was well-shaped and half-covered with rings.

'Don't be looking as if you was going to be hung, Joe, or they'll be laughing at us,' she said, coaxingly. 'Drink up your glass and take one of the girls out for a dance,' and, without a word, Joe lifted his glass and flung the contents in Mrs Joe's face.

But that wasn't all. Before she had time to wipe the liquor from her eyes, the madman had refilled his glass and dashed the contents all over the pink silk and white satin, and then he got up with a 'whoop!' and sent glasses and bottles, empty and full, flying all over the booth, while the dancers found shelter outside, and the music stopped suddenly amid the crashing of broken glass and splashing of wasted liquor. Every fresh breakage brought a shout of triumph from Joe, whose figure contortions were extraordinary to witness, until he fell down as suddenly as a man with a bullet through him, and began snoring like a double-power pig on the floor.

'Didn't I say it was a pity that the gown wouldn't wash?' shouted Jack. 'Here, lend a hand, boys, and we'll carry him to bed.'

'So that's what you expected, you rascal!'

'Just that. Joe's afraid to drink, for he always begins throwing the drink about when he gets pretty far gone, and many a row he's got into through it. Fire up, fiddlers, the course is clear for our heels now!'

There was another rather comical affair at Chinaman's Flat that may amuse some readers. On the hillside close behind us were pitched, higgledy-piggledy, a score or so of tents, and among them a very small one, occupied by the oddest couple you could well imagine. They came shortly after us, and drew all eyes by their strange appearance and amusing vernacular. The man was a twisted little wiry figure, with big joints and the hands and feet of a giant, and he was blessed in addition with a flat nose, a fiery red head, and an awful mouth that resembled nothing so much as the aperture in a frog's head. He wore coarse ribbed worsted stockings and corduroy breeches and when he was not working a tail coat that was ornamented with brass buttons, and reached nearly to his heels behind. He might have been any age from forty to sixty, and carried his head as if it grew directly out of a pair of terribly rounded, narrow shoulders.

His wife was a squat woman of about his own age, with a flat shapeless face ever exhibiting the dropped jaw and utter open-mouthed inanity of an idiot. Figure she had none. She was a square, flat surface on which was hung a stuff gown reaching to within a couple of inches of the top of a huge pair of leather boots, and a big red shawl crossed on the breast, and tied in a big knot behind. A flat sunbonnet of calico covered her head, and she had a baby of three or four months that she usually lugged about strapped up in the red shawl on her back.

Our first knowledge of this arrival was obtained by the man's visit to Grieve's Store for the double purpose of purchasing provisions and procuring information.

'And you mean to dig then?' uncle asked as he was supplying his requirements.

'Ov coorse, sur. What ud any man do on the diggin's but dig an' make his forthin?'

'But do you know anything about digging, or have you a mate who has got any experience?'

'Mate indeed! Fegs we have mate every day in the week, an' for why shouldn't we? Sure mutten is only thruppence a pound.'

'I don't mean mutton. I mean have you a friend or partner that understands digging for gold?'

'Partner inyagh! What a fool I'd be an' have to share

the goold wid him! But as for friendship, I have the best ov advice what I'm to do. Mary an' me we met an ould nabour in Milburn goin' home, av you plaze, wid the weight of himself av goold, and sure I axed him all about it.'

'What advice did he give you?'

'To get up here as fasht as we could an' watch for a rush, that was a lot of men running to where the goold ud be, an' to run then wid the best of em, an shtick four bits of stick in me ground, and as sure as my name was Patrick Deinhy, me forthin was in that bit of ground.'

Now, to the great misfortune of Patrick Deinhy, our rollicking friend Jack the Devil happened to be in Grieve's Store during this explanation, and he immediately tackled poor Patrick.

'Well, that's good advice as far as it goes; but did he tell you about jumping a claim?'

'Jumping a claim? What's that?'

'Why going into another man's ground if he doesn't work it regularly. For instance, if a man, as if might be me, was getting gold, and was foolish enough to get on the spree, why there's a chance for another man, as it might be you, to jump into that claim.'

'Ay? An' is it far to jump?'

To see the contortions of Jack's face as he tried to overcome his risible desires was enough to frighten his friends, but it didn't frighten Patrick Deinhy.

'Is it far a man has to jump, I say?' he repeated.

'That's according to the size of the claim.'

'Could *you* jump it?'

'Me? I wish I had as many as I could jump!'

'Oh, then I'm aisy, for what any man's able for I'm able for and so good mornin' to ye, an' thanks.'

'O Lord! the conceit of the little crooked anatomy!' cried Jack, as he laughed himself hoarse, 'and if I don't get up an especial rush for Mr Deinhy, I'm a nigger!'

Knowing Jack's abilities in the fun line, we became especial in watching for a new rush, as well as the movements of our odd neighbours the Deinhys. It was a regular practice of the woman's to go up the hill every

day and carry or drag enough wood to the tent to answer
the cooking purposes of the day, and while she was doing
that Patrick would lug about the wretched, puny baby
in an old rag of a shawl, or rock it mightily in the gin
case that served as a cradle; but he never for one moment
took his anxious eyes off the watch for a rush.

'I can't go out av sight av the ground,' he'd say, 'and
Mary won't take the child wid her.'

''Tisn't likely to be et wid shnakes,' she would
interpolate, 'and so I gives her every warnin' that the
minnit I sees the min runnin', down goes the babby,
av all the shnakes in Jerusalem war round the tint!'

'More shame for ye to say it,' Mary would say; but
sure enough Patrick kept his word.

Barely two days after Jack's encounter with Deinhy,
there was a sort of half holiday, of which the schemer
took advantage to get up a new rush. It was about eleven
o'clock in the day that Jack came down the street flying
with five or six other wild lads after him, each one with
a pick on his shoulder, and his mouth distended, crying,
'Rush oh!'

'Fwhat's that? fwhat's that?' shrieked the unhappy
Deinhy, as he ran out with the puling baby in his arms.

'Rush oh! rush oh!' shouted Jack, as he ran by with
his train of conspirators. 'A pound weight to every
shovelful! Now's your chance, Deinhy! now or never.'

'To the divil wid nursin'!' cried Patrick, as he tossed
the child into the box and seized his pick. 'A pound weight
to the shovel? Oh praises be I'm a med man for life!'
and off in the wake of the rush he ran.

They gave him a long run from one side of the lead
to the other, across Crampman's gully, among all the
stony ground, and up to the useless patch that then lay
near Sinnot's camp, and when poor Patrick reached the
spot, spent with fatigue and panting for want of breath,
he found Jack and his mates picking away in a ring as
if for bare life.

'Where'll I drive the pegs? where'll I drive 'em?' he
asked as soon as he could get wind.

'There isn't a bit left but that in the middle,' said Jack,

without ceasing his work – he was in such in a hurry you know, 'and you'll have to jump it. I'm going jump it myself as soon as I root out this heavy nugget.'

'Are you thin, sur?' asked Deinhy, with a sarcastical twist in his ugly face. 'By gob thin I might be beforehand wid you!' and he tore off his long-tailed, brass-buttoned coat in preparation.

'Wan, two, three!' he shrieked, and with a preparatory run the deluded man made a strong attempt to jump from the spot on which he stood to a bit of grass he concluded to be the jumpable claim, and he landed in it with an awful somersault, occasioned by a trip from that schemer the Devil.

'Ow! ow! meilla murther! me babby's gone! Paathrick! Paathrick! where are you at all, at all?' were the cries from the distracted Mrs Deinhy as, about an hour after her husband's 'rush', she returned to find both child and cradle gone. 'Wirrasthrue! wirrasthrue! arrah dacent woman, did you see e're a man or a babby rowlin' about anywheres? Arrah be all that's holy if that isn't himself coming home for all the world like a miller and the cradle an his back!'

Yes, he *was* coming with Jack the Devil 'shepherding' him at a little distance, and as they say in Ireland it was more the width of the road than the length of it with poor Patrick – that is to say, Jack had recovered him from the sad effects of his unsuccessful jump with so much of the contents of a bottle that he was staggering from side to side, and would have lost the baby and box both at every lurch if careful Jack had not securely lashed it on his back.

'You durty drinkin' slouch, where is me babby!' shrieked Mary, as she rushed toward him.

'Babby be blazed, an' you be blazed, an' every one be blazed! Stan' out o' me way till I jump for the rush! Bust ye, don't ye see what a hurry I'm in!' he shouted, as his wife seized the gin case and wrenched it from his shoulders. 'Bad cess ta ye, Mary Deinhy, av ye shtand in me way, an' I an the run for the new rush ov goold murther'll be done!'

'Iss there will!' roared Mary the irate, 'and good murther, too, if the crathur ov a child is hurted! Home to the tint wid ye, this instant minnit! Go an I say! Go up to the tint, ye shameless hang-dog divil!' and at every iteration the indignant woman laid a stick she had picked up on the road soundly and soundingly on poor Patrick's back.

'Oh, don't be so hard on him, missis; for he's met with a bad accident, strained himself with a heavy jump at the new rush you see,' this from the cunning Devil.

'I'll jump him, the hathen! Shtand up, Patrick, an' up wid you before I bate the jumpin' out o' you! Oyeh! Oyeh! draggin' the crathur of a babby to rushes an his back, and coming home wid his clothes like as a limeburner's! Go an home, ye baste!'

But Mrs Deinhy was mistaken about the baby, for when Jack had got Patrick well primed he ran to the tent for the child himself, in order to make his victim's return more ridiculous and as for the white colour on his cothes, they had only rolled him on a heap of pipeclay, that was all.

One more incident of the diggings at Chinaman's, and I wind up this paper. In shallow sinking by Bushby Hill worked two brothers who kept singularly to themselves, yet it was evident to everyone that they had been brought up to very different work and life than that of a digger. They worked early and late, and had been at several rushes before falling on the Flat, where they took up two single claims next to each other, but worked them separately. No one knew even their names, they called each other 'Brother', and when the mail came in they always got English letters.

Gold had been struck not far from them, and the ground was patchy and nuggety. Being anywhere not more than two feet sinking both had excavated a couple of square yards, when one afternoon the youngest brother, who might have been twenty or so, called out to the other who was stooping down over his work with the pick:

'Brother!'

'Yes, Teddy, what is it?' the eldest asked, lifting his head to see Edward sitting on the grass, with one leg still in the excavation. 'What is it, Ted? My God, are you ill?'

'What is this?' whispered the white-faced youth, as he pointed a shaking finger toward a lump of dull, clay-soiled something lying on the grass near his knee. 'Brother, what is it?'

'Gold!' cried the other. 'Oh, Ted, it is all over now, we may go home to mother! There must be forty pounds weight here! Oh, Teddy, hold up, you must not be sick just now when we have so much gold and are going back to the dear old home again! Ted! Oh, Heaven, have mercy! Ted! brother Ted!'

'Yes, Archie we are going home to – mother,' it was a whisper that came softly from the pale lips, as the lad's head fell to his brother's shoulder, and his last breath went out gently as the words ceased. The awful excitement, to which so many succumbed in the early days, had proved too strong for the weak frame, and a widowed mother in England waited long for her darlings, but only got one to again brighten the dear old home.

NOTES

1. A diggings three miles from Maryborough, described in James Flett's *Maryborough* (Glen Waverley, Poppet Head, 1975) as a 'hotbed of vice, hocussed drink and unchecked orgies ... the typical gold rush' (p. 81)
2. She had by this time two youngsters.
3. A diggings six miles from Dunolly.
4. Previously Con the Devil.

INKERMAN

There was a great choice of routes for those who had been disappointed in business at Chinaman's Flat; but the great attraction was heading toward Kingower, whose wondrous gold finds were already attracting great and deserved attention. Kingower, both as a place of business and a goldfield, had, however, one great drawback to the man of moderate means and that was the fact of its being entirely nuggety ground. A digger must be able to risk not seeing the colour for weeks or months, when a grand find might make him a wealthy man in one hour; and the storekeeper would find it impossible to do a business if he was not in a position to give credit when it was asked for. Grieve's Store was shifted to Inkerman, which was after all but a step on the way to Golden Kingower.

It is a singular fact, and one which I cannot account for, that my remembrance of the spot we camped on at Inkerman is more vividly present with me as I write than that of any other halting place during our days of digging life. It was on a grassy spot between the road and the creek, and it was at that time of the Kingower attraction a favourite camping ground for diggers and others bound for the Bet-Bet, Mongul [Moliagul], Dunolly, Kingower, etc., as it was surrounded by good pasture scattered over with shady trees; and one could hear the ripple of running water even as they made the fire to boil the billy for tea.

The store of goods having gone up by usual cartage, we ourselves were driven up in a trap drawn by a famous trotting horse, who was well-known at the time, but whose name I have now forgotten. His owner was a partner in a wholesale house at Maryborough, and so exceedingly proud of his animal's performances that I was truly glad to be deposited toward evening on the grassy level I have described to you. It was nearing evening, and our little round tent was already erected, as I and my young gentleman were lifted from the trap and seated among our household goods to admire our surroundings at leisure, while tea was being prepared by the men.

Four or five parties were camped there, some only temporarily, and some with an intention of 'giving Inkerman a trial', as they worded it. Only one of these parties had a woman and a child belonging to it, and they naturally attracted me most.

The woman was pale and delicate looking, though not ill; but that she was a helpless sort of creature was evident. She sat on the grass and looked bewilderedly at the meal scattered before her on tin plates and wooden boxes, and with the tea smoking in tin billy and pannikins, while her fine hearty-looking husband's whole attention was occupied in looking after the wants of the only child, a little girl of about three years. Never can I forget the beauty of that child, as, with her sunny hair in soft rings around her sweet face, she tried to interest her mother in the doings of a pet possum she vainly tried to keep all to herself.

"Ook at Possy, mamma! Possy hungry, and eat up all de cake! Peas, mamma, 'ook at my Possy!'

'Maria, dear, you are dreaming?' the husband pleaded in a low voice. 'Look at our darling, my love, and do take some tea.'

'Tea?' she repeated, as she started and turned her face toward him, 'do you call this tea? Oh, my God! Edward, why did you bring me here?' and she buried her face in her hands and groaned aloud. It was then I observed that her hands were slender and white, and that several valuable rings were conspicuous on them.

The little one stared for a moment at her mother, and then, pushing away her pet, scrambled to her feet and threw herself into the weeping woman's lap.

'Mamma ky and me ky too?' the little creature whimpered, while the father, with a pained look in his face, got up from his meal and walked quickly away. It was easy to see he was angry, and left so that he might try to control it, and I felt a growing interest in the little family I had only seen for the first time within an hour.

'Welcome to Inkerman, ma'am, an' will ye take a drop av tay for yerself an' the littly b'y till yer own'll be ready?'

These were the pleasant words that greeted me as I was absorbed in watching the woman and child, and I turned, to see standing at my side a comical looking little man with a pannikin of tea in his hand.

'Oh! there's milk in it!' exclaimed the little boy alluded to, as he greedily peered into the pannikin.

'Ay, ay! see that now! Arrah sure the crathurs o' childer misses the drop av milk worse than all.'

'Yes, and it's very kind of you to think of them,' I returned as I accepted the tea, 'it is not everyone that would deprive themselves of so scarce a commodity.'

'Oyeh wisha, ma'am, don't be sootherin' me, for it's meself that doesn't deserve it at all. Faix it's only settin' a sprat to ketch a mackerel, I am. Not that I'd begrudge the drop ov milk, God forbid, but you see the masther tells me ye're goin' to camp here for a bit, and I thought ye'd be a customer o' mine.'

'A customer?'

'Yes, for the milk, ma'am, sure I sells it. That's my tint

there beyant. Faix I'll be one ov yer nearest nabours, an 'twill be the handiest thing in life for ye to take the milk off me.'

'Oh, I'm so glad you keep cows.'

'Divil a cow thin, ma'am, savin' your presence, arrah where would the like o' me get the price ov a cow? No indeed, ma'am it's a few crathurs ay goats I have.'

'And does it pay you to keep them?'

'Why, then, I can't complain about the payin' part of it, for I can get three an' four shillin's a quart, but (in a whisper) I sells a drop o' sperrits on the sly you know, and the milk goes down very shweet that away you know. Oh, bad cess to him for a Commissioner, there he is again!'

Confounded at this sudden change of topic, I looked after my new friend as he flew toward his little tent, and dragged inside of it a goat which I now observed browsing on the grass near it. A gentleman, whom I presumed to be the dreaded Commissioner, was riding toward us from the direction of Dunolly, and as he passed by us he looked keenly at the different groups composing the camping parties. He then crossed the creek, and the hospitable little Irishman came back for his pannikin.

'Oh, bedad, he has a regular down on me, and the crathurs av goats!' cried he in answer to my questions about the Commissioner, 'blamin' 'em for what he calls deshtroyin' his garden intirely, and sure innocenter crathurs never drew the breath. He lives jist there beyant the creek where you see the hedges, an' that I may never sin, but he'll sit there watchin' the melons for half the night just as if a dacent-reared goat ud put her tooth in a melon! Oyeh! that I mightn't if there isn't poor Charley Clark and the missis and Possy!' and he ran off to join the man who had just left his tea to hide his feeling from the eyes of strangers.

But here I was introduced to another character, who has an important part to play in my reminiscences of Inkerman diggings. From a party of four seated around some smoking viands on the grass rose up a tall, dark young man, with a fine pair of dark eyes under scowling brows. He was dressed simply in loose pants and a serge shirt with a soiled scarlet sash round his waist, and a seaman's knife in its sheath sticking in the belt. It was his shout that called my attention to him.

'Hallo, Corney! here's the Commissioner! Turn the goats man! Turn them quick!'

The little Irishman turned *himself* toward the speaker, and if I hadn't seen it I could scarcely have believed his commonplace little face could possibly have expressed so much contempt as it then exhibited.

'Look here, Jim Lygon, I've tould you before that mindin' your own business is the payinest game for *you*. How mortal clever you are about my goats! Did you hear any tidin's ov Bob Dinon's horse yet?'

At the question that was put pointedly, Lygon's hand went toward his knife, but stopped ere it reached the handle, while another man beside him jumped to his feet.

'What is that you're saying about my horse, Corney? Have you heard anything of him?'

'Ask Jim Lygon,' was the reply, 'and if he can't tell you anything about the horse, come to me. Little as ye think of Corney Milligan, he's able to tell a goat from a horse any day, an' might be able to spake a word to the Commissioner, too, av he was put to it.'

'What does Corney mean?' asked the man who had been alluded to as Bob Dinon, 'what does he mean by telling me to ask *you*, Lygon? Have you seen or heard anything about the animal?'

'Confound you and the horse, too!' cried Lygon, as a perfect spasm of rage distorted his features. 'What the mischief do I know what the old rascal means? Go and ask him, and be hanged to you!'

'Keep a civil tongue in your head, mate,' was the cool reply, 'ill words don't break no bones, but neither you or any other man shall use them to Bob Dinon without paying for it!'

'Pay *me* for it, then, if you're able, you conceited whelp!' and the knife was this time seized and drawn from his belt, but before it flashed in the fading sunlight a blow was planted between his eyes, and the ill-tempered aggressor was stretched upon the grass.

He rose and swept the blood from his face. In his fall the knife had escaped from his hand, but he rose and lifted it only, however, to restore it to its sheath. He was so quiet about it that the men, who had started up from their suppers to interfere, spoke no word, only Dinon stood in a position of defence, as if he expected to be attacked.

'Oh, make yourselves easy, mates,' Lygon at last said, with a sneer, as he looked around upon the undecided faces of the men. 'I will not hurt your darling! Jim Lygon can bide his time, but by heavens you will pay for that blow, Bob Dinon!'

'I am able and willing to pay *all* my debts,' Dinon said shortly, as he turned his back and resumed his seat on the grass, 'but I will be bullied by no man living.'

I can assure you that I was a little frightened at this scene, and glad to make my way to the dear old uncle, who was busy helping the men to make all comfortable for the night ere they sat down to the now prepared supper. Corney was lingering among them, and to him my kind old relative, who had of course overheard the quarrel, addressed some words of inquiry as to the cause.

'Well, boss, you see this is the way of it. Jim Lygon an' meself worked mates at Daisy Hill, an' I caught him cheating me about the gold belonging to us both, so I tould him a bit of me mind an threw him overboard. He cleared out of Daisy Hill, an' I never sot eyes on him till I kem here and began wid the couple of goats. He's mates now wid the min you saw goin' to take me part a while ago, an' the horse you heerd me talk of belonged to the young chap Dinon. It was lost about a week ago, an' I have a good guess where 'tis gone to.'

'You suspect Lygon?'

'I just do, an' I'll tell you why, ma'am: I met an old friend of me own, that's carting on the roads, two days ago, an' he tould me he'd bought a horse from a chap of a description sech as Lygon; so, knowin' the horse was lost, I axed him to show me the brands. Well, so he did, and they wor thim av Bob Dinon's horse sure enough.'

'But you haven't told him yet?'

'No; but I will when he axes me, as he's sure to do, afther what I sed. You see the horse was gone to Daisy wid a load, an' I was waitin' to he came back, so as I cud be sartain wid the proof for Dinon's own eyes. Where I med the mistake was in not tellin' on him when first I sot eyes on him, for whin he saw I wasn't manin' to do so he began his little larks about me goats an' the Commissioner.'

'But what about the Commissioner? You haven't told me yet.'

'Oyeh! He has sech a down on the crathurs av goats that he ses aits the garden up intirely, an' he's always folleyin' me about an' watchin' me on account of 'em, that the lads are always screechin' "Commissioner" at me, for the fun ov seein' me run. Sure, he threatened to shoot the next one he sees widin twenty yards of the fence over, and he ses there's no law in the land for goats.'

'I'm afraid that the poor goats must really have been trespassing, Corney.'

'Sure, the crathurs don't know no better, an' a jontleman ought to make allowances for that; besides, he has the full of an acre of melons, an' sure he needn't begrudge a poor goat a bite out of one of 'em. Bad manners to the Commissioner, an' I don't care if he heard me sayin' it. Sure, it's run aft me feet I am thrying to hide the poor innocent crathurs whin they're thryin' to airn their livin' dacently about the creek.'

It was arranged that evening that Corney was to supply us with milk from his valued goats, and I wonder what my Melbourne readers of today will think when I tell them that our usual daily allowance was nine shillings' worth. Well indeed may we sigh as we take our pint of milk and water, and think of the golden days at Inkerman!

I rose next morning with unusual alacrity, for I was both curious and anxious to see what neighbours we were likely to have on our pretty green camping ground. The noise of hammer and saw had aroused me, and when we emerged from the well-guarded little travelling tent more than a dozen men were hard at work in erecting our own and other dwellings or places of business.

Grieve's Store was showing its full size in the rapidly fitted frame, and at but the distance of a few feet two men were erecting a good-sized tent. In one of these men I recognised the father of the pretty child 'Possy' and I saw her mother sitting listlessly on a box, and watching the little girl also sitting on the grass with the pet possum in her lap. I was never allowed to interfere with the cooking in any shape or form, so I thought I would utilise the time by making an acquaintance with my female neighbour that was to be.

'Will you play with that nice little girl?' I asked my son, as I led him to the little creature, who, with her finger in her rosy mouth, fixed her round, full eyes upon him rather anxiously, I thought.

'You are not afraid of my little boy, are you, dear?'

'No; Possy not afraid, but he mustn't touch *my* possy,' and she hugged her pet close to her with her two little fat, chubby arms.

'Oh, he won't, indeed; he will be very good if you play with him.'

'I very dood, too.'

So, under this satisfactory assurance, I left the children together, and moved nearer to the little one's mother, whom I had a better opportunity of scanning than on the previous night.

'Good morning,' I said. 'As we are going to be neighbours, I hope the children will be friends.'

'The children! God help them in such a place as this!'

'Don't you like it? Why, I think it is the prettiest place we have camped on yet. As the diggings are nearly all at the other side of the creek, we are in the suburbs, as it were, and I think it much nicer.'

She looked at me for a minute in a wondering sort of way, but when she saw I really meant what I had said, she, to my consternation, lifted her hands to her face and began to sob and cry.

As she sat there swaying herself to and fro, a woman not more than twenty-three or four, with a dress on that had once been of very elegant make and material, but was now neglected and untidy, I gazed at her silently, and, I am afraid, with some disgust, as she began to give utterance to her woes.

'To think that I have been brought to this! I was brought up like a lady, with servants to wait on me, and everything I could wish for to my hand, and now I am eating my food and making my bed on the cold ground, no better than a pig. Oh, Heaven help me! Heaven help me!'

Now I couldn't at all understand that sort of thing, and I had no sympathy with it.

'You astonish me!' I cried, and, indeed, truthfully. 'You are as young as I am and, I hope, healthy; you have your husband and the dearest little girl, *how* can you feel anything unpleasant in your surroundings? As for myself, I do think I never was happier in my life!'

She raised her face, stared at me wateringly, and then let it drop upon her hands again.

'Ah, *you* can't understand; you wasn't brought up as I was.'

'I don't know what you call being brought up,' I returned, with a red heat glowing in my face, 'but if *you* had been well brought up you would have been trying to do your duty in whatever state of life it met you in, instead of crying for nothing and making both your husband and child unhappy. Look at that little darling who was just beginning to enjoy herself with my boy, she is in tears now because she fancies her mother is unhappy.'

'Unfortunate little creature! What a life of misery my folly had led her into! Would to God she had never been born!'

'Shame on you, wife, to say so!' her husband, who had heard her, cried, as he lifted the pretty pouting baby and caressed her fondly. 'I thank God for her every hour, as she is the light of my life, and if I hadn't her sweet little face to look upon I'd have no heart to lift a tool.

For pity sake, rouse yourself, my girl! Your lot is far from being a hard one, that you had better try to be more thankful lest the vengeance of Heaven overtakes us for our ingratitude.'

'Thankful for what? – to you for persuading me to leave a comfortable, happy home for the life of a common tramp? Am I to go down on my knees and bless God for a drink of milkless tea in an iron pannikin when I might have been waited on with the best under my father's roof? Oh, yes, I have so much to be thankful for that I am overwhelmed with gratitude!'

I had risen to leave this painful scene, but the young fellow's patience was exhausted, and he set down the child upon the grass as he stretched out his hand, and an angry flash shot from his fine eyes.

'I would willingly cut that hand off if it would bring me back the day I had never seen you!' he cried. 'If it wasn't for the child I should have been mad long ago, for flesh and blood could never stand your selfish, puling ways. For the mercy of heaven, go home to your people! It isn't far to Melbourne, and I will give you every penny I have in the world to take you there, but you don't take the child!' And once more he lifted the little thing, and, pressing her close to his heaving breast, carried her away toward the breakfast his mate was making ready.

I paused a minute to see if she would speak or give me an opportunity of trying to soften her hard selfishness, but she never lifted her head, and she was sitting there when Corney brought the milk he had just brought from his favourite goat, Miss Molly, as he called her.

'Who is she?' I asked, as he seemed to recognise the woman with a comical twist of his nose. 'You know her, I think?'

'In throth I do, an' if ye expict to get any praises of her from Corney Milligan it's mistaken ye'll be. She was livin' close forrint me at Havelock, an' if I had the thraining of her it's a good batin' she'd have got long ago.'

'What is his business, Corney?' I asked.

'Waitin' an her ladyship an' nursin' the child, asthore. Oh, the sorra word of a lie in it! I seen him wid me own two eyes washing the clothes for her, an' she cryin' about the way she was rared! Business, ma'am? Sure he's a digger like the rest, God help him! But I forgot intirely – did ye hear the news?'

'No, at least we've heard nothing particular.'

'Why, thin, here it's for ye: Jim Lygon has hooked it.'

'Hooked it? What has he hooked?' I inquired, to the great delight of Corney Milligan, who laughed and stamped about till he 'most bust' himself, as he said.

'Arrah wisha, Misther Grieve, d'ye hear that! It's a reglar greenhorn ye are anyhow, ma'am! Hooked it manes runned away, an' that's what Jim Lygon done last night. But begorra, Bob Dinon's afther him. Oh, you heard it, sir? Well, I must go to the Commissioner's with the milk.'

'I wonder he takes any from you, as it seems like encouraging the poor goats he threatens to shoot.'

'Oyey! divil a shoot thin! It's all talk meself thinks, for bad cess to me if ever I saw a jontleman fonder of his taste of rum an' milk ov a mornin'.'

'It's good rum, too, eh, Corney?' uncle asked, cunningly.

'Faix, an' it is, sir; it's worth the milk any day, so long life to his honour, the Commissioner, after all!'

Even our first day in Inkerman was a memorable one, for it resulted in the disappearance of the general favourite, Bob Dinon. It appeared that he of the party had been the first to awake and discover that Jim Lygon was not in the spot where he had sulkily coiled himself in his possum rug to sleep, and a little search assured him that the man had gone for good, as a few articles belonging to him had been removed from among the others which had formed their load from Chinaman's. Young Dinon was of a quick fiery temper, and, Lygon's disappearance seeming to confirm the hint of his dishonesty given him by Corney Milligan, he started off to rout that character out and further question him.

As Corney related in evidence afterward, the young man shook him out of a sound sleep just as day was breaking in the east, and, as soon as he could understand what was up, closely questioned him about the affair of the horse he had lost. Of course Corney related to

Dinon all he knew, and was only too ready to declare that it was because Lygon was guilty that he had cleared out.

'I will follow the villain to perdition,' poor Bob cried, and his face grew red with anger.

'How can you, when you don't know which way he went?' questioned Corney.

'Oh, I'll find him! He must have crossed the creek at all events, for he wouldn't risk meeting the man he sold the mare to on the main track, and if he *has* crossed I can track him, for the dew's not off the grass yet.'

So he went back to his camp, and put his revolver in his belt, and then, without awakening one of his mates, struck across the creek by a fallen tree that did duty as a footbridge, and Corney Milligan stood at the door of his tent and watched him walking slowly across the grassy land between it and the bush until he could see him no longer, and that was the last that was seen of young Dinon's living form.

I may as well here finish the episode relating to this sad and terrible affair, though it was not in reality acted out for months after the period I write of. Corney lost one of his goats that same day, and after peering into half a hundred shafts, and making as many inquiries as he dared at the Commissioner's, who, he thought, might have impounded the animal, he fancied he heard her bleating in the direction of the very bit of bush on the way to which he had lost sight of poor Dinon in the morning.

'Oh yes!' he shouted, as he clapped his hard hands for joy, and started on the run for the sound, 'that's Miss Molly! I could swear to the Baa baa of her anywheres.'

This was toward the afternoon, and I was sitting with some sewing under the shade of some young blue gums watching, as I found opportunity, the interesting goings on within my view. My boy was delightedly engaged with hammer and nails, monstrously proud of helping to put up uncle's store, while uncle himself and his men were making rapid headway with the internal arrangements of the said store. The mother of little 'Possy' as the child persisted in calling both herself and her pet, was, in her usual listless way, standing at the opening of their nearly finished tent, while the father and child, close together, were delightedly watching the gambols of the tame possum among the leaves of a branch of green gum the man had laid down for its enjoyment. Not very near us, but still near enough for the hum of voices and sounds of pick and shovel to reach us, the diggers were earnestly at work, every one of them doubtless hoping to find beneath their feet the golden fortune he was in search of.

Amid the drowsy, pleasant air of a not too warm afternoon in the latter end of February, with the cool rustle of leaves and ripple of water, closer in these sounds were only pleasant breaks upon what had else been the loneliness of a bush life, but all at once I lifted my eyes to see that something unusual had occured.

The time had passed more quickly than I had suspected, for I saw that Corney had returned, and was standing among some men in the lead with his hands uplifted and a terrible horror in the expression of his face; but I could not hear what he was saying, as he spoke in a low tone, warned doubtless by the uplifted finger of a man I knew as one of Bob Dinon's party. A few words only were exchanged, and then the men separated for a little, going each to his tent or camp, and leaving Corney with his white face turned fearfully, as it seemed to me, toward the bush.

The bush I speak of was scarcely half a mile from the level ground behind us, and as the men went toward it in a body – there were five of them – I could see them quite plainly until they were lost in its shadows. There was a little stir, too, among the workers in the lead, and more than one lifted up his head to watch Bob Dinon's friends, but only one or two knew the truth, and my dear old uncle heard it.

'This is a sad thing, my dearie,' he said, as he came out to my side and looked toward the bush that as yet hid its secret from our gaze.

'What is wrong, uncle? I see some men going off with Corney, and one of them is carrying an axe and some rope, I think.'

'Corney has brought some bad news. In searching for his goat he has found the dead body of poor Dinon, and from what I can learn they fear he has met with foul play. I saw Merriton's face as he passed, and it looked awful.'

'Who and what is Merriton, uncle?'

'He is a miner from the Pacific slope, and a bosom friend of the dead man's. If there has been foul play, no man will ever be avenged as will poor Bob Dinon – if they had been brothers Merriton would not have loved him more.'

'I found him,' Corney, whose very lips were white, said, when they had carried the body to the public-house to await an inquest, 'lying on his face, dead, with a knife stuck up to the heft in his back. It was Lygon's knife – oh, for the love of the living Lord, don't ask me any more.'

I might here give you the evidence at the inquest, but it would be only a repetition of what Corney said to us at first. It was agreed, without a doubt, that the poor fellow had been foully struck down from behind, and that he must have perished at the hand of the implacable Lygon, for whose arrest a warrant was vainly taken out. Many and loud were the curses heaped on the murderer's head, but he did not hear or heed them, and no one ever again set eyes on Jim Lygon.

Everyone who knew him noticed the change wrought in poor Corney by his discovery of the body, for he went about as a man with a load of care upon him. I have seen him sitting at the door of his tent, and, gazing at that awful bush, suddenly rise and throw up his hands as in some horror of memory, and it was painful to see how vainly he tried to be his own old light-hearted self. All tried to cheer him up, and avoided alluding to the subject whose memory was so painful to him, but the shout of, 'Here's the Commissioner, Corney, and he's got a gun!' that used to get his dander up a bit, scarcely brought a smile to his lips for many weeks after poor Dinon's death.

Now, I told you I would finish relating the circumstances connected with this sad affair, and they will account to you for the powerful effect it had on the mind of the Irishman. Months after, and on Kingower, Bob Dinon's friend Merriton, 'Pacific Slope', as he was sometimes called, met with an accident in the deep sinking, and when he was near his last moments he called his three mates and Corney Milligan around him and solemnly released them from a fearful vow he had imposed upon them beside the dead body of his friend Dinon. It so happened that Corney and his goats had also migrated to our vicinity on Golden Kingower, and it was in his forcible but simple words that I was first told the awful story. I will give them to you as I can recall them, but they gain nothing by my relating them.

Yes, he's gone. God rest his soul an' forgive him his sins! Oh never mind me, me frinds, I can bear to talk of it now, for poor Merriton has let me tongue loose, an' he's gone himself to answer for what he done. Not that I'll say now but what it was right, no I won't; but I couldn't have done it meself, the Lord forbid!

I needn't tell ye how I ran to the lead whin I saw poor Dinon, for ye know it; but what ye don't know is what happened afterwards whin I took Merriton and Fiddler Joe and Manxman Tom to the place. I saw a look in Merriton's eyes whin I tould him of the knife (for I knew it) that frightened me, though I didn't know for what, an' I shook like a leaf whin I saw him draw out the blade and lift it up over his head.

His face was white as a sheet, and his black eyes like fire with the fury as he shouted out, 'I swear by the Holy Maker of my soul and my body that I will search for the man that did this deed until I find him, ay if 'twas for twenty years, an' that *when* I find him I will drive this knife in his cowardly heart.'

Oh, I'll never forget it! Just as my knees were bendin' under me, an' every man's eye was on Merriton, what should I see but the white face of Jim Lygon crouching in the bushes not six yards from where we war! He couldn't stir widout bein' seen, and if the word was to save me own life I couldn't have helped the hand I lifted up agin him as I stared at his face. The Lord above forgive me, for it was my hand that pointed him out for death. Merriton saw me, and with one bound he was on the murderer an' had him by the throat.

I could see exactly how it happened, for they were all on him, but seein' that Merriton was mad they tried to drag him off Lygon.

'You wouldn't kill him in cold blood, mate,' they shouted, but shure they might as well have shouted to a rock.

'Keep back, ivery one ov ye!' he yelled, an' Lygon's face was black with his grip on his throat. 'Ye have heard my oath, stand back and see how I keep it.'

'For God's sake!' the unfortunate man gasped, 'don't choke me, let me have a chance to face you!'

'One word!' Merriton said, as he loosened his grip – 'one word of the truth, and I'll let you go! Did you drive this knife into Lygon's back?'

'I did, and I wish it had been yours. Now, let go my throat and give me fair play.'

'Yes, you shall have fair play, now I loosen my grip! Die, cowardly dog that you are!'

As he said the words he had buried the knife deep in Lygon's breast, and as he flung him from him like a rag the wretch fell so that his face was within six feet of poor Bob's. There he gasped his life out, and we standin' looking at him for all the world as if it was a dream.

As the last gasp left him Merriton turned to face us, tall and hard looking as a man ready to defy his life.

'Now, mates, I've kept my oath,' he said, 'and my life is in your hands. You can do with me what you like, but if it was to do over again I'd do it a hundred times for Bob's sake.'

'He deserved his fate,' said Manxman Tom, 'and I for one will tell no tales.'

'Nor will I either,' Fiddler Joe said. 'I swear it.'

'Then my life is in your hands,' ses Merriton to me, 'so what do you say, Corney?'

'God forbid that any man's blood should be on my tongue,' ses I.

'Very well, thin,' ses Merriton, 'swear it to me – swear by the God you worship that your lips will never breathe one word of the deed I have justly done,' and we swore it as he said.

'Now,' ses he, 'we'll bury him,' an' we did bury him in a soft hollow where the bushes were tall and thick, and then we carried poor Bob home, an' you know the rest.

Yes, we knew the rest, but even to this day I don't think a dozen living persons know the real story of Jim Lygon's fate.

But having gone in advance of time, I must return to Inkerman, and to the fortunes of those among whom our lot was for the time being cast. We had scarcely settled when a load of timber and tenting with some boxes and bedding was deposited near the store, and soon a large tent was erected with a calico sign nailed across the front, and a long peeled sapling stuck in the ground, with a pair of 'halliards' [halyards] attached, ready for the elevation of the flag which was at that time the almost universal decoration of a certain class of business places.

Almost everybody took an interest in their neighbours in those days, as upon them depended the comfort and quiet of one's lives, so I was grieved at the very first sight of her to recognise in Mrs Jolly, as she called herself, the landlady of the new 'Restaurant', a woman of most repellant exterior.

She was about forty, I should say, and was a large, rather well-built woman, with a grand display of black hair, and a bold, well painted face. As a rule she was either slovenly to extreme, or dressed with a showy display of jewellery, etc., quite unsuited to her position. Of course drink was sold in the place, as it was in nearly every place of business whatever it might be called, and it soon leaked out that the 'Jolly Restaurant' was simply a notorious gambling saloon, that had been on almost every digging opened in Victoria.

She was supposed to be a widow this woman, but she had as factotum a big fellow known as Bill Bruce, and always a girl as attendant and attraction.

Now, it unfortunately happened that in the girl who came to Inkerman with Mrs Jolly the mother of little Possy recognised some acquaintance of her school days. I say unfortunately, for I attribute to that fact all the sorrow and shame that followed for the poor husband of that woman. I find I have not yet given her or him a name, [she had – Clark] but as I have a good deal now to say about them I may call her Mrs Deasy.

Their tent was within a stone's throw of us, a pretty white thing, pitched on a green rise with plenty of young trees to shade it, and the creek shimmering within a few yards of its threshold. It was behind both Grieve's Store and the Restaurant, and as my quarters were always to the back, out of the bustle, my usual seat under the verandah commanded a full view of Deasy's tent and Jolly's back door.

The first thing I noticed of Mrs Deasy's acquaintance with the girl was when the latter strolled across the grass one day and accosted the digger's wife with great heartiness and hilarity, and often after that I saw the overdressed creature coming and going from the tent, and not unfrequently accompanied by Mrs Deasy. That her husband did not approve of her intimacy was plain to me, one day, when he came home to dinner and saw the girl 'Bella' carrying little Possy in her arms as though toward Jolly's, when he followed, and took the child from her rather sharply, I thought. There were loud words between the husband and wife on that occasion, and any visiting between Bella and the wife afterwards was during Deasy's absence.

But, alas! it was soon patent to all that the unhappy woman had only too readily succumbed to the influence of those vile women; more than once I had seen her staggering back to her tent to sleep off the immediate effects of the drink she was ruining herself for, or being led there by her pretended friend Bella. At such times she would take the poor little child with her, or leave her on the grass playing with her faithful pet, and once she came to me, led by my little boy, who said that she was asleep on the grass, and awoke crying for her daddy, but there was no one in the tent.

Well, I could do little in the matter, but I was urged to do more than I dared to have ventured otherwise by a few words addressed to me by Deasy himself. I was sorry for the poor man almost beyond expression, for, as he said, it was impossible not to see that he was bitterly ashamed to have to address such words to a stranger as I was to him.

'You are a woman and a mother, and you must know that I say what I do only because I do not know where to look for help, but I cannot leave my claim, for I am getting gold; when it is worked out I shall take her and the child to my mother's.'

He had asked me plainly to let my little boy, who was a couple of years older, watch Possy, so that he might tell me if Mrs Deasy had left her, or was helpless, and I had promised all I could.

'I will watch myself,' was what I had said, 'and if things are going wrong I will manage to send for you, but you know I could not interfere between Mrs Deasy and the child and those people at the restaurant.'

So he quite understood me, and explained to uncle the position of his claim in the event of anything unpleasant happening.

After that I observed that Mrs Deasy never left the child outside the tent when she returned from Jolly's, or, when she was quite incapable, Bella or Mrs Jolly would fasten the door, and secure the child inside. The poor little thing would sometimes cry so piteously while the mother slept her drunken sleep, that my very heart was pained for it, and the little sad face that used to run to meet the patient daddy, and hide itself in his breast, grew whiter every day.

I have seen that man cry with bitterness that even I could not wholly fathom. I have seen him sit down outside his tent, with the child and her pet the possum clasped in his arms, and the hot tears dropping on her sunny curls, while the woman was standing holding on to the corner post of the fly, with her face swollen, and that idiotic expression sodden drunkenness wears ere it lapses into insensibility. He had tried everything in vain. He had appealed to the heartless women of the restaurant, to be laughed at for a fool, or bullied as a tyrant, and as for her, the mother and wife, she cared for nothing, not even the lovely little darling her conduct was destroying.

But at last the end came, an end so sad that it is remembered yet by every surviving mother who was on or near the Inkerman Diggings, and it fell the heavier upon poor Deasy in that it happened on the very last day he was to work on his claim. They had taken the last bit of 'bottom' out, and were washing off the last load, when our messenger reached him, and he was to take his darling to his mother's arms only tomorrow!

Alas for the sadness of that anticipated tomorrow that never comes! For some days Mrs Deasy had kept middling straight, and she was jubilant that soon she was to leave the hated life behind her; but I do believe that there was a purpose born of the devil in the minds of those servants of his in the restaurant that day, for they regularly besieged her as soon as her husband had eaten his last dinner under his canvas roof. With much affectation of sorrow at her leaving, they feasted her, until she, in spite of a solemn promise made to her husband, was as usual incapable of standing, yet she was not so far gone but that she was aware of her own condition, and led the child inside the tent ere she dropped the canvas and secured it.

I have often wondered since what made me so uneasy that day. I had often seen the child and mother hidden from the sun in the same way, and felt no fear; but it was the last day, you see, and I felt superstitious about it. At all events, no sooner did I hear the little one's piteous wail denoting that her patience was exhausted, than I persuaded uncle to let a man go over to the lead and tell Deasy.

By the time he came home, looking hot and excited,

there was the strangest silence around the back of our places and about the creek – it seemed as if the very air was voiceless, and not a living creature was to be seen even around Jolly's. The little white tent was closed, and I saw Deasy turn and look quickly toward me, with his hand on the canvas as he stooped to unfasten it.

He went inside, and the silence seemed to deepen for a moment, until he again appeared, running around the tent like one bereft of his senses, and then he tossed up his arms and shouted so that he was heard far around us –

'Merciful powers! the child is gone!'

As if a blow upon a hive had alarmed the busy tenants at his shout, every man and woman emerged from tent and dwelling, running, the nearest of them, to join Deasy, and learn his trouble.

'My child, my child!' he cried, distractedly, 'she is gone, she is lost! She has crawled out under the tent, and is gone, while her wretched mother is lying drunk in bed! Oh, for mercy's sake, help me to search!'

They searched everywhere, following the track up, and into every dwelling to which the little darling's feet might have carried her, yet, strange to say, there was not one foot bent toward the creek. I think that was because Bella declared that she had seen the child, after her mother had lain down, going in quite an opposite direction; but all at once the distracted father remembered, and ran down toward the not distant creek, whither he was followed by many pitying and sympathising parents – myself among the rest.

I shall never forget it. The creek was so narrow that a man might almost have jumped across it. It was so shallow, too, that the roots of the rushes that grew in it were, in many places, just only covered, but there were amid the rushes clear little pools on which the sun rested warmly, and in one of them lay dead our dear little Possy.

She was lying on her side, with the sweet little cheek resting on a pillow of rushes, in which one of the little hands was entangled. She had evidently struggled to get on her feet until completely exhausted, and then laid her head down to die. Such a sad picture of peace and

purity no mother's eye had ever rested on; but, alas! there
was no mother there to weep over the dead child.

As for Deasy, he was mad for a time, and not one
of us doubted it. He stooped and lifted the little one,
and, as he pressed her all dripping and cold to his warm
breast, he called to her with every loving word his heart
dictated to speak to 'Daddy'. It was piteous. He would
not believe the child dead until, all at once, the truth
flashed upon him, and, with an oath on his lips, he ran
with the corpse still in his arms to his own tent.

'Follow him,' was the cry, 'or he will kill that woman!'

And some who were anxious and friendly kept near
him as he ran.

Goodness knows what aroused the woman – perhaps
it was her husband's awful cry as he rushed toward the
creek – but when he came back she was standing in her
old attitude, holding on unsteadily to the post at the
doorway of the tent, with her red, bloated face, and that
general look of disorder that hangs round and betrays the
woman who drinks. She saw her husband coming up with
the child in his arms, but her face never changed in its
idiotic stupidity; she did not guess, she was incapable of
even guessing, that there was something wrong.

He held the child in one arm, and, grasping her with the
other, drew her face to face with his dead darling.

'May the sight blight you in future!' he shouted. 'Are
you too drunk to know that you have murdered your
child? O God! that it should be yours! that a thing such as
you are could once have claimed an angel from heaven!
May the great curse of a just God follow you to the
deathbed of a drunkard; that is *my* prayer for you – the
prayer of a broken-hearted husband and father.'

With the words he flung her from him, and she fell upon
the grass, nor was there one hand extended to help her up,
not even that of the wicked woman who had helped her to
make herself the murderess she, in the sight of Heaven,
undoubtedly was.

It was a sad story, but, after the usual inquiry, poor little
Possy was buried, and the wretched mother went home to
her friends in town.

PART TWO
THE JOURNALISM

Fourteen Days on the Roads

It was in reality only ten days and eleven nights I confess; but fourteen sounds better, and looks better at the head of this article, and as I have acknowledged that in using the extra number I simply consider the ornamental tendency of the word, I don't think you will have any objection to its remaining so.

Perhaps you want to know what I mean by 'Fourteen days on the Roads?' A very short time ago, and I should not have understood the term myself. It is very suggestive; suggestive of chain gangs, and stonebreaking, and a convict's dress, and guards, and all that, and yet a moment's consideration will assure you that the term is too short a one for any judge's sentence. *I* at least was neither tried nor condemned, nor sentenced, excepting by the overwhelming influence of £ s. d., to spend my fourteen days (ten) on the roads, yet there I did spend them, in the order and manner in which I am about to relate.

'I have been eight years on this road, and not a carrier

on it shall beat me off it, if my horses had to eat their own heads off!' So I heard a carrier declare during my enforced journey on the 'roads', and now you will guess that I am about to describe to you the incidents of a journey to town in a carrier's waggon. I wouldn't 'do' that time over again for – well, I'd better not commit myself untruthfully to so little purpose – but the bribe would have to be a high one, and yet I would not have lost it for twice as much.

I learned so many wonderful things! I really never knew how entirely ignorant of everything of serious consequence I was until I made that journey on the roads! But I am anticipating, and forgetting that everything has a right end and a wrong one. I can assure you that when I had been three or four days on the roads, I came to the decided conclusion that I had undoubtedly begun at the wrong end when I paid into the hands of my friend the carrier the sum of three pounds for the privilege of being transported, with all my belongings, from the agricultural district of O — [1] to the great metropolis of Victoria; but that, you know, was during my days of ignorance, and before I had learned to appreciate the value of the wonderful experience which I had been permitted to acquire at the expense of so very small a sum.

Why, my very first day's discoveries were worth the money twice told! Accustomed to be considered a thing of some little consequence as a sentient being of the weaker sex, it was of material benefit to me to discover that, in the eyes of carriers and their drivers, my comfort was not of any comparative value with the due and convenient adjustment of a loose keg or angular case. If the former was, by accident, tumbled into my lap, and lay there comfortably, or the latter fitted more agreeable to the luggage with its sharpest corner jammed into my side, nothing, I soon discovered, was more preposterous than the supposition that my comfort or convenience would be at all considered in the matter. Thus, had I only paid those three much begrudged pounds to learn to properly estimate my own value, the sum had been well disposed of.

I don't think that this is at all an unsuitable time to record the incidents of a journey on the 'roads'. In a very few years more the 'iron horse' will be conveying those monstrous loads of wool to the seaboard which are now so tediously dragged over rutted roads through the bush to their destination. The array of barrels and boxes, cases of crockery ware and of boots, loads of flooring and shelving boards, tons of iron, wrought and unwrought, that patient horses now draw toilsomely for hundreds of long tedious miles to their destination, will soon be whirled, with the speed of lightning almost, through a country no more terrible to the traveller, and without, thank goodness, interfering with either his ribs or general comfort; then, of course, those huge waggons with their complicated mechanism and obedient teams of horses, with their canvas tilts and self-sufficient drivers, will be things of the past, and I shall be relating to my grandchildren, perhaps, this story of my journey to town as a tale of wonderful adventure by 'flood and field.'[2]

My first experience, then, of a life on the roads was begun on a spring evening, just when the last rays of daylight were fading out in the west. Two huge shadowy-looking objects were looming up from the indistinct grassy margin of the River King, and near them a fire was blazing up and illuminating the faces of two men who were sitting easily upon the grass and doing apparent justice to a hissing pan of steaks and a smoking billy of tea. I was too anxious, however, to see the accommodation with which my precious self was to be provided to pay much attention to the details, and having been pointed out the particular object which was to be my residence during my journey, I prepared to ascend and examine its capabilities.

No easy matter either, and one at which it required considerable practice to become expert. First you had to make use of the spokes of the 'off fore' wheel as a ladder, and then, by a sort of 'sleight' of foot, wriggle yourself into a narrow space in front of the driver's seat. From thence you transported yourself as best you could under a heavy curtain of heavy canvas, and on this first occasion I accomplished all these feats to find myself in darkness, and with so unsteady a footing, that I was with difficulty able to strike a match and provide myself with a light.

Well, it did not look so unpromising after all. The conveyance was, perhaps, some fourteen or fifteen feet in length, and, having but a miscellaneous jumble of loose goods on the bottom, quite high enough for a person to stand up comfortably. It was quite new too, and the snowy duck, bright red and blue paint on the body of the machine, made it look cleanly as well as gay, and in comparative content I laid my mattress down upon a foundation which the carrier or his driver seemed to think quite good enough for a much superior article to a passenger.

I should like to particularise. Take three coils of heavy rope, a broken box of Epps' cocoa, two brass-knobbed trunks of unequal height, one butter-keg and a patent churn. Having procured these articles, carry them one hundred and fifty miles in a carrier's waggon, at every township requiring something to deliver which happens to be directly at the bottom of the waggon. When all this has been accomplished, and you have delivered all the articles save those enumerated, take the remainder as a resting place for your mattress, and you will have some idea of the comfort I enjoyed on my first night on the roads.

But it was of little consequence. There are many things that make a bed uneasier than coils of rope, even though they may have blocks and tackle attached.

> 'In vain does Betty perform her part,
> If a rumpled head and a rumpled heart
> As well as the couch want making.'

And it was not certainly the want of Betty's help, or the very immediate presence of the blocks and pulleys, that prevented me from sleeping that night, in spite of the soothing night-ripple of the River King and the rustle of the waving branches that shaded the waggon.

The sun had just arisen when I emerged from my elevated resting place on the following morning. A singular noise awoke me. It was the horses munching their feed out of the feed-cloth stretched on either side of the pole of the waggon. The fire was already kindled and the billy boiling when I succeeded in placing my feet once more on terra firma, and a tall lanky youth was engaged in making preparations for the first meal of the day.

His first arrangement was the careful spreading of a cornsack on the ground – this was the tablecloth. On it were placed two tin pannikins and two tin plates. A loaf of bread was flanked by a stewpan smoking and hot, and two or three round coffee tins held the butter and other condiments necessary to a bushman's meal.

I want to describe this tall lanky youth to you, and I want you to feel interested in him. Of late our colonial youth are giving statesmen and politicians – and, indeed, everyone unselfishly interested in the future of our country – a great deal of troublesome consideration. If you were to travel over Victoria from north to south, and from east to west, you would not find a more perfect specimen of the colonial youth than my friend 'Ben' and yet were all of the genus like him in every respect, the future of 'our boys' would not look so gloomy.

Tall as a reed, and flat as a lath, Ben was nevertheless strong and active beyond his seeming. His hair one could scarcely judge the colour of, so tangled was it and matted with dust. His eyes light blue, and *nothingy*, his nose nowhere, and his mouth large and unshapely. But there was a pleasant smile always ready to impart beauty to Ben's face, that made you forget its want of regularity and form.

But, alas, that mouth of Ben's! If it was *only* the never ending smoke that issued from it, or the black pipe held so persistently between teeth already destroyed by the poisonous fumes. One might be sorry that the boy of nineteen years should puff all his hard earnings away in clouds of filthy vapour, if the words were pure and lad like. But Ben could swear as loudly and as earnestly as the best driver on the roads, and when I have said so much, I need say no more.

It was an after-discovery that Ben was a perfect butt to his fellow drivers, and considered fair game to every man who fancied himself a wit, or felt sufficiently out of temper to vent some of it on Ben's unprotected head. But it was all lost on the lad – fell off him as harmlessly as water from glass; his perfect temper and childlike simplicity rendered him invulnerable to every description of 'chaff', which he was enabled to often frequently return with a point that had left himself untouched.

The simplicity of a youth who was a proficient in all the slang and oaths of a colonial 'road'! Yes, it was very strange and very unusual indeed, but so it was. Ben's wickedness, I do firmly believe, was gathered through the ear as a magpie learns his words, while his heart was susceptible of far better influences. But, alas, for poor Ben! where is he to meet with those influences? Who will undertake to provide that instruction for the lad that might enable him to judge between the evil and the good, and to eventually prefer the latter? 'Echo answers, where?'[3]

Ben's usual attire was a Crimean shirt[4] and a pair of dirty moleskin trousers, and the size of either did not seem to be a matter of importance in his eyes. An old battered felt hat, under which his shock of hair stood out boldly, and a huge worsted comforter, completed his general attire. In cold or wet weather he had an old tweed coat to drag out from under some bags or boxes or green hides, and to induct himself into, and thus fully equipped, he was the picture of an overgrown, slouching lad, whose clothes had, by some means, been arranged, as the old saying is, 'with a pitchfork'; and the general effect was not attractive.

To the best of my knowledge, the said articles of attire were never removed, day or night, save at those rare intervals when Ben considered a change necessary. Indeed, his general habits would have rendered such a removal extremely inconvenient, as, wet or dry, Ben invariably spent the early part of his night, when other people had gladly crept to the shelter of waggon or dray, stretched, face downwards, and at full length, on an empty sack in front of the roaring fire he had built to sleep by. When it died out, and the cold awakened him, he would dreamily get up and stow himself away out of sight again until the first rays of morning made attention to his horses necessary.

He drove a team of six, did Ben, and drove them with as much satisfaction to himself as the oldest driver on the road. But I was not many hours on my journey ere I discovered that a child could have done that, as, in reality, the sagacious and well-trained animals required no guidance. They were too hardly wrought, and, generally, too heavily laden, to do anything save drag on toilsomely in the track of those in advance.

But it is time for me to start. I had real pleasure in watching the process of 'yoking-up'; it was gratifying to witness the sensible deportment of each animal, as he answered to his name and took his proper place in the team. And it was pleasant also to witness the good understanding that subsisted between Ben and his charges. I saw him positively hugging and caressing one old fellow, that repaid his attentions by pretending to bite him, and showing his teeth in a most amusing manner. I took a fancy to the colonial youth from that moment, in spite of the foul oaths that he occasionally muttered at troublesome harness, etc., for I never will believe that there are real vicious propensities in the heart of that man or woman who evinces a fondness for animals, or an anxiety for their comfort.

It was so pleasant to at last start. Ben leading gallantly up the grassy hill with his team of six, and 'our' waggon following more easily in its unloaded state. I forgot to mention that Ben was loaded up to the very tilt with unmanufactured tobacco, and most lucky would it have been for me had the empty waggon been as fully occupied. But I hope it may be a warning to many as well as the writer never to trust a carrier who takes your money for a passage in an empty waggon. Commonsense might have assured me that if the man could secure a load, he would not return empty to Melbourne.

So contentedly as I was sitting in my roomy carriage, and so patiently I was determined to abide the long *six* days that I had been assured would accomplish my journey, when the conveyance was drawn up in front of a little country butcher's shop, and my troubles began. In a short space of time dirty bundles of some, to me, incomprehensible matter were tossed up into my apartment, and the driver began to stow away on my luggage or under my feet, or anywhere temporarily, a lot of filthy 'green hides', with a smell so offensive as to be almost unbearable.

'Not at all!' said the driver to my inquiries – 'I never has such an appetite as when I'm loaded with green hides, that's to say, if they're well cured – which I'm afraid these isn't,' he added, placing his nose suspiciously at the last of the lot, as he tossed it, dirty and dripping, at my feet.

That the man was sincere in his remarks I have not the least doubt, for I saw him make his bed up on the top of these very hides some time after; but, at the same time, he was fully conscious that my sentiments would not coincide with his, and looked sideways at my discomfited face with a grin of enjoyment that was most aggravating. I was glad when he mounted once more to his seat, and left me to indulge my feelings of unpleasantness without witness.

And if that had been all! But there was not a place of business, a butcher's shop, or a shanty, where, by any barter or talk, a penny could be gained, that we did not stop on that eventful and most miserable day. Hides and empty kegs were stowed away. Bags of flour and of oats were brought out and sold, and disagreed about, until the weary day was over, and we at length camped, after sundown, in a lonely, scraggy bit of bush, not more than eleven or twelve miles, I should suppose, from where we had started. I was too wearied and sick to cultivate the peculiarities of my friend Ben, and made my bed upon an aggravated array of hardware without even an attempt to soften its asperities. If I vented a few anathemas upon the acquisitive character of the carrier himself, you would not be very much astonished, would you?

The day or two following were devoted by me to the hard task of being reconciled to my uncomfortable position. I tried to feel interested in the horses and their amusing little characteristics, and while jogging slowly on to feel gratified that we *were* jogging onward, and that but a few days would put an end to the wretched experience for ever. I became more accustomed to dirt and discomfort, treated as a matter of light moment the loss of my tea when I could not succeed in getting my billy boiled before our early start, and altogether became more endurable to myself and those around me.

I learned to a penny the price of the objectionable green hides, and had the occasional pleasure of seeing the process of re-salting them, and of noticing their several defects. I found out the weekly cost of feeding each horse in the team, and the tonnage on goods which our acquisitive carrier received, and from thence deducted very pretty profits indeed; no wonder the little man grew so fat and jolly-looking. Of all cosmetics and stomachics, recommend me to a full pocket!

And then I lay upon the grass at camping hours and studied the peculiar mechanism of that most peculiar contrivance – a carrier's waggon. It may be a study yet, for all my efforts have failed to make me understand the indescribable movement with which it wriggles in and out of the deep ruts in those weary bush tracks. No other word will give you the least idea of it save that one; it simply wriggles, and it might be a centipede, or any other lengthy insect or animal, with as many joints in it as there are lines, to account for the strange motion, which is, however, so suitable to the work it has to perform.

Well, I was beginning to get used to it, as I have said, when one bright sunny midday brought us to the outskirts of the pretty township of Benalla. And it *is* a pretty township – as pretty as plenty of foliage surrounding cleanly white paint and red bricks can make it. Of course, you must suppose the red bricks built into picturesque cottages and substantial-looking business places, and the white paint on the outside of wooden houses, with pleasant-seeming verandahs, decorated with flowering creepers. But it is the many young trees – the undergrowth of the old bush – that make the surroundings of Benalla so pretty, and the 'fair, bright Broken River', winding through it like a broad ribbon of silver, that constitute its chief charm.

I saw only one thing in Benalla upon which the eye could rest unwillingly, and that was a girl with a couple of yards of dirty, disgusting looking black stuff trailing across the street after her. In the name of all that is womanly, where is the common sense of the females who wear these so called 'trains' to be found and restored to them, or must we conclude that they never possessed any? This Benalla girl was most evidently an hotel servant, and had been across the street to a shop, from whence she carried a new American broom. And there went the trailing filthy thing behind her, disturbing small clouds of dust in its way, and becoming itself momentarily more unseemly and disgusting. Heavens! I would put such women in strait-jackets, without one superfluous inch of drapery to display, and seat them in a carrier's waggon loaded with ill-cured green hides until the folly of their ways was made very evident to them!

But I had unfortunately a something infinitely more afflicting than a servant-maid's train to encounter at Benalla, and it was at a peculiarly unhappy moment that it overtook me. I was getting half reconciled, as I said, and rejoicing in each hour that passed over with the consciousness that it brought me a couple of miles nearer to the end. Let never passenger trust in carrier man again! It was thus my misfortune overtook me.

We had stopped for dinner in an open space close to a 'hay and corn store'. These hay and corn stores and convenient open spaces are quite institutions of the road. Here the hay and corn man provides water for the carrier's horses and wood for the carrier's fire, and in return the carrier buys his horse feed, and, most probably, his own feed at the hay and corn store. These spots are the *bêtes noir* of all quietly disposed passengers. Fancy a female elevated on the top of a loaded waggon some twelve or fifteen feet from the ground, and being obliged to descend, without the slightest assistance or sympathy, in the centre of half a dozen camped waggons. Fancy the same female obliged to cook at a fire, composed of a few quickly lighted sticks, and occupied by the successive billies and stewpans of half a dozen or more swearing, selfish men, and then you may partially understand the troubles of the 'road'. It is nothing out in the lonely bush, the task of fire kindling and preparing the meal is a pleasant one, but passengers on the road cannot have it all their own way or, indeed, the slightest portion of it their own way.

But I have wandered again.

'D — the wool! A pretty journey we'll have of it twenty-eight miles up the river!'

That was the observation of our driver – the man who seemed to slyly enjoy each fresh discomfiture of the 'passenger', as if it proved soothing to his own troublesome temper. He was sitting in the shade of the waggon smoking the eternal pipe, and addressed the remark to my friend Ben, who lay in the dust in his usual posture.

'What do you say?' I inquired, in terror, as I poked my head round the corner of the tilt, 'you don't mean to say that this waggon is going for wool?'

'D — it, you didn't think Ted would take down an empty waggon if he could load it! By — , he thinks too much of the tin for that!'

I leave you to imagine my feelings. It was no use complaining; not the slightest. The money was paid, and I was helpless. I had to endure the satisfaction of seeing *my* waggon disgorge *my* luggage, in company with the green hides, and of hearing the carrier himself assure me that they would not be longer away than three days. Coolly I was handed over to the charge of Ben, who was instructed to try and push the bows up a bit for my bed, and so Ben and I were led down to a pretty green spot at the back of the street – that is to say Ben and I, and the waggon and team – and there we were quietly left to camp our three days as we might.

I wonder if Mr Carrier was ever disappointed in his life. I wonder if he ever felt so miserable as I did at that moment, or if he will feel more miserable than ever he felt in his life any sooner for the fond wishes I uttered on his behalf?

'What on earth are we to do with ourselves here for three days, Ben?'

'D — if I know! The d — fool never thinks of anything! How the — am I to push them bows up, I'd like to know? Push the devil up!'

And the aggravated lad began to unyoke his horses, evincing his annoyance by giving his favourite old 'Tug' a sound kick in return for the animal's caressing movement.

'An' d — the bit of chaff either! Where the — am I to get chaff? Stand over you — , or I'll kick the — out of you. Not a stick of wood either within half a mile! Prince! back you — !'

Oh dear, oh dear, for the patience of old Job! I sat down upon the grass near my luggage, with the heap of green (very green indeed in some places) hides, forming a delightful attraction for the thousands of blowflies that gathered around them in a trice. I stared stupidly at Ben's careful arrangement of his horses' feed cloth, and mechanical arrangement of harness, and at length I saw the poor lad go off contentedly with one of the horses and a chain, to drag up some firewood. The troubles of happy-go-lucky lads like Ben do not last long.

A huge and often useless fire was a perfect hobby of Ben's, and the want of it seemed the only circumstance capable of upsetting his equal temper. I have noticed him short of tobacco, or unable to light his pipe for want of a match, and whistling apparently as happy as a prince; but when we camped where the wood was scarce, all Ben's merry laughs were lost.

But that enforced camp of three days was not lost after all. What a number of observations I made! What useful discoveries I therein laid up in the storehouse of my jumbled memory! It would take me too long to relate the one half of them, so I must content myself with telling you a few of the most prominent.

In the first place, Ben could *not* put up the bows except in an insufficient manner. The consequence was that my sleeping accommodation was of the most confined nature. The poor lad did his very best truly, but all his efforts could not make a space of four and a half feet by two into a reasonable roost for a human being and he gave it up in despair, but as perfect as good intentions could make it.

It came on to thunder and rain that night, and I was as nearly smothered as ever human being could be without actually ceasing to breathe. The confined space into which I was cribbed, and the close manner in which Ben tied down the tarpaulins, to prevent the tobacco from getting wet, made my lair intolerable. The stench of the tobacco was so powerful, and the weed was so dry, that it set me coughing until the tears ran down my cheeks as rapidly as the rain drops pattered on the roof.

Flesh and blood could no longer endure it; and, after trying, unsuccessfully, to creep out between two of the bales of tobacco behind; I, with the desperation of one nearly suffocated, tore Ben's fastenings to shreds, and poked my head out in the storm with a satisfaction I cannot describe to you.

It was a strange scene on which I looked. The sky was not too dark to prevent the bold outline of the dark box tree branches being fully observable, and they swayed to and fro around me, and groaned as the wind tossed them heedlessly about, like creatures in agony. I was so high up, too, that I half felt as if my home was no longer on earth, and the lonely sound of the rustling leaves made me miserable.

Over a stream in which the lamps of the street were reflected, I could see a part of the principal street of Benalla. Over one of the shops directly opposite were two or three pleasantly draped windows, gleaming with light and warm colouring. I did not envy the people who doubtless rested within in comfort that stormy night – not I; but I wondered if they had ever camped out on such a night, and felt it enjoyable, as I began to do.

But it passed, and Sunday morning broke sunnily over Benalla. A few hours of sun very rapidly dried up the grass, and I spread my rug in the shade of the waggon, and lying upon it, watched dreamily. I watched pale shopmen dropping past one by one, in the early morning, to bathe their weekly bath in the glittering Broken River, and return again, one by one, with a lighter step, and a look of freshness that was not all fancied. I heard the church bells begin to ring out calls as the morning wore onward, and the full rest of Sabbath had fallen over Benalla.

Hours after was the Sabbath past. A finishing mania seemed to have possessed the green township. Men with rods and lines, and boys with rods and lines, and girls with rods and lines, ay, and full-grown, fine ladies with rods and lines, and trains, and extravagant things called chignons, trooped past our camping ground, returning hours afterwards with heavier steps. I saw but one successful angler's return, and he carried with evident pride a pretty bream, of mayhap five or six pounds.

Another weary day over, and another lonely look at the silent street. It is noiseless tonight, but the rain falls not, and the wind does not blow and the moon is clear and bright, queening it in a star-gemmed sky. Huge blazes are leaping up from Ben's log fire, and stretched before it, on half a sack, is the contented and patient lad himself. Strange Ben! I lift my heavy, damp curtain often in the night to look at his recumbent figure, and find him there when the logs have burned low, and left but red embers; and, when the moon has hidden herself behind the far trees – when grey morning grows in the east, and the air is cold and the fire out, I miss Ben, and know that he has crept under the waggon, and sleeps the sleep of boyhood.

We had a grand time of it on Monday, Ben and I. There was a troublesome hide that was *not* green, but dried up stiff and incorrigible as a sheet of zinc. It was necessary that this fellow should be subdued, and Ben had placed him in the nearest waterhole, with a few stones on him, and a long string attached. It was on Monday that we dragged him once more to *terra firma*, a limp, draggle-tailed thing, with every bit of the stiff conceit taken out of him.

'He was a fine bullock, my word!' Ben remarked, as he spread it out on the grass, a red and white skin, with the white looking rather dingy. 'A d — fine killer that chap is, my word! Look at the cuts in him!'

'What do they leave the horns and hoofs on for, Ben?'

'To make them weigh heavier, to be sure. My word, if the tanner doesn't open out that chap, Ted will turn a penny on him.'

Came on that afternoon, at Benalla, the election of a member to serve in the honourable position of a member of the shire council for somewhere. It was a glorious day, and quite exciting to witness, even from our distance. Sprucely dressed 'cockatoos', I suppose the most of them were, dropped into the township in the afternoon, looking sage and responsible, as men who carried on their shoulders the fates of shire members. I wish you had seen some of them going home again. But several things came under the observation of Ben and myself before that happened.

First there was a loud ringing of a bell near a 'public house', and some hours after a number of dark forms emerged from behind an 'envious' wall, that hid the scene of the election from our view. It was some time before the distance permitted us to discover what was the tendency of the strange movements indulged in by these dark-robed figures, but anxious and interested watch elucidated the mystery.

Half a dozen unhappy horses had been enjoying a feed of 'posts and rails' during the time their responsible masters were engaged in recording their votes in the service of their country. It takes a long time to do that sometimes when the ballot is held in tempting neighbourhoods, and I hope *you* are not the man to advise that such a momentous affair should be too hastily decided upon.

But the votes being recorded, the masters of the said horses contemplated a departure sufficiently dignified to impress all beholders with the deep consequence of the business upon which they had been engaged. Do you suppose that state affairs can revolve for hours in the anxious brains of country statesmen without materially unsettling those delicate organs?

One by one, and two by two, they seized their several bridle reins, got one foot in a most tantalising stirrup-iron, and staggered back again. One, more successful than the rest, would clamber to his saddle, and, with a strange unsettlement of seat, tumble head foremost to the 'off' side of his animal. It was a work of time and difficulty, but perseverance conquered, and it was a glorious sight to behold that little body of patriots flying down the road like messengers of fate, while the labouring breath and bleeding sides of their horses told but too evidently of the consequence of the tidings they bore.

Whatshisname was elected! And the road is strewn with triumphal parcels of tea and sugar, and lollies for the little ones. It must have been strewn with heavier goods, if we may judge from the tumbled saddle that Ben picked up on the road next day, with the broken stirrup iron and the torn girth.

One privileged voter went home in a more unpretending manner. Tottering, staggering, swaying onward he came. Just at the edge of dark, with a heart-sick and ashamed woman following slowly behind him. Once he turned, with the determination of recording another vote doubtless, but his feelings overcame him, and he was obliged to lean for support against a fallen tree by the roadside, and finally to tumble across it helplessly, with his miserable head nearly as low on one side as his heels were on the other.

Such a desecration of the glossy broadcloth in which he had arrayed himself in honour of the occasion! It might have been his wedding suit, poor man, and I almost fancied I saw the wife's hot tears falling as she sat down on the log near her degraded husband, and waited as such wives must often wait.

The last glimpse I got of this privileged voter made me laugh. His fit of illness over, he turned sullenly homewards, feeling, very likely, that it would be dangerous to return again to the alluring township. Their home must have been among the cultivated fields that flanked one side of our camping ground, for the woman crept through a four-railed fence, and then turned to observe how her unsteady partner would succeed in getting through.

Get through indeed! He would do nothing of the sort, but climb over it, and let her see that he was not quite so bad as *she* thought. But it was always the way; if a man happened to get a drop of bad stuff (and that F. did keep some shocking beer on tap) the women were sure to say he was drunk.

I almost fancied I could hear every word of it, although even the pantomime was now becoming rather indistinct in the dusk of evening. With drunken gravity he climbed slowly up rail by rail, until he had mastered three; from thence he tumbled head over heels into the high growing corn beyond, and I saw him no more.

It is like a dream to me that journey on the roads after our absent waggon returned, and Ben and I were relieved from our guard over the Broken River. We jogged along, day after day, in the hot sun, and with the dust of a thousand wheels blown in our faces. We passed over deep water channels where no water remained, and over ruts down deeply worn by the winter's traffic. Sometimes the sound seeming spots betrayed us treacherously, and our wheels had to be dug out, and in some places broken felloes, with pieces of splintered spoke attached, told of troubles that had passed before us.

I became as fully acquainted with every horse in the team as I was with Ben himself, long before half the journey was over. The leaders, named respectively Duke and Prince, were sadly inclined to leave the beaten track (especially Prince), and to walk on soft places, to the great discomfort of their mates, who were often thereby obliged to travel on the new metal. And when the angry pull of Ben would force them back again, each (especially Prince again) seemed viciously inclined toward the other, and tried to vent his disappointment in severe snaps at his companion. Duke and Prince were showy animals, and glossy, but I noticed that, at a pinch, Ben's favourite old Tug was worth a dozen of the royal family.

During these long dreamy days I often wondered what the colonial lad thought of. He would sit in, or rather on, his perch, looking half asleep, and without an apparent sensation. His whip gave him occasional trouble, and in addition to a most apparent envy of the other driver's 'flash' whip, he had a boy's fondness for 'crackers', and purchased whip cord of bright colours, *ad libitum*, which he twisted and attached to his lash, and cracked in rags in sounding reports, that seemed to give him intense satisfaction.

'What will become of you when the railway is made, Ben?' I asked him one day when he was thus employed.

'Do?' he inquired, looking at me half pitifully, as if commiserating my ignorance. 'All the carriers are to be put on the line.'

'On the line! Who is going to put them on the line?'

'Government, to be sure. Not likely they'd be let do away with the road indeed, and leave a lot of chaps idle! They daren't.'

'And how do you think they'll be employed on the line, Ben? For what 'billets' do you think you drivers would be suitable?'

'D — d if I know; engineers, and stokers, and conductors, and such like.'

And Ben gave his whip a crack that sounded at once careless and confirmatory.

'To be sure,' interposed the other driver, who happened to be doing something to his harness. 'Didn't you hear that Ben's going to be station master?'

'I might,' the youth said, simply. 'There's a d — d lot of them engineers as knows no more of engineerin' than Tug does, and maybe the station masters is the same.'

For many days I had been wearying to see what the

carriers all alluded to as 'the metal'. Many an oath I heard
levelled at the metal, and at those under whom its
supervision was so shamefully neglected.

'Two pun' ten I've paid in tolls this trip, and I'll be —
if I wouldn't rather go twice over the bush tracks than
over that — metal! What do you think they're doin' now
at it? They've got a cove raking the bits of loose rubbish
into the ruts down at Wallan, and not another hand on
the road for thirty miles.'

And the man's assertion was true, for I verified it with
my own eyes.

But we reached 'the metal' at length, and my only
consolation was that we should soon be off it again, and
at the end of our journey.

Such tedious, weary days, with the hot sun broiling
down on the tilt of the waggon, and making the small
space within it quite unbearable – days when even Ben
could not endure the hot eminence of his position, and
tied his reins around the 'break'⁵ to slouch along by the
side of his horses, occasionally picking up a handful of
the metal, which he cast at some of the more sluggish
of his team, to remind them of his vicinity. The only
pleasure of the weary hours I found in the occasional
passing through one of the many pretty townships that
dot the 'old Sydney Road.' It would be invidious to select
one, and yet the old associations connected with the
Goulburn makes memory linger pleasantly on it above
all others – the Seymour of today.

The broad, placid stream and its green foliaged
banks; the picturesque bridge, beneath which lies the
old 'punt', rotten and half sunk in the destroying
water; the white houses, and their green gardens;
the rich undergrowth, where once flourished old, grim
box trees, and the perfumed peppermint; the wealth
of roses, that seem to be an institution of every
township on the Sydney Road – all form a spot that
will little recall to the old digger the Goulburn, where
his pick so often caused reverberations on the river
banks.

It is a pretty place is Seymour, in spite of the detestation of all carriers – its white toll bar.

The very last of my nights on the road we camped in an 'accommodation paddock.' I wish *I* had an accommodation paddock, for it appears the source of a very easily acquired revenue. Ten waggons in all had stopped on this night, and, including some passengers, there might have been squatted around the camp fire some thirteen or fourteen men, when a quietly stealthy foot approached, and, in the half illuminated darkness appeared a figure.

'Good evenin' to ye all; good evenin', Tom; good evenin', George. Ah! is that yersel', Ned? Always hearty – always hearty!'

'And that is yourself sure enough. D — the fear of *you* forgetting to pay us a visit. And what might be the matter tonight, Michael, eh?'

'Oh, nothin' but what money'll cure! – ha, ha. Thank ye, Jim. Yes, that's right; four, ye said. I thought ye were drivin' six now? Oh, ah, to be sure! Welcome to yer joke, gentlemen; but indeed I'm safe to trust it to yerselves.'

And so the clinking of silver went round the fire, the silver finding its way into the open palm of Mr Michael. Many were the jibes that accompanied it, but Michael, an honest and politic Irishman, returned pleasant answers to all, and gathered in his harvest with a watchful eye.

Three pence for each horse they paid for the 'accommodation' of driving their waggons within a fence where there was no water, but a stagnant pool that was odious to look at. Yes, I should like to have an 'accommodation paddock' on the 'roads' where there was a good army of carriers with large teams.

The very last night, and it passed, and morning carried us quietly into the heart of Melbourne. We did not feel the miles passing, for Campbellfield and Brunswick, and many houses between, gradually weaned us from the green country, and assured us that our time on the roads was nearly over. But I do not say *we* advisedly, since Ben's spirits all evaporated on this last day of our journey.

'Oh, Ben, the sea! There is the bay at last!'

'The bay! Where? Is that water? I never saw it before,' he said, listlessly.

'And you passing this spot so many years, Ben?'

'*I* never look. D — Melbourne! I hate the sight of it. Nothing and no comfort now till we're out of it again. I'd rather do anything than hang about town while Ted is getting loaded up.'

'Well, you'll soon be out again, and I hope I'll see you, Ben, next time you come down. I'll look out for you, be certain.'

'That's what they all say. We never had a passenger yet that didn't say I'll see you again; but we never see them again for all that.'

But you might, honest, simple-hearted Ben. *I* do not believe that we make our own fates, and yours – if bad example and rough companionship may have been thrust upon you. I shall not readily forget the only *man* on the roads who remembered that one of the weaker sex waited for her tea, on cold, rainy nights, or in hot, dusty days, while they selfishly absorbed the fire and its comfort. I shall not forget that, during my fourteen days on the roads, not one voice asked if any help was needed, or one hand was extended to even assist the woman in her dangerous descent so often during the day to be accomplished, from the top of a heavily and highly loaded waggon, save only that of swearing and rude Ben. I shall not forget all this, Ben, and some day you may remember, as may others, the fable of the helping mouse, should fate so will it.

But my conclusion is too rapid. There *was* one other man who, when carriers were numerous, tried to boil the woman's billy, and get her tea up to the elevated roost where she waited, tired and parched with thirst – one other beside Ben, and (pull your hats a little more over your faces, men of the 'Road') that man was a Chinaman!

NOTES

1. Oxley, a locality later described in 'Our Colonial Christmases' and the 1873 story 'The Second Wedding'.
2. From *Othello*, Act 1, Scene 3.
3. From Byron's 'The Bride of Abydos', Canto II.
4. A workshirt of flannel, popular in the bush.
5. A general name for the fore-part or frame of a carriage.

Looking for Lodgings[1]

Had you ever the misfortune to be looking for lodgings, and to be driven to that painful necessity on a broiling summer day, with the thermometer at ninety-nine, or so, in the shade, and a wind blowing in that aggravating way that utterly defies location? If you have, read and sympathise; if you have not, read, mark, learn, inwardly digest, and – don't look for lodgings under similar circumstances, if you can avoid it.

If one is suffering from any chronic disorder, he is not apt to enjoy existence even under its most favourable aspect; but if he groans, chronically, under that worst of all diseases – impecuniosity – I defy him to enjoy it under any. It's all very well to talk about the good appetite that devours the brown loaf purchased with the last *sous*; but I never could enjoy the most dainty viands when the bottom of my purse became unpleasantly conspicuous.

A more beautiful morning surely could not have broken than that which aroused me from a troubled dream, in which I had lost all my available funds in the centre of a crowded street, and was vainly attempting to gather up the coins again, as they seemed endowed with volition, and eluded my grasp.

'Just what I shall come to soon,' I said, as I sprang out of bed, and began to dress hurriedly, 'if I don't get out of this too comfortable hotel in no time. It's all very well, you see, and I should enjoy it all excessively, but one doesn't get style like this for nothing. Oh! thank you, my bill, eh? Ah! sixteen and sixpence, that's just about at the rate of one shilling and sixpence for each wink of sleep and mouthful of food I've had since I entered these premises yesterday morning. Six and four are ten, *and* six are sixteen, and *six*-pence. There, my friend, be good enough to carefully receipt that bill for me, and to vanish.

'Let me see, that's a five; eh! and one, two, three, five and three are eight, and six are – no, *would* be fourteen if they were 'to the fore', as Paddy says. But they *ain't* to the fore, you see, and so five and three are eight. Hum! the sooner I'm off the better, *I* think.'

And off I was in less than an hour, in that uncomfortable state of mind and body when one neither knows exactly what one is about to look for, or in what direction to look for it.

In what direction? Why, straight onward to be sure. Never deviate from the direct line if you can help it, but take Paddy's advice, and always 'follow your nose'.

And so I followed my nose, and it led me up a broad and stately street in the first bustle of morning business. Cabs were flying townward, laden with pale-faced and dressy sewing girls, and dapper, sharp men of business. Shop windows were being 'dressed' in the latest extreme of the fashion by conceited looking 'knights of the yard stick'; and fruit stalls, not quite so wilted-looking as they would be at a later period of the day, were getting finishing touches in the way of arrangement, by the addition of an orange here, and trio of very green apples there, and so the business of the day was fairly begun.

Farther up the hill, where that broad street was

intersected by a quieter one, and where the flowering shrubs that lined the boundary wall of some public buildings made a pleasant change for the eye, wearied of glaring shop fronts, more agreeable sights might be seen. Groups of little children were trotting to school, clean and tidy looking, and full of an important consciousness of the consequence they gained by the attendance. Little ones these were indeed, you know; little and innocent looking some of them, for, truth to say, there are not many innocent looking children even among the little ones of fast Victoria.

And then there were boys – rowdy boys of twelve and thirteen, ay, and nine – who varied the dull monotony of going to school by a pleasant row among themselves. It was refreshing to witness the energy with which they went into it – fists and feet, and knees and tongue. Even the school bags were not spared, and rattled about an opponent's ears joyously – nay, the very slates flew with an ardour worthy of a better cause. Fight away, young ones, and so become hardened for the great battle of life!

'Board and residence', a genteel notice this, printed on an embossed card, and hung in an irreproachable, stereotyped window – a window curtained with white muslin or netted drapery, and displaying a very pretty ornament of some kind, disposed to the best advantage on a little table inside. Sometimes it is a stereoscope placed daintily on a gorgeous mat of bead work; sometimes a splendidly bound book of a vivid hue disposed on an immaculate antimacassar; sometimes a pale bouquet of flowers in the most imaginable vase of *not* Sevres, disposed precisely in the centre of a 'daisy' mat.

I am becoming quite a connoisseur in lodging house windows, painful experience having made it quite natural to me to draw certain deductions from certain ornamental arrangements therein. Dingy and dilapidated muslin decorations are threatening, but a chair back, shoved conspicuously against the window, with an awfully open patterned antimacassar thereon, is dangerous.

'Apartments to let', small pretensions these, and a plain

card, with simple black Roman letters printed on it, signify the fact. 'Apartments to let', you may calculate on as apartments of the straitest accommodation, and as apartments whose landladies are lodging house keepers in the strictest acceptation of the term.

My first interview with such a landlady was the result of my application at a door in a quiet seeming street in Fitzroy. The house was a dingy brick house, with dingy windows, with dingy blinds to them, and there was a chair back in the window decorated with a dingy antimacassar.

'Apartments to let', was paraded in the parlour window on a particularly dingy card, that had evidently a close intimacy with any number of house flies, and the very knocker on the door was as dingy as brass can be which has not been favoured by a rub for seven consecutive years.

I expected little from this application, but I had already travelled over a weary lot of ground in vain attempts to suit myself. Most of the people to whom I applied treated me as a personal enemy, and I never entirely knew the depreciating influence of female drapery so thoroughly as I did after a search for lodgings in Melbourne. Tired, then, of my tramping, I stopped at this dingy house, and rapped modestly – *very* modestly – for I began to set a proper value on the consequence of people who let lodgings.

It was many minutes ere the door was opened, and if I had dared, I should have repeated my knock. It was fortunate that I had not done so, for a lady so fine condescended to open it that I was overwhelmed. It would scarcely be proper for me to say that this lady was as dingy as her house; however, you may suppose it so if you wish.

She was a lady of portly presence, and a commanding, self-sufficient air. She had piercing, bold eyes, as black as her jetty hair, and eyebrows to correspond. She had a rosy complexion – a very rosy complexion – which I afterwards discovered to be owing to a partiality for lime juice – a pleasant drink, harmless in its way, but which seems to disagree with the constitutions of ladies of portly presence and dark complexions. This lady was outwardly and visibly attired in a skirt of black silk, much worn, and with many suspicious looking marks, also lime juice, I should say, and a dingy – I wouldn't assert *dirty* for the world – red flannel jacket of a fashionable make.

'You have apartments to let, I perceive,' I said, in a deprecating sort of way.

How could I else address so stately a lady?

'Yes, I *have* apartments,' she replied, half closing her black eyes, and examining me from head to foot suspiciously. 'Are you in want of apartments?'

'I want an apartment – yes.'

'Oh! is it for yourself?'

The lady's mouth, as she asked this question, was so much screwed up that the words had some difficulty in escaping from it.

'For myself – yes.'

'Are you a single woman?'

'I am a widow.'

'A widow! Oh! you can walk in if you please,' she added, taking an inventory, meanwhile, of the length of my bonnet ties, and the quantity of trimming on my dress.

Doubtless the lady drew her own conclusions from what she observed, as the patronising style of her address deepened.

'You can sit down if you please,' she observed, throwing herself, with an attempt at grace, into a much worn and shiny-looking armchair, enveloped in antimacassars of a dingy hue. 'It's a very warm morning. I hope you're regular in your habits, ma'am, and a church-goer. I'm *very* particular about my church, and we lock the door at ten o'clock precisely; no latchkeys allowed.'

I looked round the room, which was a picture of untidiness – a picture composed of a worn carpet, much in need of the switch; an ungainly table, with a rickety leg, covered with a *terrible* red cover, also suspicious of lime juice, and decorated with an elegant basket of beadwork, patronised by the numerous flies. Four chairs, in addition to the one occupied by the presiding genius of the elegant establishment, and a sofa of angular propensities, macassars *ad libitum*.

I looked around this room hopelessly, I say; began to calculate internally for how many shillings paid weekly I would consent to be consigned to the society of this lady and her apartments. The very atmosphere of the place was redolent of lime juice. However, I was tired, and wanted a rest, and might as well amuse myself for a little with my consequential hostess.

'Perhaps I had better look at the apartment, madam,' I said.

'You *can*,' she replied decidedly, 'presently; but I feel a little faint just now; I'm subject to faintness.'

And a huge black head was laid back on the dubious antimacassar with a deep sigh.

Wonderful to relate, the lady's faintness did not remove one particle of the rosy hue from her cheeks or from the tip of her nose, and I was wicked enough not to sympathise one bit.

'Ah! this keeping of lodgers is a sad trial to me, I assure you, missis! One as has been accustomed to live in the first style to come down to lodgers, and their plaguey ways, is awful. And I'm only a delicate creature, and my feelings overpowers me sometimes. I must beg your pardon, ma'am, but I always finds that a drop of lime juice sets me up again; its so cool and refreshing.'

And the elegant lady got up from her seat with much difficulty, and proceeded to a cupboard that flanked the fireplace.

What *elixir vitae* she produced therefrom is best known to herself; but, as far as I could observe around her expansive person, it was of a pale hue – a very pale hue indeed – and a perfume (?) generally attributed to that berry, the juniper, was broadly diffused in the apartment.

'Ah! I feels better now,' she cried, with a sigh, 'and there's one thing I will say for my apartments, ma'am, that they're convenient in every way, and fit for any lady. There's the right-of-way at the back, you can slip out so handy for anything, and the Somerset Arms is just at the corner.'

'Well, I think I must call again, madam,' I ventured to observe, 'for you really do not look well, and the exertion of going through your apartments might be too much for you.'

And without giving her time to extricate herself from the old chair, into which she had again subsided, I went out into the dirty hall, and, opening the door for myself, escaped.

Bless us all! when shall I succeed in finding a respectable and quiet place where I can sit down with my household goods around me and be at peace! 'Board and Residence', 'Apartments to Let'. I'd give something to see one honest assurance that there are 'lodgings' to be had in a house where not a single bit of knitted or crochet work was to be seen, and where the window panes shone like crystal. But it's no use, in three-storied house and two-roomed cottage, it is all the same, there is an attempt at a grandeur which the means do not afford, and the effect is disgusting.

'Lodgings for a respectable female'. Ah! that looks something like the thing. By a considerable stretch of the imagination I might be considered a respectable female, although I needn't tell you, who know the shallowness of my purse so well, that I have no claim whatever to the term. However, I step on to the little low verandah of the little low cottage, and, by a pretty knock, try to put myself in communication with the person who wishes to accommodate a respectable female.

A fierce barking of an irritable dog, if I must judge from the animal's angry yelp, heralds the approach of the landlady, and as the door opens she stands revealed before me. A prim, starched-looking, elderly female she is, in rusty mourning, and in every wrinkle of her visage there is a frigidity and a propriety that does not argue well, I fear, for the unhappy female of respectability who may accept of her hospitality.

'You have a ticket in the window, madam?' I say in a deprecating manner.

'Yes,' she answers with a snap – 'Yes, I have – for a respectable female. Hum – um. Step in, please. That will do, Rover.' And I am shown to a seat – an angular seat, with knobs on it, and it is not very diffucult to get into that seat, considering that it is exactly two feet from the front door, and that the cottage boasts of no passage.

'What are your accommodations, may I ask?'

'Hum – are you provided with references, miss?' asks my keen hostess, looking me through as she sits down frigidly in a stiff armchair opposite to me. 'I must have references – they are quite indispensable. The last female lodger I had treated me shamefully, miss – walked off with one of my best lawn handkerchiefs, and a cake of soap out of the bedchamber.'

Well, you know there are limits to all human endurances, and the limits bounding female endurance more especially are not generally very wide. I saw that my respectability was not to be established by admittance under the roof of this immaculate virgin – of course, you will have guessed that she was an old maid – and the disappointment rendered me reckless of consequences.

'In the first place, madam, I am *not* a miss,' I said, with some little acrimony, doubtless, 'and, in the second, I would beg to inquire if you are furnished with proper references yourself? as in my case, as well as your own, they are absolutely and entirely indispensable.'

The sharp features of my lady got sharper, and the prim lips even more contracted under the influence of the indignation evoked by my impertinent words.

'References! Me, ma'am? I'd have you to know that I'm well-known in this neighbourhood – having lived in it for six years respectable, ma'am. References indeed! Though I say it, as shouldn't say it, there is no one can pass one disrespectable word of Martha Simmons. But it's no more than I might expect from what I've seen of the females of this colony; and as for expecting to get a female – a *respectable* female lodger – there!' she said, rising up in a storm of virtuous indignation, and tearing the card from her window with a swoop – 'there, I'm done with them!'

Fortunately, the door was very handy, and the simple fastening enabled me to open it with little difficulty.

'I beg of you to compose yourself, madam,' I observed, as I bowed myself out, 'and to remove that huckaback[2] towel a little farther away from my hand, it's very tempting. *Good* day,' and the street and I were once more companions.

'I wish I was a virtuous old maid!' I soliloquised, angrily – 'an ugly, frigid old thing, with a false front[3] and suspicious tendencies, and any number of huckaback towels and cakes of bedchamber soap! I wish I was that 'zinc, iron, and bottle' man, with the raggy coat and disreputable looking bag, who looks so perfectly cool and comfortable and at ease coming along there! Look at him! I'm tired and dusty, and hot and hungry, but I suppose if I were to sit down on this step and rest myself and admire him, the whole respectable neighbourhood would be shocked into hysterics!'

'Zinc – iron – and bottles – zinc – iron *and* bottles,' in a sort of 'I don't care a rap' drawl, it came out of a very dirty mouth, closely addicted to the absorption of – well, shall we say lime juice – I should think. A black face, with a leer in it, and a week's growth of beard on it, and a face surmounted by an indescribable hat, that had once been white.

'Zinc – iron – and bottles!' One foot was shuffled along encased in an old unlaced watertight, and the other followed it jealously with an old razee'd wellington. A coat so fitting as to be of no hue, was nearly covered, at the back at least, by an old raggy sack, which he carried slung over his left shoulder by one corner, and the trousers were to match.

'Zinc – iron – and bottles. Any zinc – iron and bottles?'

'No!' shouted a little girl who sat on a near doorstep, nursing a doll with one leg and the remains of a head. 'No!'

The man turned his head over his shoulder with a lazy movement and scanned the pert little maid with a grin of contempt.

'Ye might say sir, and be po-lite,' he said, with a careful syllabic intonation. 'Ye might say sir-r, and be po-lite. Zinc, iron, *and* bottles! Any zinc – iron and bottles?'

'You're an old dirt!' retorted the colonial maiden, giving her head a toss, and shaking her wigless doll triumphantly after the man – 'A rotten old dirt!'

Here came such a cloud of dust, blown upon the fierce wings of a hot wind, as shut the little girl and the bottle man, nay, even the very houses themselves, from my eyes. Indeed, it shut my eyes also for so many minutes that I began to have a vague idea that the zinc and bottle man would have eventually to lead me to some civilised region, where non-respectable females had some faint chance of being housed.

At last the fury of the blast was over, and I managed to rub my eyes clear. There was nothing in view then but a double row of 'cottages', I think they call them, and not a single card of intimation or invitation did a window in the street display. At the nearest corner was a little unpretending shop, with a miscellaneous arrangement of eggs, bacon, butter, bread, soap, starch, etc., in the window, and several bunches of leeks and turnips lying at the door.

'I must go in here,' I said, 'before I sink, and see if I cannot get rest, if not refreshment. Oh, the miseries of lodging hunting!'

The pleasantest thing – the very pleasantest thing I had seen during my long walk on that tedious morning, was that unpretending little shop, with its rows of tin cases on the shelves, and its multifarious collection of eatables and articles of domestic necessity ranged against the walls. It was low in the roof and narrow in the doorway, and the multitude of small ware hanging pendant from the one, with the heap of green vegetables blocking up the other, made the entrance and inside accommodation rather confined. But what matter – the look of the place did you good. It was the 'corner shop' and no more, and there wasn't about it even an attempt at anything but the cleanest and simplest arrangement.

There was a little low counter, guiltless of any ornament save that bestowed by soap and water and friction, and behind it was seated, in a rush-bottomed chair, a tidy, fresh looking woman, who was a picture to look at.

A picture, in which there were no long earrings, and no chignon, and no train; not even a gaudy, trumpery brooch 'relieved the dull monotony' of a full tidy bust, closely covered in the neatest and cleanest of print dresses. A fresh and rosy face it was, with a pleasant smile, and bands of fair brown hair were done up in the good old-fashioned style that our mothers affected – nay, that we ourselves rejoiced to meet on early womanhood within our school days. A simple coil of hair, fastened up behind with hidden hairpins and a well-worn shell comb, and smooth bands brought down over the temples in defiance of fashion and 'L'Imperatrice.'[4]

She was a refreshing picture to look at, that little shopkeeper, I tell you, with her clean print apron – in which the folds made by a careful iron were still fresh – and her plump little hands, with the one plain ring shining clearly on the significant finger. And what do you think she was doing? Well, she had a weekly copy of the *Australian Journal* spread carefully on her aproned knee, and she was reading it – so intently that my foot was unheard.

A little knock on the counter, though, made her start, and lay the serial away with alacrity.

'I beg your pardon, ma'am; these bothering books, if one takes them up, they forget everything. I'm sure I was far enough from the shop when you knocked. What can I do for you, ma'am?'

'I'm tired and hungry,' I said, with a smile. 'I have been looking for lodgings until I'm both foot and heart sore. Could I rest in your place, and could you give me a biscuit, or any little refreshment?'

'To be sure! Dear heart, what a day to be hunting about the streets after lodgings!'

And the pleasant little woman produced another rush bottomed chair, and dusted it down for me with her own apron. What old happy memories that simple action recalls! Memories of the pleasant visit to some cosy cottage where the old nurse lived, and welcomed the respected mother of her old charges – or the charges themselves grown into man or womanhood, and, mayhap, with little toddlers themselves to claim old nurse's caress.

'And now, ma'am, biscuits is all very well, but I'd recommend a nice little bit of fresh bread and fresh butter, and a glass of milk. It isn't every day in Melbourne as one can get them things fresh and good, but I've a girl married out at Hawthorn, ma'am, and she sends me in butter and milk fresh every morning, and sometimes a bunch of flowers, as does me good to smell.'

'Thank you,' I said, availing myself of her kindness. 'From the way you speak of these things, I should fancy that you had been accustomed to the freshness of country life. Am I right?'

'Indeed you are, ma'am. I was a servant for twelve years in a country gentleman's family at home, and I never smells my girl's roses but they minds me of the dairy. Our dairy were covered with roses and jasmine, ma'am. Many a time and often I'd pick the rose leaves out of the cream when the wind blew from the west.'

An old English servant! Ah, one might have guessed it! How neatly and deftly the clean towel is spread, napkin-wise on the corner of the counter. How delicately cut and buttered is the fresh loaf. How glossy is the white china plate, and how crystal clear the tumbler! Alas for the old servant of past days, who wore the neat dress of her class, and never dreamed of rivalling the elegance of her mistress!

'It must be change for you this little business then?' I observed, as my entertainer resumed her seat behind the counter, and took up a handsome openwork stocking she had been mending. 'After so long a country life, it is a wonder you ever dreamed of a business that would confine you among high brick walls.'

'That's true, ma'am, but we gets used to things, and it's many a long year since I left home. Well, my dear?'

A dirty trollopy-looking girl of twelve or fourteen had bounced into the shop and let her dirty knuckles fall rap on the counter. She was a disgusting looking girl, and a type of a very extensive class in colonial cities. Her tawdry dress was made so low on the shoulders, that it hung halfway down her upper arm, and exposed her skeleton, yellow neck broadly. Her dust-coloured hair was plaited up tightly, and had evidently been unopened, and, consequently, uncombed for days; nevertheless, there was a dingy scarlet ribbon tied round it, hanging in long streamers down her back, and a string of glass beads round her scraggy neck, the value of which would have purchased soap sufficient for a month's cleanliness of the dirty person they disfigured.

'I want a bunch o' leeks and a stick o' toffy,' she snapped out impudently. 'And Mrs Smart says she can't pay you till next week.'

Sticking out of this virago looking girl's pocket as she spoke was the neck of a small bottle, and as she hastily tried to hide it from 'the lady' with a fold of her torn dress, she awkwardly let sixpence fall upon the floor. It rolled under my dress, and I was obliged to get up that she might recover it, which she did without the compliment of 'thank you'. She stared at me sufficiently, however, and took a mental inventory of every article of apparel on my person.

'If all your customers treat you that way they do not deserve credit,' I remarked, as the little woman resumed her darning, and the girl had gone.

'Oh, that's just them,' she said, 'of course, you noticed the bottle. That Mrs Smart washes hard all week, and spends every sixpence she earns in gin; she owes a little here and a little there, and the husband's wages, once a fortnight, goes every penny to pay up old scores. Oh, it's just like her!'

'And is that precocious girl her daughter?'

'Daughter? no, ma'am, that's her servant, minds the child, you know, and goes for gin.'

Oh! woe to the housekeepers of Victoria if these are the growing up servants!

'And what do you think of the *Australian Journal*?' I asked, taking up the number she had laid upon the counter, and scanning its well-known pages.

'Well, I don't know, ma'am. I've done my best to like it ever since it began, three year ago, but I can't say as ever it comes natural to me like the old *Family Herald*[5] Mr Garton used to take in for the kitchen. There's some very fine stories in it, I daresay, but they're all about the colonies, and I would rather read about home any day. Unless it's for the very young people of the country, and them as never had no fathers nor mothers to tell 'em about home, I don't see what pleasure nobody can take in reading about possums, and bushrangers, and such like. However, I daresay they knows best themselves what brings in the money.'

Here such an apparition of rustling finery flounced into the shop from the back room, as nearly overturned me, and the rush-bottomed chair, and my enjoyable lunch, in a piece. A young girl it was in a short dress, and 'Marie'[6] fichu, and ephemeral bonnet and 'Benoiton',[7] and a chignon as large as a moderate-sized pillow, and a pair of crystal earrings two inches and one line in length, and a colonial brooch of the magnitude of – well, say, a small cheese plate.

I should like to describe this girl at full length to you, for the description will be that of nineteen out of twenty of the girls of a certain class in Melbourne. Girls who earn their living by machine work, or tailoring, or as milliner's assistants; or girls who don't earn their living at all, but whose parents earn it for them as tradespeople of one kind or other.

I had wondered if my neat, sensible, little woman wore such dainty stockings as the one she darned, but now the mystery was elucidated; its counterpart adorned the exposed ankle of the young person who took the shop by storm in the very middle of our discussion of the *Australian Journal* question.

I can't say that either foot or ankle were well-formed, but the boot which encased them was of the latest and most stylish mode, and furnished with the most elegant tassels and rosettes, and there was a certain exposure of open trimming, suggestive of an under garment, which fast ladies are wont to ornament and display, but which I think a really delicate woman will keep out of sight as much as possible.

And then there was a skirt of some gauzy material, gored so tightly around narrow hoops, that it is a puzzle how the fair wearer managed to walk in it. There was not a wrinkle, much less a fold, from the hem to the belt, and the entire circumference could not have been greater than five or at the most six feet. Over this strait thing, and upon it, in every conceivable way, and of every conceivable shape, hung and lay, and were disposed, tabs, and rosettes and tucks, and tails, all ornamented with braid or ribbon of the brightest hue.

Then the body was as tight as stay and laces could make it. Oh, the strength of female vanity! the endurance of which it is capable! I wouldn't have lived inside that belt for an hour, no, not for the character of respectability which the pattern Miss Martha Simmons so cavalierly refused me.

'I want a piece of paper to wrap this thing in,' said the wearer of all this finery, pertly, and giving her turned up nose a little toss that sadly endangered the safety of her chignon.

'There is plenty of paper in the room cupboard, my dear,' replied my little woman, quietly.

'In the cupboard, indeed! Do you think I'm going to carry a newspaper parcel down town? I'd look nice!' and another toss of the head and furious rattle of the long, crystal earrings. 'I want *brown* paper of course.'

'There isn't a bit in the place, Martha – not a bit. I don't see what matter it makes though you carry it in your hand just as it is.'

'Stuff!' with a look of vicious disdain at her mother, 'pull some of the paper off that rubbish on the shelf there, and be quick about it. I'm sure to be late.'

The little woman did as she was commanded, with an air so utterly blind to the disgraceful and undutiful address of her daughter that I was disenchanted.

'Alas!' I soliloquised, 'if girls could only know and mothers only realise the disgust that such behaviour, on the part of girls towards their parents, creates in the mind of every sensible observer, there would be more respect on the one part and a stricter watch on the other!

What can be expected of a girl who has no more respect for her own mother than if the woman who bore her were the dirt beneath her feet?'

I rose, and followed the pert miss out sadly. Of course, I did not do so without settling with my kind shopwoman, and offering her an abundance of thanks; but I did so sadly, as I have said, remembering that the off-shoots of the unpretending old English servant had degenerated into something infinitely less useful than brambles from want of proper training and pruning.

'Poor girl,' I thought, as I followed her affected footsteps down the pavement of the narrow street. 'There will be no reminiscences of a homely, breeze-swept dairy in your old age, should you live to see it; nor will the smell of an Australian rose recall the blush leaves that floated on the yellow cream.'

It was nearly dark when I at last turned my unsuccessful steps hotel-ward. I was tired and discouraged when I came by accident in the vicinity of the house where resided my morning lady of the lime juice. Mere chance it might have been most certainly, yet a fortunate chance I must ever consider it, as the ludicrous sight it brought under my observation cheered me up and made me forget my weariness in its enjoyment.

Without recognising the locality, I had got into a right-of-way, which appeared to have no visible outlet save the gates of the various residences, or rather yards of residences that abutted on it. It was evening, as I have hinted, and the sun had been down for some time; but it was just the time most enjoyable to children, and half-a-dozen of them were jumping and dancing at one side of the right-of-way around some object that appeared to be on the ground.

'Oh, crickey!' shouted one little scamp with a huge pocketful of marbles, and a wry nose, 'Oh, crickey, here's a go!'

'Run, Bessie! run fast, and see Mrs Rash on the ground! an' her bottle broke. Oh? oh!'

A glimpse of a scarlet jacket, and a black skirt, and a black head, that was strangely familiar, made me step curiously forward to look over the excited children's heads, and there, sure enough, was my lady of the lime juice, so completely overcome by her feelings and favourite beverage, as to be utterly at the mercy of the urchins who laughed and jeered at her. She was so close to her own back gate that one additional step would have placed her beyond their reach; but, unhappily, she had made that step falsely, and found, as many another silly woman has done before her, that she could not recover herself, and so she had lodged in a mud hole, and was squatting in it like a frog.

A number of angry ducks that her slip had dislodged from said hole were quacking and flapping their dirty wings behind her, and she herself propped up against the fence, with her hair hanging in disorder, and her scarlet jacket displaying a deplorable rent, was abusing, to the best of her ability, the dancing, and screaming, and hallooing children, to whom she persisted in ascribing her disgrace.

'A set of dirty little wretches, as don't know a lady when they sees one,' she mumbled, 'like their mothers, oh, yes! Get on with ye for an aggravating lot, running and racing and upsetting decent people as they comes in their own right-of-way?' and here she made a terrible scramble to get on her feet vainly.

'Let me help you,' I said, taking pity on the woman and her footless condition. 'Get up, now do, and go out of sight. See, there's your bottle quite broken, and fortunately; now don't you take another drop of lime juice tonight.'

'Thank you, ma'am.' She did not recognise me. 'Them troublesome imps as ought to be taken in hand of the police, which there never aint one about when they're wanted!' And she scrambled up, and got in the gate which I opened for her. 'And to say a woman can't go round the corner to the Somerset Arms – as I'm troubled with a weakness, ma'am – to get a drop of something strengthening – and   ducks – dirty   drabs – lime juice – respectable – drat it!' and so I shut in a jumble of sounds indescribable.

That last vision I had of Mrs Rash's right-of-way gathered in a circle of dancing brats, holding high jubilee, and performing a sort of war dance around the fragments of the broken gin bottle.

'I smell brandy!' shouts one.

'And I smell beer!' screams another.

'And I smell gin!' yells a third, while a regular chorus is ringing in my ears still as it died away in the distance, with a crash of broken glass,

'Brandy, and gin, and beer! and brandy, and gin, and beer! hooray!'

NOTES

1.   A sequel, 'My Lodger', appeared in 1870 and is reprinted in *Eclipsed: Two Centuries of Australian Women's Fiction*, eds. Connie Burns and Marygai McNamara, though they give its date, incorrectly, as 1869.
2.   Huckaback was a stout linen fabric.
3.   A hairpiece worn at the temples, to stimulate a fringe.
4.   The Empress Eugenie, wife of Napoleon III and dictator of fashion for the period.
5.   A British periodical, published from the 1840s.
6.   Marie (Antoinette) fichu: a long shaped scarf worn around the neck, the ends crossed over in front and tied with a bow at the back.
7.   Benoiton: woman's elaborate coiffure, the hair parted in the middle, smooth on top, with a chignon and curls at the back. Three gold chains, or sometimes garlands of flowers, were worn on top of the head, and hung in dangling loops under the chin.

HOW I SPENT CHRISTMAS

Christmas brings nice times for some people, I daresay, but I can't say that my personal experience has ever favoured me with many 'merry Christmases'; and, as for the 'happy New Years', well, they have been, as far as I am concerned, entirely mythical. This, however, is the first Christmastide I have spent in a 'great city' for, let me see, fourteen years, I should say; so it ought, at least, to have been a change for me.

And so it was. I often wonder how people feel who have at their beck all the good things of life, and can enjoy them surrounded by hosts of relatives and friends; but, vivid as is my imagination, I cannot fancy myself placed in such a position. My strange lot has almost been like that of poor 'Topsy',[1] who believed she 'growed', as I never knew either mother or sister or brother; but I never *did* feel so utterly lonely and thoroughly a 'waif', as I did in this great city of yours on Christmas Day.

It was quite impossible to avoid imbibing some portion of the spirit of holiday making which ran rampant in

Melbourne during the week previous to Christmas. If you had it not jostled into you 'down street', where crowds ran into each other, and cabs, laden to the roof, threatened to crush you flat at the crossings – if you were unimpressible as stone, and passed carelessly those gorgeous placards, in which the wonderful pantomimes were depicted in alluring colours – if you could gaze on Robinson Crusoe in his island cave, or recognise the wonderful flight of Sinbad the sailor, in charge of that strange bird, the Roc, without feeling that *your* Christmas was approaching, then you must be akin to the Topsys and the Waifs, and I am not so kinless after all.

And then the grocers' shops, and the confectioners', and the fruiterers', for the gourmand, young and old! and the drapers' and the jewellers' for womankind, young and old! and the Christmas presents, and the New Year's gifts for everybody, which we saw in the windows, and which made our mouths open, and our eyes sparkle, and our hearts beat, everytime we went down town, and one of which, when Christmas *did* come, we did not get! *Eheu!*

If you escaped all this, I say, without realising the approach of holiday time, surely it overtook you on Thursday morning, at the Eastern Christmas market.[2] Did you get up and go down to see it? did you get burned up with the most distressing hot wind I have felt in the colony, and hustled along in such a crowd as I never saw anywhere, and return with a vivid impression that you had been *kneaded* and rolled and baked in a very hot oven, and were, in consequence, worthless, to all human intents and purposes, for the space of at least eight consecutive days? *I* did, and I am truly glad that Christmas *does* 'only come once a year'.

I was always a remarkably hard subject in the early morning, in so far as getting out of bed is concerned. No one, I hope, knows better than I do how beautiful and revivifying is early morning, and how utterly impossible it is to replace the early hours in value by any others of the day. *N'importe: I can't* get up unless some great object is to be accomplished, or somebody else will be inconceivably disappointed if I indulge my usual weakness. Both these stimulative circumstances made me start from my rest at the untimely hour of six a.m., on that Thursday morning, and induct myself with alacrity into my 'vestments'.

I wish I had done nothing of the sort. I wish I had stopped in bed until the sun burned in at my window, and rendered the blind a thing of no account whatever. I wish I had stayed there until the flies had held their Christmas revels on the top of my head, and performed any number of waltzes and polkas and quadrilles, not to speak of an innumerable amount of racing, and hop, step, and jump, on my face, until I had been driven to hide under the sheet, or in desperation arise.

I wish all this, I say, and that, finally, I had not gone to the market; for, although such a scene will not be 'on view' again for twelve long months, which will not be all holiday to any of us, I am open to confess that the intolerable hot wind, and the unfragrant crowd and their effects together, dearly bought the novelty of the sight.

And, early as it was, there were very many sensible people returning as I went down; returning laden with many strange good things, but principally, I think, long wilted fern leaves, that were to do duty over many a doorway, and around many a picture, in place of the old holly and ivy, and time-honoured mistletoe. Alas! for the old glossy and prickly holly, and the haunted green ivy! Is it the hot wind, do you think, that makes one's eyes so dim when the green of far away Christmas is recalled?

But if your eyes are dim as you near the top of Bourke Street, you had better rub them up, you know, as the sight is worth looking at with every bit of their power. At the left-hand side of the street, from the intersection of Spring Street downward – yes, from the very top of Bourke Street, a row of vehicles of every description are backed into the pavement. You could hardly drive a good-sized wedge between the wheels, while the pavement itself is bordered with so various an assortment of green and living produce, that a buyer must be puzzled where to choose.

There is an attempt at green decoration too, that would bring that disagreeable dimness into your eyes again were it not impossible for sentiment to exist in the neighbourhood of so many ludicrous sights and words. From the dirty-looking man that sells little, dirty, fat pigs, to the owner of that cart piled with sprays of quickly-fading fern leaves; beginning at those heaps of fruit, and ending with those screaming geese and bags of potatoes, there is scarcely a face but has Christmas in it, or a lip which does not curl with either a smile or a word that causes one; it is so easy to smile at Christmas you see.

And so much easier when the chink of coin is in your ears. Even though it be going out of your own pocket, and filling that of the pig man, or the fruit man, it is so well to feel that you *have* it to spend at this Christmas market; always, however, with this reservation, *that it is your own* to spend. I wonder if among all these laughing, chatting, hustling stream of people, there are any who spend the money which does *not* belong to them, and which *does* belong to the baker or the butcher or the draper? Shall I again repeat that *eheu!* or pass on in silence?

I wish I *could* pass on in silence. Such a babel of tongues was surely never heard save on such an occasion. At Paddy's market, on Saturday night, you know it is principally the vendors who make the noise, vociferating their fanciful, and generally hideous, cries at the very utmost strength of their lungs. Here, however, it is everybody who talks and everybody who laughs, and everybody who crowds and pushes, and acts with the usual selfishness of crowds. This morning, I congratulate myself on the possession of a *very* angular basket, which is of invaluable service to me. Sometimes insane people imagine a possibility of retracing their steps, and resolutely stop with the evident intention of forcing a way backward through my insignificant person; well, I edge forward the sharpest corner of my basket as near the region of the simpleton's ribs as possible, and the effect is magical; we push, and squeeze, and jam, and shove forward once more.

Once fairly on the pavement in front of the market, and I defy you to get out without 'moving on'. The Eastern Market on this memorable morning is a receptacle so full to overflowing of carts and people and produce, that it surges out crowds of all into the neighbouring streets, having no room whatever for another object within its precincts. It puzzled me to understand how a person could stay long enough in any one spot to spend a shilling. In one desperate effort which I myself made to purchase a flower pot, with something green it, I was obliged to seize my prize and literally toss the coin representing its value into the man's hand as I was hustled forward.

'Go on! what the mischief are you jamming up the way for? Maria, wait for me! Oh! do wait for me.' 'Don't Maria,' urged that useful corner of my basket, and Maria obligingly passed onward.

'Praises be to goodness!' ejaculated I as I found myself wriggled out of the market, at the upper end of Little Collins Street, with my hat awry, the fastening of my jacket broken, my pot of posies looking withered and broken, and my own face scarlet with heat, and, I fear, a little ill-temper too. 'Praises be! I'm out, and if any one catches me in again *ever* – well!' – and that was my first introduction to Christmas.

And the next was Christmas morning; a promising morning too, with no indications of hot wind in it, and I rose with about as rebellious a heart as it was possible to encourage in a human breast. *I* didn't want to go out holiday-making, and I had no idea where *to* go and holiday-make if I had the inclination; nevertheless, out I *must* go, for I am simply flesh and blood, you see, and ordinary flesh and blood could not be expected to endure the vicinity of a regular family Christmas gathering without feeling its own loneliness a hundred times more.

And so I hurried, and got ready to go out, I knew not where, before I should hear the arrival of the son from up-country, or the married daughter from Tasmania, or the merry-voiced lads from the distant school. I didn't want to see even the big goose stuffed, or another stick placed under the pot which held the great plum pudding, and so I hastened and fled as one who flies from a crime.

Where to? where shall we go? Shall it be Brighton by the sea! No, there are too many *fine* people there for us. Let us go and see something that will make us strong and reflective; let us go to Sandridge and see the ships that 'do business on the great waters'.[3]

The train is pretty full, but by no means so full as we had anticipated, and we have no time to amuse ourselves with any of the characteristics of our fellow passengers. How short a time it appears until we are standing in a bewildered sort of a way on the very spot where I myself landed more than twelve years ago, and wondered at the inhospitable look of the sandy shores of the Golden Land.

Let us follow the crowd; we are not tied to time, and can afford to go where the stream leads; and, in this instance, it is, I think, leading us in the right direction, viz, towards the pier. Yes, these people are going down the bay in one of those little puffing steamers; but we go no farther than the ships, and there they lie in stately rows at either side of the wooden pier.

With many a piece of bunting flying in honour of the day, in addition to the proudly floating ensigns of the several countries that have sent out these ships to do business on their behalf in the great waters. It is all of those twelve or thirteen years since I last saw a ship, and my companion has *never* seen one, and how does the sight affect the one and the other.

Very different. The younger face is flushed by excitement, the eyes sparkle, the step is light. Wonder is flowing in words from the parted lips, and curious questions are being propounded. *I* am choking; my face is paler than its wont, I know, and my knees tremble; there are big tears in my eyes, and my heart has got the pain of long ago in it. Would you know the reason? Read it in golden letters on the stern of that stately vessel, it is but a simple word, but it is the name of 'home'.

A home lost fifteen weary years ago – a home where Christmas did not find a lonely wanderer, but an envied member of a happy home, where the shadow of death had not yet fallen. A home, where musical sleigh bells danced to the music of friendly wishes, and where Christmas morning awoke to greet a country covered with pure snow, that sparkled like miles of diamonds in the brilliant sun glow. And from that very spot has come this noble vessel, the names of whose owners are almost as familiar to me as my own. I can almost picture, as vivid as a reality, the very spot on the wharf to which she will go back. She will lie at the foot, or rather, opposite to the foot, of 'St Francois Xavier Street', where one may see, passing to and fro still, the old French 'habitant', with his coat of 'Etoffe du pays' and his scarlet woollen cap, and eyes will rest on these very timbers – ay, and on that same word in golden letters, that need but pass with a breath to see the glorious shores of the 'L'Isle Jesus', and the broad waters of the regal St Lawrence. Oh, let us pass on and forget it all! I shall see it again no more!

You would like to get *into* a ship? well, here is a very convenient gangway, and a very nice-looking vessel. She is large too, and does not feel the influence of the wavy water so much as the other ships. See how they rock gently, as the strong breeze flutters the ensigns, and how strangely looks the moving spars and shrouds against the background of pale, sunlit sky. This vessel carries the 'flag that braved,' etc.[4] too, you see, and that man who walks steadily, and rather sulky-looking backward and forward on the main desk is doubtless the mate, from his appearance.

'May we take the liberty of looking around your ship, sir? This little gentleman has never been on board a vessel, and is curious.'

'Ye-es you can take a look round,' and with a sharp, uncivil look under his brows at his troublesome visitors, the man turns on his heel in continuance of his walk.

Hum! my dear fellow, I truly sympathise with your disappointment in being reduced to this most disagreeable necessity. Doubtless it *is* aggravating to be confined to this 'beat', when all the world is holiday-making but yourself. Doubtless, also, your captain is a selfish old tinker to go and insist upon your keeping charge of the ship while he went rollicking 'on shore', and you are a very ill-used individual indeed.

Nevertheless all that agglomeration of ill-usage on the part of an insensible beast of a master does neither excuse or necessitate your unpoliteness to my humble self, and you must permit me to add that a man of one country alone would be guilty of it. It was not necessary for me to hear your voice, my dear friend, to know that you belong to that said land, and in the face of your most unsailorlike conduct, a very short 'look round' in your vicinity will satisfy me. *Good* morning, sir, I am truly sorry that your captain is not on board.

A little farther on, and nearer the fresh breezy end of the pier. Yes, my lad, that vessel is deeply laden, and lies low in the water. She, too, has got the 'flag that braved', etc., flaunting at her peak, and, as she catches the full power of the breeze here, she is heaving up and down considerably. There is a treacherous looking space, too, between the pier and her side, and creaking groans come up strangely from the chafing wood.

'Ahem! would you like to come on board and see the ship, ma'am?'

Ah, you are an Englishman, and you look anything but sulky either; indeed, I should gather from your countenance that you are really anxious that we *should* 'come on board', and cheer up your dull Christmas day a little. But how is it to be accomplished? From this elevated spot to that most unsteady craft of yours, how, in the name of wonder, is a transit to be effected? And then the trouble?

'Trouble! Oh, no, ma'am; quite the contrary, ma'am! Two of these planks, you see. Yes, pretty heavy, ma'am, certainly; but we'll manage it – there!'

Hum! again, and very hesitatingly this time. We *may* manage it certainly, and, so far as you are concerned, you *have* managed it successfully. But pray, how am *I* to manage it without running the risk of an intimate acquaintance with that grinding of wood down there in the water? Ah! that's it, and not so bad either. What *of* a torn dress and soiled kids, when there is such an evidently gratified face to reward the little inconvenience.

'And you will come into the cabin, ma'am, if you please, and have a glass of wine and a biscuit? And the young gentleman will have a bit of plum pudding? See here, my lad – that's my locker, and plenty of good things in it.'

Eureka! The very first invitation I've had from gentle or simple this merry Christmastide! The very first 'thank you' I have had the pleasure of saying for the offer of 'broken bread and salt' among a whole city full these heart-opening (?) holiday times! And if I do say no, my kindly-disposed entertainer, pray believe it is from a perfect incapacity to eat at this moment. Oh certainly, stuff the young gentleman until he cries hold if you like, and thank you for all.

'You see, ma'am, the captain wouldn't let me leave the ship today. Someone must stay on board you see; but he left no end of good things. I'm sorry he's not on board himself, ma'am, for I'm sure he'd insist on a glass of wine for the lady.'

Wine! Good gracious bless us! I say, little gentleman, that pudding doesn't seem to agree with you, eh? You're getting rather *less* rosy than – than – my good friend, *will* you let me into the air as quickly as possible, for I don't feel just the thing somehow. Why, I am seasick! as sure – as sure –

'Ah! it is a little rough, ma'am. Nothing like a little brandy and water for it ma'am, I assure you – pray be advised – last voyage – chartered with tea – Fow-Chow – Hong Kong – four hundred and seventy tons – oh! you'll be all right in the air, ma'am, but I wish you *would* try a little brandy and water!'

Oh, it's all very well for you, you know, but I run upstairs for it, although I have *not* got 'my sea legs on', and leave the 'young gentleman' with a huge slice of pudding arrested half way to his mouth, and a very white face. He is swaying strangely to and fro, and wondering very much if there is poison in the pudding?

And there is a pig! 'Oh yes, ma'am! And he'll follow

me down the hatchway if I'll let him. Yes, ma'am, very
good company indeed, and comes in quite handy for
a bit of fresh meat in a long voyage. Disagreeable to kill
him after being such a pet ma'am? Well, yes, ma'am it
does make a bit of a mess about the deck, but there's
no want of water ma'am, you see, although it *is* salt.'

And so while my companion's memory is sadly
bewildered with a string of names, into due acquaintance
with which our friendly entertainer has been trying to
drill him – while he is wondering why one belaying pin
is iron while another is wood, and trying to recollect
whether the 'main-tops'l hal'yards' was something
connected with the capstan, or one of the inviting things
in the edible line down below in the steward's pantry.
I am looking ruefully *up* at the pier, and sadly speculating
on the possibility of getting on *terra firma* once more.

Oh, I'll never do it, you know! There was a reasonability
in my sliding down that inclined plane, but sliding *up*,
you know, is – well, you do it! And there go those
dangerous planks, shifting and sliding, and
accommodating themselves *so* agreeably to the
movement of the vessel. Oh, I say! *would* you be *so* kind
as to pull me out of this?

And so I secure the services of two passers-by. Very
pleasantly too they *do* pull me up, and very grateful I
am to them for their assistance. I do not forget my civilly
disposed entertainer, you may be sure, and try to make
him too believe that I am grateful; and once more we
'move on'.

Hungry are you? Well, I suppose it is about dinner
time. Well, where shall we eat *our* Christmas dinner? I
saw somewhere, let me see, a 'Family Hotel'; ah! there
it is, and a very nice family hotel it looks indeed.

And we are just in time for the 'ordinary'; for certainly
we cannot pretend to miss the soup on this bright warm
sunny day. There are but a few persons seated at table,
in a large cool dining-room, this Christmas day, and these
few, with the exception of the landlord, you may well
believe, have not *chosen* to sit down to a hotel dinner.
I should feel sorry for them all, every one, were it not

that I firmly believe they are almost more than contented with the fate that has cast them around that mahogany.

The landlord himself is a gem of a landlord. He is neither obese, or consequential, or rosy faced. He is, *au contraire*, a small, dark-faced, slender, and gentlemanly man, with a conciliating manner and a keen bright black eye. On his right hand is seated the most perfect opposition to himself that could be produced, and I do believe, the very happiest one of the party.

And this man was a jolly, red-faced, weather-beaten, and hearty-looking sea captain – one who had 'doubled' *all* the Capes, I know, and 'weathered' so many gales, that he thoroughly despised them all. A perfect man of his class too, full of information, which he had gathered, however, in his own sharp eyes and ears since he first served, a little cabin boy, in the old ship *'Lightning*, you know,' and an information which he was fond of sharing with every man, woman, and child, with whom he came in contact.

I never knew a genial good sea captain who was not garrulous. Did you? And this identical one took a great delight in laughing at his own incapacity of holding his tongue; as you will see presently, but I must pass on to the other diners at this our Christmas table.

Our jolly captain had crept as close to the landlord as the corner of the table would permit, and told his anecdotes, and looked into his face for approval; but a young gent – that is the only term for him – a young gent sat on our landlord's left at a respectable distance, with the air of one who knew his own consequence, and was determined to keep it uncontaminated, at all risks and inconveniences to himself.

Heaven send me inspiration to describe this young gent and his conversation and manner to you. I know it will be a difficult task, for, often as I have written of 'Young Australia' this was the very first specimen of his class I ever came in contact with. Forefend that I ever should with another! unless it should be in that empty monkey's cage in the Botanical Gardens.

A young 'gent' who was, if we are to judge from his

'downy' face, about twenty-one or two, but if from his self assumption and imagined knowledge of everything, he must have numbered at least one hundred and fifty. This young gent absorbed the talk as much as he possibly could, and instantly silenced every attempt to differ in opinion with such an overwhelming audacity of experience as is indescribable.

Yes, he was the only disagreeable object at a very agreeable dinner-table; yet an object it was worth encountering to convince one's self that such objects were truly encounterable. And yet the appearance of the learned young gent was passable enough, if it had not been so thoroughly and entirely saturated with the quintessence of conceit.

He was above the middle height, I dare say, and dressed as well as any youth of the present age. He had so dark a complexion, that had it not been for the certainty of his long colonial experience, I should have located him in 'L'Isle de France'; he had dark curly hair, also suggestive of 'L'Isle,' and his scarf tie was carefully disposed, and fastened with gold.

In short, the lad's – I beg his pardon – appearance was well enough, but the air and manner ruined it. I have been wondering ever since what combination of circumstances had 'raised' such an ineffable self-conceit, so perfect a specimen of self-assertive youth. Surely such young gents are *not* the work of unassisted nature, nor have they emanated from any ordinary arrangement of matter or mind.

This young gent's *role* then was the perfect ease of a man-of-the-world, and his idea of perfect ease consisted in the most perfect self-assumption. He *was* particularly troublesome to the waiter, and gave his orders in an off-hand undertone, that was very impressive.

I was delighted with our landlord's treatment of this young gent. Our landlord was a sensible man you know, and had evidently taken the measure of Mr 'L'Isle' to an inch. He listened to his forward interruptions to the conversation between himself and the captain with a patient air, and head slightly on one side, and when they were temporarily at an end, bowed and smiled, and restored his attention to the captain. I wonder if any suspicion that he and his experience were both boring to a degree to everyone that sat around that table, once entered that young gent's head.

'Thank you, no! No ale for me' – with his hand placed on the top of the glass – 'I haven't taken a drop of ale for four years – doesn't agree with – *never* did. Waiter! Pale brandy. *I* believe in P.B. at dinner.'

'All taste, sir,' said the jolly red-faced captain, drinking up his ale with gusto. 'I tell you what it is, young man, when you have been at sea for twenty-eight years, you'll find yourself able to drink anything.'

'Captain, a *leetle* more goose? Ah, that's it. Ma'am, *may* I assist you? Waiter, green peas to the captain. Yes, New Zealand *is* in a fearful state now, and the natives appear to be thoroughly aroused.'

'They must be exterminated, sir!' declares our young gent, in a determined manner – 'exterminated to the last man! The New Zealand Government, sir, has shown such a spirit of pusillanimity as will be remembered as a beacon to the governments of ages hence! Yes, sir, they must be crushed, stamped, obliterated out of the country!'

'They're a fine race of chaps,' interjects our captain, shaking his head, as he had another pull at his ale.

'A fine race of devils!' cries the young gent contemptuously. 'The man who would take their part with one word deserves to share their fate!'

('L'Isle' manners let us hope, dear reader.)

Our landlord looks quietly at the young gent, whose face is getting very red and fuller of consequence than ever, but he takes no notice of his remarks, and believing it to be for the general good, immediately starts another subject of discourse.

'Bad times these for the sheep owners; what with the reduction in the price of wool and the shocking drought up-country, they are in a bad way.'

'Well, they must reduce their breeding power, that's all,' says the young gent emphatically. 'Nothing else for it, sir, and they're fools that didn't begin long ago.'

'Do *you* think so?'

I hope our captain is not beginning to fancy this young gent *too* clever, as he asks him this question in a wondering sort of way, with his knife and fork suspended over his plate.

'Think so? *Decidedly*! What else *can* they do, sir? Boiling down won't pay, and the land is overstocked. Depend upon it, sir, there is nothing for it but to reduce their breeding power!' And considering the affair as settled for ever, the young gent proceeds to carve himself a very delicate slice from the baron of beef before him – carves it daintily, sir, with his chin in the air, and his little finger extended, to the great reduction of *his* power in the carving way I should say.

'Well, we'll have a glass of champagne!' cries our landlord, as the waiter places a bottle by his side. 'Christmas times, you know, captain. By-the-bye, where will you eat your next Christmas dinner?'

'Lord knows!' cries our hearty captain, wiping his face with a huge bandana handkerchief. 'I've had three summers this year! Yes, as sure as my name is Dickson, I've eaten cherries three times this one year. First we were at' – blest if I remember the place, reader – 'in their cherry season, then my ship was chartered for England, and I was in the middle of the cherries *there*. Then we ran out here, and blowed if the first thing I saw in the street wasn't cherries! What do you think of that?'

'Very strange, captain; but now come, your glass for the champagne.'

'No champagne for me, thank ye,' with as sober a look as that face could ever wear, I'll be bound.

'Nonsense! Come, captain, I'm sure a glass of champagne won't hurt any man,' urges the generous landlord.

'I *can't* drink champagne – haven't tasted a drop for six years.'

And so serious the jolly man looked, as he shook his head solemnly, that I was prepared for a story.

'I'll tell you why, if you like. I was wrecked six years ago in the brig *Wave* with a full crew of hands, and a mixed cargo. We had six hundred dozen of champagne on board, and ran out of water. For thirty-four days, sir, we had nothing but champagne to drink and d — little to eat, and by that time there was two or three of us beginning to long for a draught of hot blood by way of a change! And, we'd have had it too if it hadn't pleased the Lord to send a barque to us in the nick of time. No, I can't drink champagne.'

'No, I should think not,' from our landlord.

'Nor I – it doesn't agree with me at all. During fourteen years' experience in these colonies, I've never altered my opinion that it's the most unwholesome drink made.'

The expression of sadness that seemed so ill to agree with our jolly captain's face faded out like magic, and it was replaced by a stare of the most utter astonishment. The knife and fork which he had resumed fell from his hands to the plate with a loud clatter, and with great round distended eyes he stared from under his brows at the young gent of experience opposite to him.

How easily I could imagine his thoughts – honest, simple straightforward son of the sea! 'Fourteen years' experience! *by* gosh! That young son of a gun! And this is young Australia! God help us!'

But he spoke no word, only turning to his ale once more he heaved a great sigh as he lifted it to his lips.

And as for our landlord, he only smiled; but the smile was more satisfactory than the longest speech could have been, as it expressed the opinion of the man truthfully.

And so I had to leave our agreeable and courteous landlord, and our genuine, hearty captain, and I should have left them less reluctantly had it not been that our young gent was getting more assertive, and consequential, and dogmatic every moment. My opinion is, still, that brandy and water, as well as champagne and ale, did not agree with him, even although he himself might have had fourteen years experience to the contrary.

His voice followed me through the passage and out into the street. He had been half abusing the landlord for refusing to permit him a 'game of billiards' on Christmas Day.

'Do you think there will be no billiards played in Melbourne today? Faugh! I'll tell you what, sir, I want a new suit of clothes, and I'm open to a bet of a new suit that your licence does not prevent you from having billiards played in your house any day. I tell you, sir, the days are all the same to me, and when I was up the country, a little ago, the young ladies and I used to go to church twice a day, and spend the interim in playing and singing, not sacred music either, sir, but songs, and all that. Bah! That Sunday business is all bosh, air – all bosh!'

Our return to town was early, but not too early for the holiday to have taken effect upon some choice spirits who were returning too. In the carriage behind us, during the early part of our start, and before the engine had got full way on, a jolly time was in full swing. Heaven knows who was the party, or of how many it consisted; but the wild 'hurrahs' and loud laughter, and occasionally snatches of song, assured us that it at least considered itself a merry one. My companion wished much to wait and see the carriage disgorge them; but I begged to be excused, and went from the platform.

And up Elizabeth and into Bourke Street in search of a suitable cab, when a new idea presented itself.

'Why, you know, *we've* had no fun at all; can't we go and see the waxworks?'[5]

The waxworks! To be sure. Well, I declare, and I never thought of it! Oh, by all means, the waxworks. That pleasant looking bill-sticker in the window has been tantalising me for ever so long, not to mention the elegant 'bearded lady' at all, at all.

Yes, this is where we pay our money; one shilling for me and a sixpence for you, so, and here lies the splendid exhibition before us. Bless us all! did ever anyone before see such a collection of odd caricatures? Well, they're nothing else. Do you mean to tell me that the dislocated figure to the left there, and the lugubrious visage with the twist in it, bears *any* resemblance whatever to our good old Sir Walter Scott, whose genuine portrait we are so familiar with, and near whose home – beautiful

Abbotsford – is the old home of *our* forefathers? My most respected friend of waxwork notoriety, you could not make me believe it were you to argue over it for a month.

And if that is Solomon – well, all I can say is that I am very sorry you, my little gentleman of the poisoned pudding, should have seen it. Why, all your preconceived ideas of the splendour, and greatness, and majesty of that wise monarch with whom you are so well acquainted in that well-thumbed Old Testament of yours, are now certain to be scattered to the four quarters of heaven, where, I wish to goodness, some tidy person would scatter the dust off poor Solomon's dusty vestments, and off the tip of his begrimed nose.

And there, at the other side of the door, squat Burke and Wills, and the more fortunate King. They have got a few veritable gum branches dried up around them, I believe, and a veritable bit of old, dried log also; but, alas! what shocking lazy-bones they must have been! We can well believe that in that 'dry and parched land where no water is'⁶ wild dust storms should arise, and leave the dense clouds to subside on every log and leaf. But did those poor fellows let it settle down on them also in such volumes that every fold of garment, and crease of hat and figure, rested thus under half an inch of misty dirt?

And as we pass along (with the most perfect disgust, I confess it), shall we wonder on which figure to confer the palm of absurdity? Shall it be on Mrs Yelverton's⁷ stiff, angular, prim figure, that has not one iota of the woman's energy in its waxy face; or on the almost ditto form of Madeline Smith⁸ at her elbow? Shall we select one to crown, from among this hideous row of things attired in (apparently) attire from the 'old cloes' shop, or lay our wreath upon the brows of that 'sleeping beauty' in which there is neither the semblance of beauty or of sleep? For mercy's sake, help us, among such a galaxy, to select the *one*!

Oh! we are to pass them all, are we? In the name of absurdity, do you mean to tell me that there are more absurd things still? Well, I give in; you are right, for this 'out-Herods, Herod'[9] indeed!

'Her most Gracious Majesty Queen Victoria' in one corner in (I presume) a chair of state, and 'His Royal Highness the late Prince Consort' in an opposite corner, looking as if he was thoroughly ashamed of himself, and was trying to keep out of sight as much as possible. Now, if there was nothing else to settle the matter to my own perfect and most entire satisfaction, this separation would be quite enough. *Would* anyone who knew anything put her Majesty, even in wax, a whole room apart from the husband whose loss she has never got over to this day, and attire her in gorgeous (dusty) apparel, while *he* was shoved into a corner in a plain suit of black, that had not been brushed since it left the premises of Moses Aaron and Co.?

But from all those stiff, lay figures that represent the royal family let us turn to this one directly in front. I want to have a look at this wonderful young prince,[10] who turned all your heads in Melbourne a year ago. Well! at any rate the artist (?) has had his revenge, and *turned* the prince's head out of spite.

I hope it wasn't out of a 'chunk' of gum log he turned it. No, it looks waxy enough that face, sure enough, and 'cheeky' enough, to all intents and purposes, and if that royal blooded lad carries his three-and-twenty years with such a coarse visage and unrefined figure as that, I should advise Elliot York,[11] or some of them, to put him under a course of acidulation to tone him down.

As for O'Farrel,[12] standing behind him there, with an overgrown horse pistol in his fist – as for him, I say – why we are going up to the 'chamber of horrors'.

Now, when I entered the door of this establishment, I had no idea whatever of visiting the collection of amiable ladies and gentlemen who decorate the chamber of horrors, for my nervous temperament is highly susceptible – in short, I am a coward; but, after reviewing the mock figures down below, I think I can go through the ordeal 'like a brick' and without the slightest danger of them being repeated in my imagination during the 'wee sma' hours ayont the twal'.

Nevertheless, I stand cautiously at the head of the stairway, and directly in front of a furious-looking, sitting figure, with a coil of rope in his hand, and a decoration of dusty gum branches around him. In his company are three other gentlemen, whom I discover to be, including the gentleman with the rope, the four murderers of New Zealand notoriety.[13] In the corner of this sylvan retreat stands a figure who represents Sullivan, the informer, and the sight of his unknown visage and unlike figure, with both of which it was my hap to have been acquainted, freshens up my courage to proceed.

Come, I say, we may venture further, my little gentleman, for I am decidedly of opinion that we shall find here simply another lot of the most indubitable caricatures.

And so they are. My imagination is tolerably lively and vivid, and I can at a pinch become terrified enough at the scenes of my own creation to insist upon the lamp burning all night; but I could not get up a single shudder in the midst of all these wooden-looking figures – not one, for the life of me, although I leaned with my back against the rail separating that delightful chamber where two wooden Chinamen are cutting a wooden girl's throat, with her face hidden in a wooden-looking pillow, and to which horrible scene I dared not have turned my back had there been the least evident vitality in it; I leaned against this, I say, and tried to fancy all these criminals alive, and myself in the same apartment with them.

But it wouldn't do; I could not fancy anything of the sort. The things had all waxy-looking, unreal faces, with staring eyes, and their bodies were all hard-looking and disproportionate. The boots were all drawn over angular wooden sticks, I am convinced morally; and the limbs *must* have been of ditto formation, so 'draggy' looked the trousers, or else these men must have been, one and all, very ill 'nourished' indeed during their respective sublunary campaigns.

Only one subject in that room created a sensation for good or ill within me, and the secret of that one is its reality. In the centre of the apartment is an oblong box, with a glass lid, and under that glass lid lies a 'mummy'. The explanatory card tells us that it was once an aboriginal who climbed up a tree, where he was shot, and remained hanging over a branch until he was sun-dried into the object remaining. And there that object lies, a doubled-up, fearful thing of dried bones and parchment skin. The hair yet partially remains under the grinning teeth, and the claw-like fingers are far more suggestive of humanity than those waxy things behind you there. Little gentleman with the open mouth, is it not a strange, a solemn thing to think that you and I shall some day be something like this? Ah! there is a veritable shudder at last; come, let us go home.

A ride home, then, be it; and here stands our cab. Now, my good man, I am not in the least hurry, and you may stop till your cab's full if you like.

'I'll drive you up for two shillings, ma'am.'

Oh! you will, will you? By way of returning me thanks for my unselfish thought of your interest, my ungrateful friend, I suppose? And for your usual fare of threepence you will take the next comer, who is in a hurry, and bouncible, to the very end of your beat, eh? Thank you. There, our places are vacant in your delectable cab, and you may fill them at your earliest convenience with fares at one shilling a head, if you can. *Good* evening.

Well, I don't know but we are just as well walking after all. The streets are not inconveniently crowded, and yet there are quite a sufficiency of pedestrians to amuse the eye as we go homeward. Cabs are rattling past, but not overcrowded either; and, by the way, there is one cab coming in dangerous proximity to the gutter, with two little boys on the back seat, and a gesticulating cabman.

'Take ye up now, ma'am, usual fare, ma'am. Take ye both up for sixpence, ma'am.'

No, sir, you will *not*. You will neither take me 'in' or 'up' at any time from this henceforth and for ever. Not even, sir, if you should pay me your *un*usual fare for the honour of my company in your conveyance. No, sir, let me but once discover that my confidence has been misplaced, and Sir Walter Scott's wooden body, on view at the exhibition of waxworks, lately honoured by my patronage, is not harder than I am.

I feel better after that. I feel as if I had my revenge on that old scamp of a cabman. Yes, he *had* white hair, and I am gratified to follow him with my eye, far up, and to see that he does not gather up the ghost of an additional 'fare'. And then I chuckle to myself at the nice touch of the sixpence I have saved, and, passing *my* stationer's shop, I invest that very sixpence in the last weekly paper, which I carry home triumphantly in my hand.

And that periodical is a great comfort to me over my nicely-flavoured tea (tea which tastes unusually good when I remember that I have earned every penny of the money that bought it, myself); nor are my slumbers one bit less sound on that identical Christmas night in consequence of the fact that I do not owe a single 'thank you' to one of my kind friends (some of them famous promisers, too,) for an offer of treat or hospitality; nay, for even an expressed kindly wish during these festive times. God bless ye all, my dear friends, and grant me continued independence!

'Oh – oh – oh! the rope's breaking! Oh – oh – oh!'

In the dead of night it breaks on my ears, as a sort of nightmare, until I am thoroughly roused and wide awake.

'Oh! the rope is breaking! It'll fall! Oh! And there is that black man! Oh, it's Morgan!'

Bother that plum pudding, I say. Young gentleman, are you aware that you have tumbled out of bed, and that your head is at this present moment in dangerous proximity to the water jug? Ah! there it is, capsized! Well, the cooling application will be the very best thing for you. There, jump into bed again and go to sleep.

NOTES

1. An irreligious young slave in Harriet Beecher Stowe's *Uncle Tom's Cabin*.
2. The Eastern Market (Paddy's Market on Saturday nights) in Bourke Street, on the site of the Southern Cross Hotel.

3.   From the Psalms, CVII, 23, 24.

4.   From Thomas Campbell's 'Ye Mariners of England' (1800):

Ye Mariners of England
That guard our native seas
Whose flag has braved a thousand years
The battle and the breeze

The ship is therefore English.

5.   The waxworks at 95 Bourke Street, owned by the phrenologist Philemon Sohier.

6.   'in a dry and thirsty land where no water is', from the Psalms, LXII, 2.

7.   Maria Theresa Longworth (1832?–1881) a nurse in the Crimean war, plaintiff and writer. In 1857 she married William Yelverton, afterwards fourth Viscount Avonmore, in a Roman Catholic ceremony. The following year Yelverton made another marriage, and she sued him for restoration of conjugal rights. The litigation lasted nine years, with her marriage being declared invalid by the House of Lords. Her slender fortune was consumed by the legal costs, and she turned to writing to support herself, travelling widely and publishing books about her journeys.

8.   Madeleine Smith (1835–1928) whose trial in 1857 for poisoning her lover with arsenic ended in a sensational verdict of 'Not Proven'.

9.   From *Hamlet*, Act III, Scene 1.

10.   Alfred, Duke of Edinburgh (1844–1900), second son of Queen Victoria and Prince Albert. He toured Australia in 1867–8.

11.   Eliot Yorke, the Prince's equerry, rebuked by Marcus Clarke for his poor grammar.

12.   Henry O'Farrell (1833–68) a paranoid and Fenian, who had earlier that year attempted to assassinate Prince Alfred during his Australian tour. Despite his obvious insanity, he was hanged.

13.   Richard Burgess, Thomas Kelly, John Sullivan and Phillip Levy, who in 1866 murdered five travellers on the New Zealand goldfields. Sullivan turned Queen's evidence, and the other three were hanged. Sullivan had previously lived in Wedderburn, near Kingower, where he was involved in various disreputable activities, including a wayside grog-shanty. No doubt it was here that Mary Fortune and he were acquainted.

Down Bourke Street

'Well are you going down Bourke Street tonight!'

'Down Bourke Street? What for?'

'What for?' With a wide, open stare, and the most plainly expressed disgust at my verdancy, 'for a walk to be sure, and to see Paddy's Market. Why, *every*body goes down Bourke Street of a Saturday night.'

And one might almost believe the broad assertion. If you want to get a fair idea of the crowds that do go down Bourke Street on a Saturday night, just go up to the back of the Parliamentary reserve and take a look at the streams that are pouring down the flagged channels that cross it from one suburb to swell the tide of people who go down Bourke Street. It puzzled me to keep in the channel, that is to say, *on* the flags, among the moving crowd of rustling, clattering, chattering people, of all sizes and shapes, who hurried along the path; and it is very fortunate for all concerned that nobody was silly enough to fence in that flagway, or to even provide it with a kerbstone.

'You might a knocked me over with a feather – when I got that new belt and the – bottle of gin that she never paid for – Oh! I never! – past the Haymarket[1] with such a thunderin' – lie! I said so! – ma'am, I'll trouble you to stand off my gownd!' were some of the scraps of conversation that rewarded part of my passage through the Parliamentary reserve; and for as give the whole of them, I might as well try to write Chinese.

If it were for nothing else that you had been pushed and dragged in the greatest of Bourke Street crowds for two consecutive hours, save to get five good minutes look at that identical street, from its head in Spring Street, you would be amply rewarded. I cannot at this moment recall to recollection a more noble and beautiful street among the many noble-looking and beautiful streets it has been my wandering fate to see.

Of course we must all rejoice that the early closing movement has placed so much valuable time at the disposal of those hardly-wrought young men whose unenviable lot it is to stand behind counters on bright sunny days and dull wintry ones, and to humour the trying whine of women who very often do not really know what they require; but we nevertheless, that is, we who walk down Bourke Street in the evening, miss the brilliantly-lighted windows and doors, the broad sheets of decorated plate glass, and, more than all, the magnificent *coup d' oeil* that used to await us when we emerged from the Parliamentary reserve, and paused to let the streams of people diverge to right and left of the gleaming thoroughfare.

And a brilliant spectacle it still is, though only now on Saturday night. On that last night of the week floods of light are pouring from door and from window. Did the lamps not stand out independently, and the pavement width away from those blazing gasaliers, their lights would fade into an insignificance unworthy of that broad street. But, stretching away down in brilliant star-like rows, and sweeping up the distant acclivity where Bourke Street West leaves the noble Post Office behind, and creeps away into the far distance, those brilliant lamps stand like dusky soldiers with radiant helmets guarding the wide thoroughfare, and the wealth-full emporiums that line its sides.

Light in broad glares from broad, colour-lined windows – light streaming out from narrow doorways, and up from barred areas – light glowing strangely in great, round, red, and green, and blue, and golden balls through chemists' windows – and light, sending vividly illuminated letters out into the gleaming darkness. Light, battling with night's darkness in a hundred different forms, and gaining the victory down in Bourke Street! Light, in squares – light, in balls – light, in circles – light, in stars! Light, streaming, glaring, glowing, flickering, blazing, for a long mile of a vista almost worth coming to the antipodes to see.

Choose your own side of Bourke Street on Saturday night, but if you follow me you will turn to the right. At that side you will find the most vivid gasaliers, the most tempting windows. It will be impossible for you to go down that side without stopping to admire and to sigh – that is, if you are one of the sex, naturally weak in mind as in body; and, indeed, though you should proudly wear a 'bell-topper' *could* you pass those attractive gentlemen's emporiums without wishing to try 'a suit off this piece, newest style, at three guineas?'

First, you will pass that well-known letter receiver. Will you wonder, as I often do, how many sighs and broken hearts in words lie at the bottom of it? If there are sharp, bold business letters, or ill-spelled, vulgar, scrawls, or scratchy, angular words, meaning nothing but folly, waiting, in the dark recess of that dumb receptacle, for that smart, scarlet-coated official to gather them up in the early morning?

But you won't have either time or patience to think anything at all about it; for, on Saturday night, at all events, you *must* 'push on'.

Certainly you must, and whether you like it or not; for you are getting into the stream now, and such a stream of forms, and colours and noises, as was never seen flowing between the banks of any stream in the known

world. Little girls – growing girls – full grown girls and
women – old and young. Pups of boys and fops of
men – tall and short – young and old. Fat and lean; rich
and poor. Flaunting in all the colours of a lighted prism,
or hanging in dirty tatters of no colour; all bodies moving
and talking, and all going down Bourke Street.

Before you get very far down Bourke Street, there is
some possibility of your being able to pause and indulge
your curiosity at the attractive windows, without the
imminent danger of being pitched head foremost into
that brilliant sea of plate glass, and its islands of 'loves
of bonnets' spread out before you. As for myself, being
naturally an arrant coward (where my pocket is
concerned), I never can enjoy, as I otherwise should, a
full, delightful examination of those ravishing concoctions
of tulle and ribbon and lace and flower and feather. Horrid
visions of being precipitated into that maze of colour
by some vindictive enemy, and of finding myself borne
by fierce drapers' assistants into the clutches of some
vicious policeman, while the real criminal has hurried
away in the hiding crowd, rises up between me and the
distracting view, and hastens me onward in affright.

Here, however, can you pause, you will see two dowdy
middle-aged matrons, carrying market baskets, or,
perchance, the more genteel bag, on their arms, lost in
a serious consultation about the form, colour, external
and internal arrangement, of a bonnet that is to adorn
the sandy head of one of the ladies, and has already
created virulent symptoms of the green-eyed monster's
presence in the bosom of the other.

'I think as I'll have it blue, Martha; with a few small
roses and a couple of feathers. And if the ties was blue,
I'd have 'em fastened behind, and that 'ud show my
new earrings, you know.'

'Ay, so it would, Mrs Perkins; but I'm afraid that the
blue and the roses wouldn't become your complexion,
ma'am. You see you're rather sandy, ma'am, an' for my
part I thinks that when a female comes to the likes of
your age, Mrs Perkins, the less she 'sposes her wrinkles
the better.'

'To hear *you* talk, Mar'hy! 'pon my word, one would think you were about twenty yourself, and a born beauty in the bargain, umph.' And Mrs Perkins tosses her head with that indescribable sniff of disdain so full of expression and meaning.

I wish I could write down some resemblance to that so frequently heard sniff of disdain which can*not* be written. I should take out a patent for it. But alas! I have tried it all ways in vain. How can one write down a sound which is simply an expulsion of air through the nostrils, and not a sound formed by the combination of any letters? No, I give it up, and class it with that other unwritable click of the tongue against the palate, and which means almost anything.

But this is not going down Bourke Street; and we are still at that absorbing draper's window. Do you see that trio of giggling and conceited girls, who are, in appearance, any age from twelve to twenty?[2] Perhaps I am not quite correct at the present time in calling them a giggling trio, as they are too deeply engaged in a consequential discussion of millinery matters to giggle just at present. Look at the aping chignon and the frizzled ringlets; mark the dangling, valueless eardrops! and the flaring brooches; notice the disgusting fast airs of these poor children and wonder with me what on earth the mothers of Australia are about!

'Now, which would you like best, Maria, if you had your choice? Oh! isn't that a beauty; that one with the sweet feather and the coronet? Look. Ellen! there's one, I declare, just like Fanny Glen's; a nasty thing, I call it.'

'Well, I'd rather have the green one, Clara, it would be more becoming.'

'Oh! I say (this latter in a loud whisper) – there's William Ray and George Hopwood behind! I hope they'll see us!'

Again, if I could write that sound, expressing disgust, of which I spoke a little ago, I should put it at the end of that last paragraph; not as 'sic' you know, but as a private expression of my own private feelings.

'Move on.' It is dangerous to linger here, and the crowd

thickens. We are getting on famously. Passing, oh, such appetising confectioners' shops, with their tempting buns, and seed cakes, and iced plum cakes, and tarts. And those lolly shops, where the little ones dare not stop, else would their little hearts break. 'Lemon drops, one penny per ounce,' coconut tablet, one penny ditto; and that tantalizing Everton toffee, at ditto ditto! This latter is the stuff for the boys, who, boy-like, will invariably patronise the dirtiest of all dirty sweetness.

Go on! Why we shall never get down Bourke Street if we stop this way. But here is a jeweller's; is it within the power of woman to pass that array? Does even male moral courage resist this fresh temptation?

I think not. I have often noticed the gentlemen more frequent examiners of jewellery than the ladies, and invariably, I think, with a more practicable object in view. You will see the *youngish* ones examining the array of signet rings, or wrist-links, or scarf pins. These gentlemen are bent upon the decoration of self, you may perceive, while older and quieter-looking men are examining the jewelled rings of small circumference – the sets of brooches and earrings and bracelets – or the pretty miniature watches, intended to decorate the belt of some fair lady. It is no difficult matter to guess that, when you see one of these gentlemen entering the enchanted premises of the jeweller, he is about to purchase a present for some fair, and, perhaps, beloved friend.

Apropos of the simplicity of being able to put two and two together and make four, I saw, on Sunday last, and in Fitzroy Gardens, a serious and sensible-looking gentleman lying under a shady tree in a quiet spot engaged in the intent perusal of a letter. I quite sympathised with him in his search for quietness to enjoy an evidently absorbing communication, but, as I passed onward it was impossible for one of my observing character *not* to observe that the letter contained a photograph, at which he gazed frequently. On the following day I happened to visit a jeweller's shop, and there I saw that same gentleman purchasing a handsome gold locket, a gentleman's. Do you think the guess that it was intended to enclose that portrait was very far wide of the fact?

And if I may confess a personal weakness, it is for the windows of those aggravating jewellers' shops. Bonnets or dresses have no temptation for me. Lollies are an abomination, and pastry beneath my notice; but a jeweller's window is my weakness.

And the weakness of many wiser than I, we may judge. What frequent hushed pauses are made at these windows by the passers-by! And is it not strange that they *are* hushed pauses? You will hear a great deal of talk going on in the glaring front of a draper's, but those very same talkers cease to speak when they pause in front of a jeweller's window; or, at most, they speak in subdued tones, as if there was something awe-inspiring in the wealth that lies in such small compass, and in such beautiful forms, in those unostentatious rosewood cases.

Jewellers do not indulge in much *glare* either; their wares are sufficiently valuable in themselves to prevent any adventitious aids to show being necessary. There are no tickets in these windows with the shillings in large, black letters to attract your eye, and the pence (nearly always eleven) in small pencilled ones, to deceive it. There is no necessity here for huge placards to insult one's own judgment by the assertion that some trumpery article is the 'latest style' or the 'most recherche' or the 'choicest mode' for diamonds, and emeralds, and rubies, and onyx are always in fashion and always 'most recherche' and always valuable; and so, were I not Caesar, you know, I would be a jeweller.

But, for mercy sake, go on or we'll be crushed flat! Do you see that man standing there by the pavement, with his eyes fast closed and a placard on his breast? That placard asks you to 'Please assist the stone blind' and I should like to assist the stone blind, and be sorry for him but the world is so full – so very full of humbug, that I dare not. It would be a different thing, you see, if the coin he asks for would be unmissed by me or mine, for I could then afford to be charitable, and risk the humbug; but, as it is, the innocent must often be punished for the sins of the guilty.

Two or three yards further on you will see a fruit stall at the corner of an intersecting street, and on it a placard, declaring it also to be 'for the benefit of the blind'. Now, that looks like *mean* humbug, for certainly the women attending it are keen-eyed enough, and also quite strong enough to work for the blind. I wouldn't buy an apple or an orange from that stall on any consideration; far better would it be to deposit the value in the placarded man's box, as he at least begs for himself openly.

We are getting almost bewildered now, for as many seem to be coming up as going down Bourke Street. There seems to be a general, but by no means invariable, tendency to take the right, and many are the collisions between the ups and the downs. Oh, bless us! do you see those chignons – those *frizzes* – those trains? Heaven help us with brains! Do you observe the eardrops, and the ribbons, and the glittering jet ornaments hanging in and on every conceivable, or at least perceivable, article of attire?

Are you not overpowered by the bewildering charms of these bedizened women, and oppressed by the loud, vulgar laugh, and – the smell of stale, inferior *eau de cologne*? I am; let us move on quickly.

Stale *eau de cologne* indeed! Why, this is infinitely worse. We are passing the 'Royal' now, at least we are being bodily hustled past it, and there is only one word – which I dare not write, you know – that can at all describe the odour with which you are so nearly poisoned. Heaven knows who the loafers around the door of the Royal are; I don't; but I know that they smoke vicious tobacco and drink poisonous spirits, and that you must endure it until you are wriggled past the creatures, or not attempt to go down Bourke Street at all.

Turn back? Yes, I think we have had quite enough of it. That tall man who goes onward as straight as he can, without looking to right or left, eh? 'Oh I thank you infinitely, my friend; *my* pocket is on the other side, and there is no purse in it.' *That* is your tall, gentlemanly looking man, who takes not the slightest notice of anything as he passes onward. I should like to pick *his* pocket some day.

We will cross over here. Although at night we have still some little danger of being run over by cab or carriage, but nothing in comparison with what we should meet with during the day. Now, don't you find this side quieter? But just wait until we get in the vicinity of 'Paddy's Market'.

A good deal devoted to feeding the public is this side. Lots, heaps of oysters here, and big, knobby cray fish. Pie shops occasionally, and everywhere the inevitable 'public'. 'Drinks at threepence' very frequently, and (astonishing to relate) a flower shop. Bouquets are here, looking wonderfully fresh, considering all things, and suggestive of the stalls.

Ah! I thought so. Here is the old Haymarket Theatre, you see, and what do you hear! Bedlam – or all the bedlams of the universe amalgamated, or Glasgow Green on a Fair night. Well, Paddy's Market does bear a faint and small resemblance to that wild festival, Glasgow Fair by lamplight.

'Daily *Age*!' 'Daily *Argus*!' 'Daily *Argus*!' 'Daily *Age*!' '*Evenin' Star*! only one penny! All the latest news by the Panama mail.' 'Just arrived! All the latest news from Panama and New Zealand; latest news of the week – *Leader! Australasian*!'

That is what you hear, in all tones, as you pass the Haymarket, and just ere you turn the corner into Paddy's Market. In all tones, from the most 'profondo basso' to the very shrillest of altos; from little, cute-looking, town boys, and from tall, grown men; from each and every one of these you may purchase the very latest news.

Here we are, amid crowds of people, and in an atmosphere redolent of fish. Faugh! let us get out of this as quick as the crowd will let us, for I never was a fish eater, and most determinedly detest the stench of it in any shape. 'Fish alive O! fish alive! All alive here, *and* kicking! Come, try and buy, and buy and try – anything under a bushel for fourpence! – Alive O – alive O! – Fish alive! fish alive!'

'Cherry ripe – cherry ripe! fresh as daisies and sweet as sugar! Cherries at twopence a pound! Twopence a pound, ripe cherries! Here, ma'am, give a fellow a turn! There's not finer cherries in the market. Come, taste 'em, I say. Cherry ripe – cherry ripe! Two pence a pound! Cherries at only twopence a pound!'

'Strawberries! – fine ripe strawberries! Turn in and try the strawberries! Roll up, and buy the strawberries! That's it, missus; they're fit for anything – pies and puddin's, and jams, and all sorts! Fine ripe strawberries – fine ripe strawberries!'

'I'll trouble you to keep your elbows out o' my ribs, mister! Drat the man! Look at my gown torn to shivers.'

'Cherry ripe – cherry ripe! All alive and kicking – fish O! Fish O! All live at twopence a pound! Roll up here – roll up!'

Oh, no! You must not get bewildered, or disgusted, or stunned, and feel like flying for bare life into some dark street leading away from the noisy spot; nor must your head ache 'like to split' or your limbs give way and want to deposit you on that heap of green, limp vegetables. By no means; you must 'do' Paddy's Market from one end to the other; you must go up one row of stalls and down another, until every inch of it is covered, and until you are 'ready to drop' and until, in short, you are as sick of it as I am.

Look at that tempting array of glittering trash. There are at least eight square yards covered with it. 'The choice of any article for one shilling' or 'the choice of any article at sixpence'. Could you ever conceive such a brilliant collection of shining, glittering glass and tinsel ornaments? Yes, nearly all ornaments, and ornaments for the female person. God help the mechanic who has a wife fond of worthless finery, if she should happen to drop on this stall at Paddy's Market! Why, there are gold and jet chains (fine long ones, that will rattle and loop, you know) to be had for one shilling, and what's the matter of a Sunday's dinner in comparison with *that*!

Stalls of rich, ruddy fruit, mountains of cherries, piles of oranges, and mole hills of strawberries; stalls of cabbages and new potatoes, and of onions dry and green; stalls of boots and shoes, not by any means tempting these, but strong and serviceable-seeming; stalls of villanous, rancid bacon, and shocking cheese; and stalls of 'old cloes! old cloes!'

A veritable bundle of the articles themselves attends to this latter stall – a bundle well filled out, and not particularly graceful in form, or lady-like in deportment. As she dives between a half dozen of suspended 'gowns' of no particular hue or material, and in distressing condition, and leaves nothing visible but a pair of huge ankles and slipshod feet, not intended for exhibition, she looks – well, funny.

A magnificent array of crockery ware and general ironmongery, spread out broadly and attractively on the ground, will be sure to attract your eyes as you are crowd-driven past. Here examine and bargain, sensible and generally sturdy-looking women, who value an extra chimney ornament, or new pudding dish, more than a long 'jet' chain 'at one shilling'. There is much higgling about the prices, and many assurances that 'the last one as I bought from your wor cracked, missus,' etc., etc.; but if you wait long enough you will see the bargain concluded, and doubtless with perfect satisfaction to both parties.

There, you have reached the pleasantest spot in the whole market. Surely you will never complain of headache here, where there is nothing unpleasant in either sight or smell, to remind you of disagreeables. Here are baskets of all shapes and sizes, and articles of all shapes and sizes in basket-work. If I were rich I would spend money on this spot – such a lot of money as would astonish you; and I should go home rich in basket-work of multitudinous uses.

I should have jolly market baskets, and pretty little knitting or crochet baskets, and baskets of plain willow, as well as baskets coloured and varnished. I should have baby baskets, and waste paper baskets (and help to fill the latter eh, Mr Editor!) and clothes baskets. I should have baskets with lids and baskets without lids, and square baskets and round baskets, and oval baskets; and I should have baskets neither square or round or oval, but of shapes only imaginable and not describable.

And I should have chairs of basket-work fit to ornament any drawing-room, and little suggestive chairs for the baby. And I should have high chairs for the pretty little boys and girls to sit on when they were admitted to the honour of dining with big people; and I should have half a dozen glorious cradles for the baby. Bless your heart, if I had plenty of money, I should take a waggon load of basket-work away from Paddy's Market.

Just look at the crowds of people pushing, and driving, and elbowing one another; and do you observe that cherries are an institution of the market tonight? Every man, woman, and child appears to be supplied with a paper bag containing cherries, and such munching goes on as you would hardly credit. It is beginning to be dangerous for lightly shod ladies to walk on the pavement, so numerous are the cherry stones scattered about. But what business have lightly-shod ladies in Paddy's Market?

There is a steady-looking mechanic in front of that stall, you see, and by his side is a comfortable-looking woman, carrying a fat baby, who is making insane attempts to push a whole tangled bunch of cherries into its gaping mouth. The father is supplying two little ones, who stand around him with upstretched hands, from the paper bag of cherries he holds in his hand. The eager delight pictured in the little, anxious faces is worth waiting to see; but will they cry for more when those are done, like big children, or will the fruit make them sick, poor little toddlers, and very cross and troublesome, as they go home from Paddy's Market?

Here are three schoolboys gathered around another paper bag full of cherries. There they stand, a triangular group, keeping their ground in the middle of the moving crowd and in spite of it. Indeed, they are oblivious of the crowd, so far as their privacy is concerned, and as thoroughly comfortable as if they were in the quietest right-of-way in Melbourne.

'I'd rather have lollies – owed if I wouldn't! By golly, ain't they sour!'

'You be jiggered; they's fine! Now, you, Jim, you're pitchin' away the stones; half's mine, you know!'

'Rat the stones! Why, there's bushels of 'em lying about. I don't care; I've got seven hundred and twenty in my nut bag. I'm tired of that game. I wish 'cherry nuts' was out; don't you, Jack?'

'Blowed if I know. I wonder what'll be in next. Marbles, I guess.'

So you see that the 'cherry nut' game[3] is 'in' now among the town boys, and marbles is for the present 'out'.

'Cherries ripe! All hot – cherries all hot!' What a facetious chap, to be sure. 'Cherries going – going – and nearly all gone! That's it, my boy – twopence a pound – as cheap as dirt. There you are! Sold again, and got the money!'

Next pleasantest thing to the baskets in Paddy's Market is, in my humble opinion, a dainty little stall where white muslin ready for embroidering is sold. It is simply a table, or some such contrivance, surrounded by a tolerably high rail, which is covered, as well as the table, with specimens of clean, white muslin, covered with cut-out patterns. There you may have your choice of chemisettes and collars, and strips for trimming anything. Of all widths and of all patterns, white 'slip bodies', white vandyking[4], and white frilling – everything pure looking and attractive, even amid the noises and stenches of Paddy's Market.

It is pleasant to see a woman stop here, although I am sorry to say that as far as my personal experience goes, not many *do* stop. Better the odd pennies spent in a strip of English embroidery, to be worked pleasantly by the home fireside, and to afterwards decorate the little one's petticoats, than three yards of the most conspicuous chain to hang with rattling elegance from the most stylish of chignons. Good luck attend the vendor of muslin whose wares are disposed of without noise.

'The celebrated soap which will remove stains from all sorts of linen and cloth! An invaluable boon to the public! Removes kerosene and oil of all sorts from all clothes!'

This crier is elevated a little higher than his wares; but from his manner of enunciation I should judge that *he* is not the immortal inventor. Because why? He doesn't seem to care much whether he sells his celebrated soap or not; and draws out his words heavily, as if they were lies(!) and choked him. Over and over again he repeats his parrot-like lesson, pausing between each word to permit of its due effect upon the audience, of whom he takes no more notice than if they were in China.

It's a pity that man has to open his mouth, for it is most evidently a great trouble to him to do so. It would doubtless be more satisfactory to him if he could sit up in a little box and masticate cherries, like poor Jacko there.

What is it? Why, don't you see it's a monkey, and a monkey for whose appearance and characteristics I have the most unbounded respect? He presides over some sort of a lottery arrangement, by which small quantities of lollies find their way into the stomachs of young Australia, and large quantities of copper coin into the pockets of the proprietors. No, I don't think poor Jacko benefits much by the profits; his imitation of a jacket, and the short petticoats that pretend to cover his miserable bits of legs, are very raggy and tawdry.

Bits of pink and white calico they were originally, and of the same material is the flat pretence of a cap that is tied on his head, doubtless to his great discomfort. Poor Jacko! how wretched an object he looks, and yet look at the cool content of his expressive face! He's not the size of a small cat, you see; and his box, turned on its side to form a frontless house, is barely large enough to hold him sitting on his haunches; but Jacko little cares; he is resigned to his hard fate.

Yes, that is the expression I admire in poor Jacko's face – its perfect resignation. He looks as if he had been so hardly used that fate had nothing worse in store for him. See how he munches his cherries and manipulates them actively with his long fingers, as the soft pulp is greedily abstracted from the stone. His cap has slipped down – a round, puckered frill of pink, glazed calico – and it now hangs on his right shoulder an objectless article.

And his keen, restless, observant eyes, they range over the moving crowd, in front of his dwelling, as sharp and quick as if there was reason and speculation in them – now here, now there; sometimes resting for a second on a lad who offers him some more cherries, only, however, to pass him without a sign; and always manipulating his nut, and munch-munching with his funny jaws. Poor Jacko, I should like to see you up on the highest coconut palm tree in your native land.

One last look at the glowing stall overspread with heaps of lollies of aggravating appearance. How attractive is this corner to the boys! How lovingly they linger around it! Watch the eager delight of these two lads, happy in the possession of threepence between them. If the fate of empires depended on it, could they be more anxious in their selection of a favourable investment? What is it to be? Coconut ice, pink and slushy, or almond tablet, firm and durable! Shall the purchase consist of lozenges or drops, bulls' eyes or peppermints? Little lads – will it matter fifteen minutes hence when the lollies are devoured?

Here we come again in contact with the most piteous objects we have seen in Paddy's Market; and they are neither blind, halt, or lame, hungry or thirsty, cold or ill-clad – they are simply young and silly. Two girls they are, who have been wandering purposelessly up and down and in and out of every alley in the market; for surely we cannot call a plain anxiety to be seen a lawful purpose for two poor girls, of thirteen or fourteen. Look at the taller one's hair, frizzled so absurdly as to resemble a very ill-used mop; and the other's dark ringlets tossed about her shoulders with each affected toss of the wearer's head. Mark the silly giggle and the conscious swagger as they fancy the observation of every male eye in the vicinity to be upon them. Have these girls no little brothers or sisters at home to wash, and tuck snugly into bed on Saturday night, so that the little ones may waken, clean and rosy, in the morning, and lighten the Sabbath morning's work? Or have they no brothers to accompany them to Paddy's Market, or no mothers, to order their stay at home? If this latter question can be answered in the affirmative, what then, ask we again, are the mothers of Melbourne about?

In comparison with these precocious girls who sweep past him with elevated chins, that boy is a useful and respectable member of society. His object is a lawful and laudable one, at least, if it is not in reality what it seems to be, viz, the explosion of himself. His wares consist of cabbages. You see only cabbages; and yet if they were jewels of price, he could not be more anxious to trumpet their virtues. With an extended palm at either side of his mouth, he is shouting, as if in storm, until his cheeks are at the point of cracking, and each as red as a peony.

'Cabbages! Cabbages!! Cabbages!!!' There is no variety, you perceive, and the boy is evidently not afflicted with a powerful imagination. He has but one idea, and he is determined to carry it. That idea is to make a louder noise in his legitimate profession than that gruff-voiced opponent of his; and he is doing it – more power to the lad! Shout on, my boy! *You'll* never stick in the world for want of perseverance, and thrive none the less for the want of the originality which prevents your framing a more taking puff about your wares than your neighbour. I wish to heaven, that in every trade lying advertisements of all sorts – including tickets labelled 'latest style' and 'most recherche' etc. – were put down by our wise government, and that every vendor was restricted to the simple declaration of the article in which he dealt. Wouldn't it be quite refreshing to read and hear, as you went down Bourke Street, every window and every tradesman reiterating one simple word – 'Tea!' or 'Bonnets!' or even 'Cabbages!' like my boy of the market?

Are we nearly out of the din at last? Well, just let us have a look at the butchers' stalls before we cross that dim Stephen Street. Now, that is a pleasant sight, if you like – a very pleasant sight indeed, and a cleanly. There is no noise here. People will buy meat without much coaxing, and they soon find out the best shops, and stick to them. One could not imagine much room for artistic arrangement in a butcher's shop until they had seen a town one, and then they will believe that even with so unlikely a material as dead bullocks, or dead sheep, or dead pigs even, so beautiful an effect could be created. But there is room for taste in every walk of life, you know.

How wild it looks here in the shadow of the market, with those glaring and unshaded gaslights driven about by the night wind. There is a regular dust storm sweeping down Bourke Street just now; and clouds of white rolling dust are rising up into the darkness far above the lights of the street and the din of Paddy's Market. They look like volumes of white smoke, or of wreathing steam bellowing out progressively against the background of dark sky above the house tops. Higher up and higher, until lost in the darkness; even dust, then, has a tendency to mount skywards has it?

Whew! how cold it is sweeping round this corner, blowing the flaring lights under the dim stalls out one by one, and leaving them still dimmer in Stephen Street. Let us get over the way and home, for surely we've had enough of Paddy's Market.

But what is this strange object coming noiselessly around the corner? Is it a phantom? It shows no horses, and yet it moves – a black, huge thing, with imps behind it. Bless us all, what is it?

Dare you go nearer to see? There is one bigger demon than the rest tossing black bags out of it now, for it has stopped; and there is another performing some strange mysteries behind – quietly though, and with a matter-of-fact air. I don't see his eyes blazing in the dark, nor do any flames belch out of the mouth of this attendant spirit; I think we might venture a little nearer.

A long cylindrical object, not black on nearer inspection, but green; an object on four wheels, with an aspiring chimney standing sturdily in front. On its side, in proud letters, may be traced as it opens its huge eyes, 'Young England'. Why this is, as sure as you live, the wonderful

'Hot potatoes and saveloy engine' that has commenced a new era of street cookery in Melbourne.

Its huge eyes? To be sure; it has three, I think – a red and a green one down by its sides, and a furious white one up behind its chimney. Well, of course, they're lamps – can't I see that for myself? and can't you understand a poetical way of talking when you're favoured with polite company?

Well, let us watch 'Young England' a little, although if that is not a strange misnomer, I don't know one when I see it. You perceive that those jumping imps behind are simply a few little boys looking out for fun and hot potatoes – anxious and impatient for the latter, if one may guess from the eager watch they keep on the dispenser's movements.

And a great many movements there are. First, those big lamps have to be hooked into their place, and the silent monster fed with one of those black bags full of something – coke, I should be inclined to guess from the sound it made as it was tossed on the ground. 'Young England' is just getting up you see, after having reposed all day in some unknown region, and they are giving him his breakfast as soon as he opens his eyes.

Nay, he must have had an early French breakfast in bed I think, and this is a second. Lo! there is heat and cookery in his back premises. And now that dark man opens and shuts two or three little doors behind in a manner that leads one to suppose he has been accustomed to practice the shuffling art of legerdomain; and now he flings an observation to the audience, which is highly interesting to the main portion of it, viz., the boys:

'All hot, gentlemen, all hot! Potatoes and saveloys, all hot!' And, in reply to unheard (by me) orders, click goes the little iron door, and in and out pops the speaker's hand, dispensing supplies of some eatable to the little lads behind him.

What is he dispensing? I am sadly disappointed. In the first place, I am very doubtful if this much-talked of steam engine does anything but cook potatoes and saveloys; and in the second, I am afraid it doesn't cook them according to my preconceived ideas of the management, which is, you must acknowledge, a very unfair proceeding on the part of the proprietors toward – myself. From newspaper descriptions, I had fancied a smart engine, puffing, and screaming, and revolving its own wheels through the streets of happy and benefitted Melbourne, whereas I am sadly afraid that someone shoves it behind.

And I had fancied steam-cooked potatoes, snowy and floury, and melting in one's mouth; such potatoes as I have seen in the days of old cooked in our own kitchen range. Alas! what, then, are these black shrivelled things that this man fingers out of his iron door that clicks, and has no one any objection to their being fingered? And what, in the name of curiosity, are saveloys?

Well, I'll be blessed if I can tell you. Suppose we invest? Come now, you need not be particular in the dark you know, and as you are the cheekiest of the two (hem!) I'll find the cash if you'll go and purchase. Is it a bargain! Well, there.

'Ho! ho! sixpence worth of potatoes and a saveloy! All hot, gentlemen, all hot! Potatoes and saveloys all hot!' The potatoes in your cap, eh? and the saveloy in a bit of very dirty play-bill? Well, never mind, the one is, I dare say, not much dirtier than the dispenser's fingers; and as for the play-bill, well, it's good enough for the looks of the saveloy anyway.

For it looks a dried up, shrivelled bit of pork sausage, that's what it looks like, my friend, and its cost is twopence; there, you are quite welcome to it. I assure you, and 'may good digestion' etc., etc.

One, two, three, four, and four. Eight hot baked potatoes – black, soapy, sticky potatoes, that you would be expatriated for selling in fair Ireland twenty years ago. 'One halfpenny each for hot baked potatoes, to be sold here a bargain at three a penny!' No, 'Young England' I may be prejudiced I know, but I cannot conscientiously recommend you to the patronage of Young Australia.

And so we really go home at last, enjoying with delight

the comparative cool and quiet of the streets. Across the Parliamentary reserve there still flows a thin stream of people, mostly homewards though, and more silent than they were a couple of hours ago. The most delightful enjoyment tires people at times you know.

What is that building to the left there, shadowy and ghost-like in the darkness! There is a long tunnel-like vista through it, illuminated with a solitary dim lamp, hung far up; is it among the rafters? Ghosts of vehicles are there in the obscurity, defying one to define their forms or ages, and far in – away through the tunnel – things are moving obscurely. I should judge the whole affair to be a livery stable of some sort, and the moving objects to be faraway feeding horses, were it not for a strange object that performs strange motions in the middle distance of this strange picture.

Under that dim and solitary lamp it is; a dark, distant figure, or rather shadow of a figure, for so it seemed in that dim space, surrounded by ghosts of carriages. Mopping and mowing it was, twirling and twisting, and performing the strangest antics that was ever performed by humanity – if the thing was human – in the dim light of that tunnelled lamp. Was it really only in reality some stable boy performing a *pas seul* for his own delectation and amusement, or as an exercise conducive to the warmth of his toes?

But hush! we are coming near holy ground; not from the vicinity of St Peter's at all, but from the thrilling warnings that are thundered there in the darkness every Saturday night. Now, if you want to hear eloquence, and see a performance such as would do credit to a professional gymnast, go by all means, and stand within sight and hearing for five minutes. If you exceed that space of time, then I've done with you, and set you down as a decidedly irreligious person, although you have been listening to a sermon.

And for this reason, that any reverent person must be thoroughly disgusted with the man's roaring, blustering, sing-song desecration of the subject on which he pretends to discourse. The advisability of street preaching at all I do not attempt to deal with; it is, I suppose, a matter of opinion. But if we must be waylaid in park and street, let it in mercy be by people of education, who will neither destroy the Queen's ordinary English or shock our preconceived ideas of reverence as connected with religion. Of course, he gathers an audience. If I myself were to go into that selfsame spot and shout 'Cabbages!' like that lad in the market, I should in fifteen minutes have a larger audience than ever listened to his psalms and hymns!

Just look at the man's antics! Could Lola Montez – were she in the body – rival that pirouette, or equal that bound! It is to take in the circle with a regular sweep. You see, that he pirouettes out that fearful warning; and to fix upon the minds of his hearers the immutability of their sentence that he brings his heels down upon the pavement with such a crash.

'O O-O! my friends, look at the lake of fire and brimstone! Think on your fate be-*fore* it be too late. O-O-O! repent! O-O-O! my friends, repent before it is *too-o o* late. A-And cry out in the be-ewtiful words of the poet – 'none but' (shall we say David?) 'none but – !'

Please move aside, my absorbed and, doubtless, repentant friend, I wish to pass on. Being a person of hardened disposition and most unimpressible temperament, I infinitely prefer the performance of my friend in the livery stable over the way, and have some intention of returning to witness it again, to take 'the taste of this' objectionable 'one out of my mouth'.

Here we are at Victoria Parade and here comes a swirl of dust along it, that momentarily obliterates lamps and illuminated shop windows.

But here is another orator doing *his* performance of religion! I can hear the stentorian bellow from where I stand. Hope to mercy the dust *won't* fill his mouth up so 'chock' full that he won't be able to open it for a month, eh?

NOTES

1. A theatre in Bourke Street, next door to the Eastern Market. It was renamed The Duke of Edinburgh in 1868, in honour of the royal visitor, but the name evidently did not catch on.

2. Marcus Clarke, in his account of Bourke Street by night, also noted 'the number of sewing girls and milliners' apprentices that haunt its pavement. These girls, neatly and sometimes handsomely dressed, will pass and repass for hours, either for amusement or for the purpose of making assignations. There are nearly 2,000 girls, from the ages of fifteen to twenty-five, employed in Melbourne, and in their manners and mode of life they are daily assimilating themselves more nearly to the Parisan *grisettes*'. (In L. Hergenhan, ed. *A Colonial City: High and Low Life: Selected Journalism of Marcus Clarke* (St. Lucia, UQP, 1972), p. 102). John Stanley James ('the Vagabond') was blunter: 'the state of morality amongst the working girls of Melbourne is worse than in Paris, and they commence their downward course earlier' (In Michael Cannon, ed. *The Vagabond Papers* (Melbourne, MUP, 1969, p. 29).

3. Cherry nuts or cherry bobs, a game in which a circle was drawn in the dust, a hole in the middle, the object being to flick cherry nuts from outside the circle into the hole. The large number mentioned here may mean that the losing players forfeited their bobs.

4. Chemisettes were lace or muslin panels made to fill in the open front or neck of a woman's dress; slip bodies were camisoles; and vandyking was fabric cut in imitation of the collars worn in portraits by Van Dyke.

TOWZER AND CO.

Being still, as you know I always was, the most unselfish being in existence, it is not to be wondered at that I hasten to introduce you, dear public, to three of the most interesting characters it has been my lot to come in contact with for some considerable time. Perhaps it is because my circle of observation has become unusually, but, I devoutly hope, temporarily limited of late, that I have devoted no small amount of time in amusing myself by contrasting, and speculating upon the several characteristics of my new friends; but you know that I was always sadly addicted to that sort of thing, as well as to recording my conclusions for your behoof.

Well, then, under the roof which has the present honour – an honour which I fear it doesn't sufficiently appreciate – of sheltering me, reside the three individuals to whom I allude. That is to say, the said roof, surmounting some walls, is supposed to be their habitation; although two of them locate themselves during the night watches in a roofed box in the yard, and next door to the hen house, while the third – dirty fellow! – displays an undoubted preference for a bed in the coal house. Even under these debasing circumstances, however, I expect you to be interested in my three friends; and it is not today that you are told for the first time that even in worse places than fowl houses and coal holes you may find material for observation and reflection.

My three new friends are animals of the canine species. I might have said dogs at once; but I am fond of fine writing, you see, and never make use of a plain expressive English word when I can introduce a five or six syllabled one, expressive of nothing but my own want of common sense. But what would you have? We must swim with the stream, and nobody would accredit me with any refinement whatever if I used ordinary words on ordinary occasions. Bless you, this is an age of refinement; and, as one of our dailies remarked the other day, we have reached that pitch of it, that there isn't a woman left in the country – they are every single one of them *ladies* of the first water!

For my part, and *en parenthese* once more, I wish we had fewer ladies to deal with, and some more honest, downright, straightforward women to encounter. In the sense in which the term is ordinarily used, I should take it as a decided insult to be dubbed a 'lady', and some day I mean to give you my idea of the several divisions of the same lady species, but at present I am a chronicler of caninity, and so –

The eldest of my dog friends is named Keeper, and he is the remains of a not thoroughbred Newfoundland. I say the remains advisedly, for most assuredly is poor old Keeper the remains of his former self. You couldn't help feeling sorry for him, did you see him in his pitable state of decay, and hear, as I do, many tales of his old prowess and faithful attachment.

Keeper is very old for one of his species: he has been for some fifteen or sixteen years in his present home. He is black and white; that is to say, ought to be black and white, for I am sorry to say, it is he who selects a resting place in a deep bed of coal dust. Pray excuse him; if you were old and helpless, and had no woolly blankets and soft beds to curl your frail limbs up in, perhaps you, too, might become neglectful of appearances, and root for yourself a hole in the ash heap of the coal hole, even though the contact might soil your white hair, if you had any left.

And poor Keeper is deaf – 'as deaf as a post' and he looks piteously at you with his dull weak eyes, as he stands swaying in the sunshine on limbs that will hardly support him. Long ago, legend tells us that he accidentally, or otherwise, received a gun charge in his hindquarters, the effects of which are added to his age in paralysing, or partially paralysing, his poor limbs. When he walks he shuffles along, in a pitiable sort of way, with his head hanging, and his long dirty tail drooping inertly, and sadly reminds me of some old trembling man, who goes slowly on his friendless way, without one supporting arm or whispering word of cheer.

Little use it would indeed be to whisper words of cheer to old Keeper. You may shout if you like but he will not lift his heavy head from that sunny spot on the verandah. And you may scold him – if he is in your way, and you have the heart to do it – but he will gaze helplessly into your face with so touching an air of imbecility, that you wonder when the poor fellow readily obeys your pointing finger, and removes himself out of your path into his patch of sunshine.

I wonder if old Keeper thinks. I wonder if he feels that he is diseased, from the crown of his head to the sole of his foot; and is offensive to even his most pitying friends. I wonder if, when he lies with his huge head on his flaccid old paws, and watches the ducks and the hens blinkingly, he meditates sadly on the past or has any hope in the future. I wonder if, when he sleeps in the sun and lies stretched on his side, as nerveless looking as the thing without strength which he is, and when he utters muffled barks, and moves his old feet spasmodically, I wonder, I say, is he dreaming of long ago days, when he was young, and bounded in the full enjoyment of animal vigour, after his beloved master's footsteps. Poor Keeper, is it a pity that one dare not believe in the doctrines of Pythagoras for your sake?

Be introduced to Towzer,[1] one of the most perfect epitomes of dog cheekiness that you could discover in a month's search, even if you are a 'dog register' himself. Towzer is a well grown mongrel terrier, in colour a sort of iron-grey. He has got no hair, I venture to assert; the article which represents it being so nearly assimilated to bristles, that it stands up from his body in an aggressive manner entirely descriptive of his character. The remains of his ears, too, are erect, and *qui vive* looking; and so, most certainly, is his stump of a tail, which sticks out at an angle of, say, forty-five degrees from his back, in all seasons and weathers. Indeed, the whole general appearance of Mr Towzer is characteristic of stiffness; his little short legs are stiff, and the hair upon them is stiff; and he trots along in a jointless manner, that suggests the idea of a wooden dog, with the hinge in the small of his back, upon which he turns and twists as a vessel to the swing of her rudder. In short, Towzer is a matter-of-fact looking dog, and sentiment could not possibly exist within a considerable radius of him.

And a politic dog is Mr Towzer. There isn't a dog in Melbourne that knows better than he upon which side his bread is buttered. Oh! a regular time server he is, who will sneak into your good graces about dinner time, and muzzle the first poor little dog that has the misfortune to venture within ken of him. A splendid man of business would Towzer make. It would require no very special stretch of my imagination to picture him in an erect posture, with a pair of business-like inexpressibles covering his scrubby legs, and with a coat declaring the man upon his stiff back. I can fancy I see him at this moment, with a flower in his button-hole, and a bundle of papers – scrip,[2] of course – sticking out of his pocket, and trotting down under the verandah, with a ready notebook in his hand. Why, his very air of *dogged* impudence would be a fortune to him; and silly speculators would study his firm, determined looking trot, and conclude that he, at least, knew where he was placing his feet. His air of indomitable self-satisfaction would, I say, be a fortune to Towzer & Co., for Towzer would be sure to have a 'Co.' for selfish reasons of his own, which, even as a dog, he at present indulges.

And now for Towzer's 'Co.' If you ever saw a miserable little cur, with the very stamp of helpless imbecility in the drop of its tail, you would recognise the character, or rather the want of it, in Towzer's 'Co.' A poor little trembling, yellowish-coloured mongrel, so nervous that a look is sufficient to set it shaking from 'stem to stern' is this nameless waif of caninity. It is nameless in that it crawled – off the street, I suppose – into its present quarters, and, having apparently found its vocation, will not leave them for any inducement. You may wonder what is the vocation of this poor little shaker; and when I tell you that it is to keep Mr Towzer warm in the cold weather – to lie at the kennel door and keep off the rain in wet, to form a pillow of support for his highness when it suits him, and toady him in a hundred ways, and to feel happy in the privilege of being permitted to do it, need I state to you the sex of selfish Towzer's 'Co.'

If you admire, between the sexes, an exhibition of the old simile of the oak and the ivy, doubtless it would delight you to see little Nameless muzzling around Mr Towzer's bristly neck, and, after some vain attempts to relieve his lordship of some of his insect lodgers, lick his elevated nose as he, the consequential recipient of these proper attentions, blinks sleepily at the fire; and if you are one of Mr Towzer's fraternity – in the sex way, of course, I mean – you will doubtless try and secure just such another 'Co.' of your own, and blink indolently at the fire while *she* fusses around you, and studies your every shade of countenance and your smallest amount of taste, as a future guide for her own willing slavedom. I wonder if you will today find such a 'Co.' my dear sir, or if the race has not nearly died out with the straightforward, sensible womanly fashions and ideas of our grand or great grandmothers?

But however one may try to admire the idea of a dependent and helpless femininity, one must rebel at times, for the honour of the sex, against too abject an exhibition of it, even in a dog. It is aggravating, to say the least of it, to see an animal cower to the ground in the extremity of trembling terror, when you extend your hand toward him with a bit of beef in it for acceptance; and yet you could not follow your first inclination of giving him (or her) a turn over with your foot, when you meet the poor little imploring eyes, and recognise in the prostration the utmost of humility as well as of cowardice; and so you simply call little Nameless a fool, and fling the beef at it (generally for Mr Towzer to pick up and devour).

I wonder if any person could furnish me with a psychological reason why females all admire courage in the opposite sex, and inwardly look upon the coward as something wholly despicable. In this one feeling, at least, I am a very woman (not 'lady' I beg you to observe), and recognise nothing so contemptible as cowardice, meet it in whatever shape or form it may exhibit itself. And yet, as we think a little over the position of poor little Nameless, we cannot help extending much of pity toward her to mingle with the occasional disgust her conduct inspires. It is, in reality, a homeless little stray, and only retains its present position by the most abject toadyism of Mr Towzer. Should his lordship choose to take to burrowing in the coal hole, like old Keeper, and so be able to dispense with the warmth of his present 'Co.' or should some other of the little canine waifs of this great city usurp the place poor Nameless at present holds within his dominions, woe to the future of the helpless little animal.

And, besides, who can tell how far the instinct of the intelligent race can go? Does Nameless know anything of that terrible dogman, and tremblingly anticipate the possibility that its services to the favoured Towzer may not be considered worth the yearly sum of five shillings?[3] Does it (I hate to call it *she*!) while Towzer is dozing by the fire, or lolling his lazy weight upon the poor, frail little carcass, speculate hopelessly as to the sad end of homeless and houseless dogs who may be driven from the shelter of a roof for the paltry sum I have mentioned? Alas! Little Nameless, for how many of *us* – the great human race – would a friendly hand be stretched out, with five shillings, to save from the same homeless condition that you may dread?

Take a leaf out of friend Towzer's book, ape his consequential strut, and cultivate his thorough and unmitigated selfishness. Fly at the beck of your master, and affect to fully believe him when he calls out 'Rat! rat!' in inconceivably odd moments, and most out-of-the-way places, and take out your revenge by bullying all the dogs smaller than yourself that may be unfortunate enough to fancy that it is a free country. Be irrepressibly impudent, and don't allow yourself to be put down by anybody whatever. That's the way to get on in the big world, my simple little friend. So fully do you now believe in Towzer, who condescends to extend his sceptre to you, and to permit you to bask in the light of his august countenance (weak little 'Co.'), that you do not hesitate to follow in his wake, assured that whatever he does is right; but you must act upon 'your own hook', little Nameless, if you wish to become independent of Towzer and the dogman.

The study of character is at all times an amusing and instructive one, and the idiosyncracies of those around us afford an unlimited source of gratification to one prone to such amusements, but they cannot be indulged in with pleasure at all times. A keen sense of the ridiculous is a troublesome aptitude to carry about with you, and it is grievously hard to wear the mask of a deaf and dumb person when, some absurdity being enacted or spoken, makes you want to fly out to the back premises for a genuine good laugh. Thus it is that I so enjoy the observation of my three new acquaintances; for I can make as many grotesque faces as I choose in watching the smug individuality of Mr Towzer, or the helpless self-abandonment of poor little 'Co.'

Have you all heard of the minister's man, John, and the 'inference' he drew from the text furnished by his master? 'Ye've been a long time wi' me noo, John,' said the minister; 'I daresay ye could preach a pretty fair sermon yersel'.'

'Weel,' said John, in reference to the everlasting custom of Scotch ministers of winding up the firstly, secondly, and thirdly, etc., etc., with 'From this we may infer,' before the final 'application,' 'I think I could draw a gey guid inference.'

'Weel, noo, John, what inference would ye draw from the following text: "The ass snuffeth up the east wind"?'

'I'd infer, maister, that he'd no get very fat on it.'

Now, in humble imitation of the minister's man, John, I wonder if I could draw any 'inference' or make any 'application' of the lessons I at least *ought* to have learned from my comparisons of the several characteristics of my three friends. But morals are hateful things, as we all know; and should I be silly enough to moralise in the pages of the *Australian Journal*, Othello's occupation would soon be gone.

Still, it might be admissible for me to say that I should far rather be old and worn out, and my past spoken of in terms of grateful kindness as one of duty faithfully performed, than be irrepressible, and impudent, and selfish, and a thorough bully, like my acquaintance with the 'Co.'

But, irrespective of all that, there is nothing in Towzer's present life to envy, for his is no sinecure, I do assure you. It cannot be pleasant to be caught 'by the scruff of the neck' occasionally and held under the pump, or to be incarcerated and howl by the hour in the small tenement which does duty as a kennel. If he had a spark of honest independence, he would take his swag on his back and earn an honest living elsewhere, or, in default, drown himself in the big washing tub; but he hasn't, you see, and so he coolly trots into the drawing-room after his bath or his imprisonment, and impudently coils himself and his dirt up in the best armchair, and, of course, poor little silly follows him, as in duty bound, and keeps his back warm.

Well, such is life. I do not offer you this as an original quotation by any manner of means; but such really *is* life, all the world over. All over the world, and to the end of that strange thing we call Time, there are, and will be, Towzers and old Keepers, and silly nonentities that are only suited to be 'Co.'s' and, having no separate individuality of their own, must live, move, and have their being in that of someone else. That someone else will not always be a selfish, bouncible, bullying, and aggressive Towzer, to be sure; nor will, it is to be hoped, in the interest of future nameless, characterless waifs, those poor, soft unfortunates always be in terror of being evicted from even such a home as our little 'Co.'s' by any destiny, be it in the shape of the 'dog register' or any other shape whatever.

Towzer, having retired to his box (with the 'Co.' at his back, of course), and having resigned himself to hideous dreams of a huge rat, in form somewhat resembling a pump, who is pouring icy streams of water on his wretched scrubby back; and good, helpless old Keeper, having betaken himself to a fresh hole in the ashes, where he utters muffled barks at an aggravating dog he was acquainted with twenty years ago, I may cease to try and interest you on their behalf. Should you meet old Keeper some day trying to shuffle along Collins Street, in my wake, and observe him staring in a bewildered manner at some fine ladies who are 'doing the block', I beg that you will excuse him. He is an old-fashioned fellow, you see, and in his day there were *women*, and they did not appear in public attired in a style which might suggest an asylum.

NOTES

1. A favourite name for dogs in Mary Fortune's writing, see the crime story 'Towzer's Teeth' (*Australian Journal*, February 1891).
2. Share certificates.
3. The price of a dog licence. The period when these fees were collected was the subject of her article 'The Dog Days' (*Australian Journal*, April 1869).

THE SPIDER AND THE FLY[1]

'WANTED, HOUSEKEEPER: Position of trust.'

That's the advertisement that set so many female hearts in a flutter in and around Melbourne; and as I was very much personally interested in a mythical 'place of trust', I myself was among the number of 'ladies' who donned their best bibs and tuckers and repaired to the place appointed, at or before the time appointed.

It is astonishing what different ideas of full dress are possessed by different women; and if you want an illustration of the fact, I could not recommend you to a better observatory than one of the said places of appointment. And while upon the subject, I should like to draw your attention to the number of advertisements you will meet in *the* daily, making some hotel or other the place of rendezvous.

I have lately had some little experience in, and opportunity of, taking notes upon the way these affairs are generally conducted, and my conclusion is, that no hotel whatever, be it as respectable as it may, shall ever be honoured by the light of my countenance in search of a place of trust. I may be mistaken, as you know we are all liable to be, but I am more than suspicious that a good many of these advertisements are simply hoaxes.

It is easy for any person at all conversant with one of the many varieties of fast human nature masculine, to imagine the delightful 'fun' it must be to see forty or fifty gullible women flocking to their call, with faces more or less anxious, and with every pin in their several attires arranged to make a favourable impression upon the enviable 'gentleman'. I could have guessed all that without having seen the advertiser I am going to tell you of, so thoroughly enjoying himself and his levee.

I said forty or fifty, did I not? Well, that was about the number that, as the hour of two p.m. approached, managed to locate themselves in and around the side door of one of the first hotels in Melbourne. I have no doubt that many of the females felt as awkward as I myself did at applying in such a place, and would not have showed face near it had it not been well-known as a first-class hotel, and a noted rendezvous for country gentlemen.

Well, as I arranged my bonnet-ties, and put upon myself generally as attractive an air as I could muster, I entered the side passage, to find myself in the company of seven or eight females, every separate one of whom seemed as thoroughly uncomfortable as any woman could be. Some of them were making inquiries through a window into the hall of a barmaid, who in vain attempted to keep her countenance, and whose very face was quite a sufficient declaration that she at least considered the whole thing a most absurd farce.

Well, having received a reply from the said barmaid, the several applicants looked around for some place in which to dispose themselves until their turn came to be ushered into the presence of the great autocrat of their fates. There was little choice. On one side was a private sitting-room, already crammed with 'ladies' possessed of sufficient impertinence to intrude there. On the other, a door opening into the bar itself, on the seats of which were disposed some half score or so of persons very available for places or positions of trust.

Some vacillated between the bar and the sitting-room, afraid to encounter the number of excited persons who occupied the latter, each jealous and envious of the other, and disinclined to make so little of themselves as to seat themselves in the public bar. Indeed, there were 'ladies' who seemed to take it as a personal insult that the bar door had been left open for their accommodation, and turned up their nose visibly at those who availed themselves of it. I observed that every one of these ladies had furiously red faces, and about half-a-stone or so of mock jewellery on their persons.

I did not feel inclined to face the ladies in the parlour, and I could not hang about the doorway in the public streets. Certainly I might have followed the example of some confused and forward applicants, who pushed open a glass door leading into the more private portion of the hotel, and there stood congratulating themselves, no doubt, upon the more comfortable position they had obtained.

But I didn't – I had a fancy for seeing all that was to be seen, you see, and I walked straight into the bar. Once there, I seated myself between a gentle-looking woman in deep but rusty mourning with a little pale-faced girl on her knee, and a brazen-faced lady with a 'diadem' bonnet, three-quarters high, upon her head. And then I began to enjoy myself thoroughly in my own especial way. Opposite to me was the bar, and inside the counter the barmaid; the latter was affecting to arrange her glasses, etc., but her risible faculties were not under the strongest control, and sometimes overcame her altogether.

And no wonder. If you had been there you would have laughed too; that is to say if you had not been one of the 'unco guid'[2] folk of poor Burns. I was fortunate in having the advantage of the poor girl, seeing that I could observe every movement of the ladies in the mirror behind her, without being observed; while she was obliged to face the crowd, and answer the hundred and one questions put to her by fresh arrivals.

Behind the bar went one applicant after another, and returned, some looking particularly sheepish, and some bold enough to terrify a troop of dragoons. It was evident that the sanctum of the wonderful and interesting gentleman who required the person of respectability for a position of 'trust' was somewhere inside in a corner, and do you know that for the life of me I could not help thinking of that favourably-known composition, 'Will you walk into my parlour? said the Spider to the Fly.'

And such a great choice of flies had that hidden spider, that I began to have a decided curiosity to see him. I wondered if he was a huge, bloated spider, with small eyes and a grin, or a slender limbed black, sharp chap, that seemed on all sides at once, and with long crawling limbs, that were ready to grab any fly foolish enough to put herself within his clutches. And there was such a choice of flies, too, that I can fancy the spider, of whatever stamp he might be, aggravated to death that he could not grab them all at one haul.

There was a buzzing, restless mosquito, and the ubiquitous housefly, of changeful hue and indomitable perseverance in attack. There was the ugly and disgusting big brown blowfly, and the active and detestable, yet seemingly pretty bluebottle. There was the miserable little midge, and the silly moth, all gathering at the invitation of Mr Spider. And he was not long invisible to me, seated in the bar parlour in a charming state of excitement, and licking his lips in a delightful state of anticipation, I could well imagine. Charming old Spider! Little he thought how open to inspection was every one of his movements, through the unpoliteness of an angry fly (of the bluebottle species), to whom his highness would not extend the top of his sceptre.

This fly was of ample proportions, and had a face of the hue of port wine stains. A number of tremulous red flowers, a profusion of metallic green silk, and blond, and beads, was raised above a quantity of shining black bepuffed hair, in the form of a bonnet wondrous to behold.

A tight jacket of dark blue velvet stuck to her stout figure; and her skirt was a changeable silk, of chameleon hues. A chain – a watch – a brooch – a locket – rings upon an ungloved, puddingy hand, and *voilà*! the most dashing-looking bluebottle fly you can imagine!

'You a gentleman!' she cried, bursting from the sanctum, and dashing the intervening door open against the wall. 'A good lambing is what the likes of you wants. Gentleman indeed! Advertises for respectable ladies, and then insults 'em.'

'My good woman,' remonstrated the invisible Spider, in a deprecatory tone of voice, which had no chance amid the thunder of indignation launched at him by the parting lady.

'A position of trust, indeed. Do I look like a person to do your dirty cooking and washing, and what not? Faugh!' And, amid an indignant rustling of silks and shaking of agitated red roses, evanesced that disappointed fly, leaving the door wide open behind her.

Now I could well understand why the occupant of the bar parlour left the door open. To close it, he should have been obliged to expose himself to the eager gaze of many dozens of eyes – eyes now in a state of snapping curiosity as to the occasion of the departed female's anger.

So the door remained open, and the Spider behind it, in his corner, exposed to my delighted watch, reflected in the mirror opposite the door of his den.

There he sat, I say, and in a state of unpleasant excitement, as recipient of the lady's abuse. He *was* one of the bloated, cunning-looking spiders, with small green eyes; and he had grey bristly hair, that now stood up from his low forehead, most likely where he had desperately run his fingers through it at the moment of his late attack.

He grinned, and he shuffled in his chair, and he listened; and then he tapped at the bar partition, a signal that seemed understood by the barmaid, who had not yet recovered her gravity, which had been completely upset by the bluebottle's exit.

'You can go in now,' she at length managed to articulate,

indicating at the same time one of the females in the bar.

'That she won't!' exclaimed a prim conceited-looking woman, attired in a stuff gown, a black shawl, and an old straw bonnet. 'I've been here full an hour before her, and it's my turn, whether you like it or no,' and, suiting the action to the word, the dame pushed her way into the autocrat's den.

But she was a very unattractive fly, that elderly person with the old bonnet and the wrinkled face. The Spider required but a single glance to convince him that his web would be wasted in catching a 'lady' so unsuited for a 'position of trust'.

'I have engaged a person, ma'am,' he said, with a stiff nod at the woman, as she put her screwed-up nose around the door.

'Oh!' she said, with an indescribable toss of the head, as she emerged with a vinegar visage, 'He's engaged, ye needn't wait any longer.' And she too went out of the door, shaking, I have no moral doubt, the imaginary dust from her shuffling feet at its threshold.

At this instant a loud rapping from inside assured the barmaid that our gentleman required her instant attendance. From my post I could see that his highness was exceedingly irate, and soundly rated the barmaid for something or other. When she emerged, too, she shut the door, and I think I never saw so great a want of tact as that girl displayed in a position that she doubtless felt exceedingly awkward.

'Has the gentleman engaged?', 'I never heard the like! Before he saw half the applications!', 'He had no right to do it!' etc., etc., were some of the questions and observations with which she was assailed.

The girl looked hither and tither, and feigned to perform some extraordinary feat under the counter, casting all the time furtive looks from one to the other of the excited applicants. It amused me excessively to observe the way in which the poor girl was obliged to twist and turn her mouth to prevent an open exhibition of her merriment; while her face was perfectly scarlet from suppressed laughter.

At this awkward juncture arose a young woman, attired cheaply in an extravagantly fashionable style. I need not describe her – you may see her type every day on the street, and the impudent stare and conceited air are not attractive. She was one of that class of foolish young ladies who are happy in piling pads and bows of ribbon on their heads, and in trailing a yard of cheap material after them in the dirt, and in walking upon boots two sizes too small for them, and upon heels less comfortable than stilts. No need to describe her, is there? You know, by sight only, I hope, a round hundred of them.

Influenced by her movement, doubtless, stepped also forward an old frowsy woman of about fifty years, determined, as it would appear, not to lose any chance that might present itself of admission to *the* presence.

'I suppose I can go in?' she did not question, as she attempted to push aside the barmaid, and enter; while the fashionable 'young lady' stared at her insolent rival as if she would wither her with a look.

Again came that rap at the partition, and the poor go-between's face grew redder than ever.

'The gentleman is engaged, ma'am,' she half whispered to the frowsy woman, 'and it's no use for you to see him. He's engaged a person already.'

And she winked – yes, winked visibly with her left eye at the 'young lady'.

Another 'Oh!' from Mrs Frowsy, and out also went she, muttering as she went.

'Isn't it true that he is suited, then?' asked the smiling fashionable of the also smiling attendant of the bar and the Spider.

'Oh, he only says that to some he doesn't like the appearance of,' replied the maid. 'You can go in.'

And in swept the delighted young lady.

Now came the chief fun of the whole business. In the front door of the bar crept the most ludicrous figure you can well imagine in search of a 'position of trust'. I do not generally find much difficulty in describing to you such characters as make a forcible impression upon myself, but in this instance I confess to a fear of failure, so immeasurably beyond 'all my fancy painted her' was this old lady's absurdity of appearance, and conceit of manner.

She was tall and thin, and attired in the sparsest manner. From her appearance, it was to be judged that her dress consisted totally of the scrap of dirty black skirt and voluminous long cloak that she drew tightly about her shoulders, always excepting the filthy muslin cap and old greasy, blackish bonnet, that but partially covered it.

Every line in her face had a downward tendency. From the sharp nose on her ash-coloured face, to the wrinkles at the corners of her thin mouth – even her flabby cheeks, or rather what remained of them, dropped visibly, as in a vain search to discover their proper level. But, in spite of all this, there was an impudence and a temper that asserted itself in the elevation of her sharp chin, and the twist of the most flexible nose I ever beheld in my life.

As I have said, she drew the voluminous but thin cloak tightly around her shoulders, and she drew it with both hands under her chin. That is to say, that with both hands concealed under the cloak, she clasped it across her flat chest, so that nothing remained exposed to view of her skinny person, save the ash-coloured face, and the narrow angular outline revealed by the tight black covering.

She moved toward the bar in such a noiseless manner, and with such suspicious looks at the 'ladies' in the place, that one might have come to the conclusion she had come on some errand in which she feared the intervention of the police; and as she curled up her nose, firstly at one, and secondly at another, and finally at myself, in proper person, it was but too evident that she looked down upon us separately and collectively with the most perfect contempt.

After disposing of us to her satisfaction she leaned her old, wretched visage across the counter, and accosted the retreating barmaid in a stage whisper.

'What sort of woman does he want, my dear?'

'I don't know, indeed; he's inside with one now,' was the reply, as the speaker seized her apron and hid her face from the old hag.

It was impossible to stand it any longer – the old creature was the last straw on the risible faculties of the woman, who nearly choked in an attempt at coughing to hide a laugh, in which every one of the applicants joined as silently as they could.

'Housekeeper, eh?' in another stage whisper.

The speechless girl nodded again. 'Oh-nm!' and the old face was turned at us over her shoulder, as she once more examined us with a grin of ineffable disgust. 'Oh, I know what he wants! An' if i'd a known afore I cum here, you wouldn't a seen *me* wid the likes!'

And the old creature drew her drapery still more tightly around her, to avoid contact with the 'ladies', who could not help laughing aloud as she made her stately exit.

And in a few minutes forth came the 'fashionable young lady', all smiles and pride, and announced to the envying applicants who waited 'at the gate' that she had been engaged by the 'gentleman'. There is no knowing what might have been the symptoms of some of the irate and disappointed women in the bar; for sundry tossing heads and mutterings, such as, 'A person of trust indeed!', 'Pretty person for a position of trust!' were beginning to be seen and heard, when to the rescue pops in at the door the old head of the skinny old woman.

'I told ye so!' she nodded and grinned at the barmaid. 'Ha, ha! I knew what he wanted – he, he! ho, ho!' and she was gone.

Retired we all discomfited. Retired the poor widow and her pale-faced child. What impudence she had to suppose that one without youth, and with sense, would be eligible for a position of trust under a bloated old Spider! Retired the barmaid, to laugh heartily behind the scenes, and to repeat the whole story to the hero of the hour, who called for a glass of brandy, and chucklingly began to consider if the silly fly, who had engaged with him would require a very intricate web to entrap her.

> Will you walk into my parlour? said the Spider to the Fly,
> 'Tis the prettiest little parlour that ever you did spy;
> The way into my parlour is up a winding stair,
> And I've many pretty things to show you there.

But I shall ever hereafter, in connection with a 'position of trust', remember the miserable old skinny face that chuckled through the doorway, and said, 'I told you so! Ha, ha! he, he!'

NOTES

1. This narrative was the first Mary Fortune story to be reprinted since early this century, in Fiona Giles' *From the Verandah*. The title comes from a poem by Mary Howitt (1799–1888), sister-in-law of the Godfrey Howitt mentioned in the first instalment of the memoirs. The piece is highly unusual in its subject matter, though Mary Fortune had earlier addressed the theme of women's paid work in her 1866 novel, 'Dora Carleton'. One scene of the novel is set in a women's Labour Office, although the exploiter is not a man, but the female proprietor of the Office.
2. Rigidly religious – from Robert Burns's poem 'Address to the Unco Guid'.